Digital Borders

Digital Borders

The New Geography of Control

By

Ayaan Chowdhury

Vij Books

New Delhi (India)

Published by

Vij Books
(Publishers, Distributors & Importers)
4836/24, 3rd Floor, Ansari Road
Delhi – 110 002
Phone: 91-11-43596460
Mobile: 98110 94883
e-mail: contact@vijpublishing.com
www.vijbooks.in

ISBN: 978-93-47436-93-2 (HB)

ISBN: 978-93-47436-72-7 (PB)

ISBN: 978-93-47436-04-8 (eBook)

This book was developed using advanced writing tools to support the drafting and ideation process. All content has been thoughtfully curated, refined, and reviewed to ensure quality and relevance.

Contents

Introduction

The World With No Outside

The teenager holds a phone above the crowd, its camera struggling to stabilise against the surge of bodies and the push of riot shields. He is not a journalist, not a politician, not even old enough to vote. Yet he believes that if he broadcasts what he sees, someone, somewhere, will know the truth. The stream goes live. For a moment, the connection holds. In a neighbouring country, viewers refresh and refresh again, only to be rewarded with a buffering wheel. A continent away, a platform's recommendation system quietly replaces the footage with a cheerful clip about civic harmony. Three audiences, three realities, none able to verify the others. The map says they live in the same world. The network insists they do not.

This is not science fiction. It is the quiet normality of a planet where borders are built in code, sovereignty is negotiated by algorithms, and visibility is distributed like a privilege. A decade ago, the internet was sold as a universal commons: one space, open to all, where ideas flowed freely and geography lost its grip. Instead, we inhabit a digital archipelago, fragmented by national firewalls, commercial content regimes, payment interruptions, and identity credentials that determine who may speak and who may simply watch. The lines dividing us no longer sit on maps. They are buried in submarine cables, fibre conduits, app stores, and opaque terms of service that no constitution ever ratified.

The borders returned. They just changed shape.

This book is a map of those invisible frontiers. It attempts to make legible a world in which the most decisive barriers do not look like barriers at all. A firewall is a law, a cache rule is a checkpoint, a recommendation engine is a customs officer with suspiciously strong opinions. Few of us notice, because these borders rarely announce themselves. They disguise coercion as technical fault, censorship as a network outage, exclusion as a business decision. What fails to load might simply be "unavailable in your region". What vanishes from a search result might merely be a prudent adjustment to "local sensitivities". And when something spreads like fire while something else sinks without trace, we are told the algorithm knows best.

Yet digital borders are neither natural nor inevitable. They are made. And what is made can be remade.

The aim of this book is clarity: a durable framework for understanding how digital borders work, who builds them, and what they mean for human freedom. Clarity is not a luxury. The health of public discourse depends on knowing whether a missing message is a technical glitch, a national restriction, a corporate fear of regulatory reprisal, or an automated policy designed to optimise "engagement". Too often, we are left guessing. That ambiguity is not benign. It erodes trust, fuels conspiracy, and quietly normalises the idea that access to information is a conditional gift rather than a civic right.

To read digital borders properly, one must first acknowledge that they are layered. Some are constructed by states—overtly through legislation, covertly through licensing pressure, or discreetly through partnership with carriers and platforms. Some arise from corporate incentives: the desire to control costs, appease advertisers, or protect brand reputation. Others emerge from code itself: protocol choices that prioritise one type of traffic over another, or ranking systems that elevate particular voices while burying others. These layers overlap like geological strata, creating fault lines and pressure points, shaping what people see and what they are permitted to say.

Historically, borders were physical. They could be touched, argued over, defended. A passport confirmed one's identity; customs officers rummaged through luggage; declarations were stamped and signed. Movement was slow, frictional, visible. When the internet appeared, many believed physical borders had met their match. But the lesson that technologists and governments slowly learned is that digital space can be controlled more quietly and, in some respects, more absolutely than land. To deny entry to a country, one must patrol its gates. To deny entry to a website, one only needs to adjust a list. And where a wall can be climbed or tunnelled beneath, a blocklist can be updated in an instant. Control scales.

So the border adapted. A visa stamp became a login token. A customs search became packet inspection. A deportation became a silent account suspension. Where once states controlled who crossed into territory, they now control which packets cross into networks, and which ideas cross into minds.

The great irony of digital borders is that they did not emerge to keep outsiders out. Many were installed to keep insiders in: the citizen who tries to send money abroad; the journalist who attempts to share footage; the student who seeks information beyond a national curriculum. Some borders are not built to forbid, merely to discourage—to slow a stream until it becomes useless, to degrade a video until the story fades, to add just enough friction that only the determined persist. A border can be a checkpoint. It can also be a delay.

That subtlety matters. Democracies and authoritarian states alike employ digital borders, though for different reasons and with different levels of transparency. Even countries that champion openness encounter moments when the temptation to restrict proves strong: to combat disinformation, to stabilise markets, to protect children, to prevent panic. The rationale shifts. The powers stay.

Meanwhile, corporations—not just governments—have become gatekeepers of global movement. A handful of platforms control visibility for billions of people. App stores behave like customs authorities, approving or rejecting which tools may operate on a device. Payment processors determine whether activists get funded or whether a news outlet can monetise its audience. What appears to be "content moderation" is often something more consequential: a border policy crafted in code.

The power to permit or deny is the essence of sovereignty. And much of that power now resides outside elected institutions.

We are, therefore, in a peculiar moment. The world depends on digital infrastructure as if it were a global utility, but that infrastructure remains a patchwork of private incentives and national ambitions. It has the appearance of universality, but its reality is contingent. Some nations build their own platforms, their own clouds, their own content models. Others outsource digital sovereignty to foreign companies and hope that their values survive the transaction. Some seek total control over information. Others try to balance freedom with responsibility, only to find that the border keeps shifting beneath their feet.

This is not a treatise against borders. Borders can protect. They can secure systems, limit abuse, and prevent exploitation. They can compartmentalise failures and preserve stability. The problem is not that digital borders exist.

It is that we struggle to see them clearly, ask little about who draws them, and have even less say in how they evolve.

The point of this book is to provide that visibility.

The chapters that follow treat digital borders not as abstractions, but as engineering choices, business strategies, security measures, and political tools. Each chapter examines a different frontier: identity systems, payment rails, national firewalls, platform moderation, data localisation, diaspora networks, and the emerging institutions that might, one day, bring accountability to the entire system. Throughout, a simple analytical framework appears: every border, whether physical or digital, performs three basic functions. It identifies who or what is crossing; it inspects or classifies; and it enforces permission or denial. Ports, protocols, platforms. Identity, inspection, enforcement. Once you know where to look, borders reveal themselves.

Some readers may ask whether this story is merely a tale of creeping surveillance or digital authoritarianism. It is not. There are reasons for cautious optimism. New forms of openness are emerging: decentralised platforms, transparent standards, interoperable tools, and civic pressure for fairer processes. Digital borders can entrench power, but they can also distribute it. They can confine speech, but they can also protect vulnerable communities from harassment. They can restrict information, but they can also create alternative spaces where marginalised voices thrive.

The challenge, then, is not to abolish borders, but to build better ones: borders that are accountable, reversible, proportionate, and open to oversight. Borders that serve people, not merely states or corporations. Borders that do not disguise censorship as design.

To reach that point, we must first name the forces reshaping the world.

Why is the topic urgent? Because digital borders determine who counts. When a platform demands a real name, it implicitly decides who may speak under conditions of vulnerability. When a payment processor cuts ties with a news outlet, it decides whether journalism survives. When a state throttles video quality during protests, it decides what citizens will remember. When undersea cables are rerouted, when app stores are split by geography, when search engines return different realities to different populations, a border has been drawn—even if no one announces it.

These borders do not simply govern movement; they govern imagination. They affect what people believe their society is, what conversations seem possible, what futures appear thinkable. A citizen who cannot see protest footage may believe there was no protest. A voter whose feed is sanitised may conclude that dissent is marginal. A student who is denied scientific resources may inherit a narrower world. The border does not need to block everything. It only needs to block enough.

And unlike their physical counterparts, digital borders are elastic. They tighten during unrest and relax in calmer times. They vary by device, by identity, by location, by inferred risk. Two citizens standing beside each other may see entirely different worlds. Not because of censorship in the old sense, but because adaptive filters calculate one as safe and the other as suspicious. Rights become personalised. Freedoms become conditional.

That is a profound shift in the philosophy of citizenship.

There are also deeper historical echoes. Empires once controlled trade by sea lanes and choke points. Modern states protect territory through checkpoints and visas. Today, control moves to the layer of code: routing tables that divert traffic, protocols that throttle data, rankings that amplify and erase. The old merchants of maps have been replaced by engineers of default settings. The new cartographers are standards bodies, cloud providers, and app stores whose decisions redraw access routes without the ceremony of legislation.

History teaches that borders are rarely static. They expand and contract with political philosophy, economic interest, and technological change. When printed books emerged, authorities tried to license presses. When telegraphs arrived, states sought to control cables. When radio became powerful, frequencies turned into regulated airspace. Digital networks are simply the next chapter, but with a twist: scale and subtlety. Never before have borders been so granular, so fast to update, so hidden from public scrutiny. A single line of code can restrict millions.

This is not a call for paranoia. It is a call for maturity. If digital space is now a site of governance, then citizens deserve transparency, due process, and meaningful rights. If platforms exercise power over speech, association, and economic life, they must be held to standards comparable to public institutions. If governments rely on private companies to implement policy, there must be oversight. Without that, we risk drifting into a border regime built entirely on convenience: easy for states, effortless for corporations, suffocating for individuals.

A recurring motif in the chapters ahead is that of the "gate". Gates are mundane structures. They are neither inherently good nor bad. They can protect, organise, or exclude. What matters is who controls them, how they are used, and whether those who pass through have any recourse when the gate malfunctions or is misused. Today's digital gates are login screens, content flags, traffic classifiers, payment tokens. Some are public, others private, most invisible. But begin to see them, and a pattern emerges: a global architecture of control that is improvisational, unaccountable, and immensely powerful.

Yet there is also agency. Citizens build counter-borders: VPNs, mirror sites, diaspora relays, encrypted channels. Technologists design decentralised protocols that resist capture. Lawyers challenge extra-territorial jurisdiction. Journalists expose abuse. Activists demand transparency. Even within governments and corporations, there are principled actors who recognise that a society held together by hidden borders is a brittle one.

The stakes are therefore not only political or technical. They are human. Borders affect dignity. When someone is silenced without explanation, denied access without recourse, or misclassified by a system they cannot see, the harm is not abstract. It is personal. Freedom is not simply the absence of constraint; it is the presence of fairness. A digital border that cannot be challenged, questioned, or appealed becomes a form of quiet domination.

The coming chapters seek not to criticise from the sidelines, but to offer a vocabulary for building something better. A vocabulary that treats digital governance as a craft, not a mystery.

As you read, you will encounter a world both troubling and hopeful. You will see how states assert sovereignty without geography, reaching into servers located continents away. You will see how platforms create borders through policy, sometimes intentionally, often accidentally. You will see how money moves—or fails to move—across payment networks, and how that shapes journalism, activism, and everyday life. You will see why data localisation promises security but can undermine resilience. You will see communities that behave like virtual nations, complete with rules, rituals, and governance. You will see institutions that attempt to restore accountability and designers who build for dignity.

You will also see that the future is not foreordained. Digital borders are being negotiated now, in legal offices, data centres, product teams, civil society circles, and diplomatic meetings. The choices made in the next decade will determine whether the internet matures into a space of civic possibility or calcifies into a patchwork of walled gardens and silent corridors.

So the questions that animate this book are practical. What counts as a fair border? What rights should travellers of the digital world possess? What standards should govern the blocking of a website, the throttling of a video, the suspension of a person's voice? What protections should exist when algorithms make mistakes? How much power should private companies wield over public life? And how do we design systems that do not collapse the first time a government or corporation decides that certain ideas are inconvenient?

These questions are difficult precisely because they sit at the intersection of security, commerce, ethics, and human rights. But difficulty is not an excuse for resignation. It is an argument for clarity.

The teenager in the square believed his livestream would be seen. He believed that truth could outrun suppression. Perhaps he was right. Perhaps enough people used VPNs. Perhaps the footage spread through diaspora networks. Perhaps mirrors appeared within hours. The point is not whether he succeeded. The point is that he had to circumvent borders that did not exist on any map.

This book is for those who refuse to treat such borders as an inevitability.

It is for citizens who sense that something is broken when a government can silence speech by leaning on a payment processor. For lawmakers trying to regulate without crushing innovation. For engineers who do not want to build systems that quietly exclude. For designers who believe dignity is a feature, not a luxury. For anyone who believes that digital spaces are not mere entertainment platforms, but civic arenas where culture, politics, and daily life unfold.

We live, now, in a world with no outside. Everything connects. Everything flows. But not everything crosses. And that is where the story begins.

Chapter 1

From Lines on Maps to Gates in Code

An airport once made borders visible. A traveller stepped off a flight and entered a choreography of documents, stamps, and glances. Luggage moved through scanners, passports through readers, bodies through queues. The state's authority was expressed in the theatre of inspection. You could feel the border: its texture, its waiting, its scrutiny.

Today, borders can be crossed without a foot leaving the ground. A blogger in one country posts a video; viewers in another watch it instantly. A business shifts capital across continents with a few keystrokes. A student collaborates with classmates she has never met. At first glance, movement seems frictionless, too swift for gatekeepers to keep pace. Yet the freedom is illusory. The border has not vanished—it has dissolved into the infrastructure. A silent checkpoint lives in code, deciding what travels and what does not. Most of the time, we do not notice. It is only when something fails to cross that the border suddenly becomes real. A website will not load. A payment declines. An app quietly disappears from a store. Like a door that locks only on certain visitors, the network enforces boundaries without ever raising its voice.

Ports. Protocols. Platforms. These are the new border posts. Imagine trying to leave a country only to discover the roads have been rerouted beneath your feet. In digital space, such redirections happen every day. An internet service provider blocks a domain name. A messaging app is removed from a national store. A video platform limits search results inside one country while amplifying them in another. To the end user, it appears technical, even accidental. To those who understand the machinery, it is border control by design.

This chapter explores the architecture behind those decisions. It shows how the physical gatehouse evolved into a networked apparatus capable of admitting, delaying, or blocking information with silent efficiency. To grasp this transformation, the reader needs a new mental model of borders—one that works not on land or sea, but at the level of packets, permissions, and platforms.

Start at the first layer: the port. In the physical world, a port is a coastal gateway where goods and travellers are inspected. On the internet, a port is a numeric channel at a service provider, controlling how information enters and leaves. A government that once needed embargoes, patrol boats, and customs officers can now ask an ISP to restrict a handful of ports, severing access to a service halfway across the world. The difference is speed. A naval blockade takes weeks to enforce; a port block propagates in seconds. No uniformed guard appears. No warning is issued. The server simply responds with silence.

Next comes the protocol. Where ports determine *where* data travels, protocols determine *how* it travels. They prioritise some traffic, throttle others, and decide whether a packet deserves fast lanes or slow queues. A protest livestream may be relegated to a trickle while entertainment flows freely. Technically, nothing has been banned. Practically, the story dies in buffering. Blunt censorship becomes unnecessary when delay can achieve the same effect with none of the spectacle.

Then the platform. Unlike ports and protocols, platforms do not simply manage traffic; they shape discourse. They write the rules of speech, decide which applications can exist on their devices, and set the terms for monetisation, promotion, and removal. A state might ask a platform to take down a post; a platform might go further, altering recommendations, disabling features, or automatically cleaning up search queries. When a social app disappears from an app store, the border has not been sealed by soldiers; it has been sealed by software. The citizen feels isolated, not policed. The platform calls it compliance. The user experiences exile.

In physical borders, identity is conferred by documents. Online, identity is a login token. A state that wants to know who is speaking no longer needs to interrogate suspects; it can demand real-name policies, SIM registration, or identity-linked accounts. Inspection, once a physical act of rifling through bags, becomes packet inspection—machines examining traffic for forbidden signatures. Enforcement, formerly an officer stamping exit denied, becomes an automated blocklist or a geo-fence: invisible, impersonal, absolute.

This triad—identity, inspection, enforcement—forms the core of digital border power. It is the logic of movement reimagined. To cross, you must prove who you are; your message must survive scrutiny; the gate must choose to open. Governments have understood this. So have companies. The result is an ecosystem where power is distributed across engineers, regulators, compliance officers, product managers, and algorithm designers. Each adds a brick to the border, even if they never think of themselves as border guards.

Once, borders needed maps. Now they need architects. The new cartographers are not surveyors or generals, but standards bodies, cloud providers, app stores, and network operators. When they adjust default settings, they redraw continents of access. A standards committee decides that a certain encryption method should be deprecated. Overnight, older devices cannot connect. Security improves; access shrinks. A cloud provider restructures its infrastructure. Graciously or not, traffic that once flowed through one jurisdiction now passes through another, bringing it within range of new laws and new pressures. No citizen voted for this. Most never hear about it. But the shape of the digital world changes regardless.

If physical cartographers once determined where a nation ended, digital cartographers determine which services reach which people. When a platform enables a feature only in select countries—perhaps a payment tool, perhaps a messaging upgrade—it has drawn a line not visible on any map. A critic may call it censorship. A shareholder might call it prudent risk management. The effect is the same: rights fragment by region, and citizenship slowly develops tiers.

Of course, this border-making is not solely the work of private actors. States encode their preferences into algorithms. Recommendation systems can be tweaked to promote national content, demote foreign sources, or elevate approved narratives. Risk scores can categorise voices as trustworthy, questionable, or dangerous. When a platform optimises for local compliance, it may over-correct, removing lawful speech in anticipation of pressure. Governments rarely need to issue explicit commands; a raised eyebrow from a regulator, a vague clause in a licence renewal, or a public hint of new legislation often suffices. The algorithm moves before the law does.

Call this phenomenon *algorithmic nationalism*. It is softer than propaganda, more subtle than a ban, and far harder to detect. The user believes they are seeing a neutral feed; in reality, their content landscape has been tailored to satisfy legal sensitivities, advertiser comfort, and platform incentives. A patriot might welcome the outcome. A dissident might despair. Neither can see the boundary lines.

Why did borders migrate from the physical to the digital? The answer is not a conspiracy; it is an evolution driven by economic logic and national anxiety.

Revenue is one motivation. If money flows through foreign platforms, states worry about taxation, capital flight, and domestic industries hollowed out by global competition. Regulating ports, protocols, and platforms lets governments tilt the playing field in favour of local services. Network control becomes industrial policy by stealth.

Narrative management is another. Rulers have always sought to influence what their citizens hear and see. But controlling newspapers and broadcasters proved easier than controlling a global torrent of user-generated content. Digital borders restore leverage. Block the site. Slow the video. Demonetise the journalist. Pressure the platform. Each step can be justified as moderation, safety, national interest, cultural preservation. Censorship without fingerprints.

Then there is infrastructure defence. When transport, energy, healthcare, and finance rely on networks, states cannot afford unfettered openness. Distributed systems bring resilience, but also risk. Malicious traffic must be stopped. Foreign surveillance must be resisted. A government that appears heavy-handed might genuinely be protecting public safety. The challenge is distinguishing protection from suppression, security from pretext.

The point is this: borders moved because they could. The material world is stubborn; the digital world is pliable. Fences are expensive; filters are cheap. Guards require salaries; algorithms do not sleep. A country that once struggled to control its frontier can now enforce restrictions at the speed of code. And unlike physical borders, digital borders do not need to be consistent or visible. They adapt to target individuals, not populations. Two users in the same room can face different gates.

As this chapter unfolds, the reader will meet the engineers of this new frontier. Some operate machines that classify traffic. Some govern the markets through which software travels. Some write the standards that shape encryption, routing, and identity. Not all exercise power intentionally. Many do not think of themselves as political actors. But the border does not care about intention. It cares about effect.

To understand digital borders, we must abandon the fantasy that the network is a neutral corridor and recognise it as a governed space—one where rights are allocated, policed, and, at times, withdrawn. The question is not whether borders are wrong. The question is who controls them, and to what end.

By the time this chapter reaches its close, ports, protocols, and platforms will no longer feel like abstractions. They will appear as gatehouses, each capable of reshaping what people can know, say, and build.

For now, the gates are quiet. Their mechanisms are subtle. But step through them with care, and the architecture of control begins to reveal itself.

Ports, Protocols, Platforms

A website disappears. Not with a grand announcement or a police raid, but with a quiet adjustment to a routing table. One day the address resolves; the next it hangs, spinning endlessly, as if the internet itself has forgotten that the site ever existed. No soldiers, no sirens—just silence. The disappearance feels technical, almost accidental. It is not. It is border control executed through infrastructure, precise and bloodless.

The internet's promise was unimpeded flow. Anyone could publish, anyone could read, anyone could speak to anyone else without asking permission. That promise never quite matched reality. Beneath the surface, the network has always relied on gatekeepers. As the medium matured, those gatekeepers grew in power and sophistication. The physical border's checkpoint—visible, bureaucratic, slow—became a constellation of digital gates: ports at service providers, protocols that shape speed and priority, and platforms that control who may speak and who may be heard. These gates do not look like walls. They look like ordinary functionality. That is their advantage.

Ports sound innocuous, too dull to inspire controversy. Yet they are the internet's front doors. Every online service occupies one or more ports, and every packet destined for that service must pass their threshold. Blocking a port is the technical equivalent of shuttering a harbour. A government that once needed battalions of customs officers now needs a handful of network directives. A single order to national carriers—*do not route port 5228*—and a messaging app goes dark. To the citizen, it feels like a glitch. To the operator, it is closure. Blocking ports requires no ideological justification, no courtroom, no public spectacle. It masquerades as engineering.

The sophistication goes further. Ports can be shaped, not just closed. A state may prefer subtlety: slow down traffic to a video platform during demonstrations, but leave entertainment untouched. The change is plausible deniability disguised as congestion. Activists complain of throttling;

authorities claim "increased demand" or "technical issues". In truth, the checkpoint has shifted from visible frontier to invisible gate, exercising control not through prohibition but through time. A delayed message can be as effective as a blocked one. A frozen livestream is a border, every bit as real as a guarded crossing.

Protocols add the second layer of control. If ports dictate whether traffic enters, protocols dictate how it travels. They decide priority, shaping the experience of communication. Video calls may glide smoothly while politically sensitive content stutters. Nothing is formally barred; everything is formally permitted. But some things crawl. Others sprint. The user perceives inconvenience, not interdiction. This is the genius—and danger—of protocol-level control. It preserves the emotional illusion of an open network while engineering real-world asymmetry.

Protocols also enable more surgical interventions. Deep packet inspection allows machines to classify traffic by signature or behaviour. A constitutional society that would recoil from police rifling through private letters often accepts network inspection as routine maintenance. Few realise that inspection can be used to hunt encrypted tunnels, block proxy traffic, or downgrade connections that appear too anonymous. The digital border guard does not wear a uniform. It wears a regular expression.

Yet ports and protocols, for all their power, pale beside platforms. Platforms sit at the top of the stack—the layer that feels closest to everyday life—and for that reason their influence is both the most visible and the most normalised. People understand what it means when a social network removes a post or suspends an account. They feel the border personally: their voice disappears, their audience erodes, their history vanishes. Even so, the mechanics of that border remain opaque.

A platform's rules operate like law, but without the rituals of lawmaking. Terms of service become constitutions; content policies become statutes; moderation teams become magistrates. In a world where billions communicate inside a handful of platforms, these pseudo-legal frameworks wield immense authority. If an airport passport officer denies entry, the traveller at least knows which state acted and why. When a platform deletes content, the explanation may be automated, ambiguous, or withheld. Appeal processes—when they exist—often unfold in silence. The state does not always need to censor speech directly; it can lean on platforms, and platforms will pre-emptively align themselves with risk-averse priorities.

App stores illustrate this dynamic with particular clarity. They behave, functionally, like customs authorities. Every application attempting to enter a device must pass inspection. Review teams scrutinise code, content, partnerships, and business models. A rejection does not merely impede distribution; it erases entire products from market. A state seeking to block a secure messaging app need not legislate against it. It can simply persuade—or pressure—the platform to delist it. The effect is forensic. As soon as the app disappears from the store, updates cease. Users remain stranded in outdated versions, vulnerable to exploits, unable to communicate securely. No doors have been slammed shut in public; the border has simply withdrawn its welcome.

Domain name takedowns capture the same principle in miniature. The Domain Name System is an address book for the internet. Remove an entry, and a site becomes unnameable. The content still exists, technically. The server still runs. But for most of the world, the address has been erased. It is exile by deletion. And because domain names reside in a complex hierarchy of registries, national authorities can exert control through pressure upstream—again, without visible confrontation. A packet dropped by border guards of code is no less potent than a book burned at customs.

These examples reveal a structural truth: digital borders are flexible, rapid, and reversible. They can be activated for an hour or a year. They can target a single service or an entire country. They can disappear without trace. The border has become software, and software obeys whoever controls the update.

Yet the mechanics alone do not explain the power. The most consequential shift lies in the cultural normalisation of gatekeeping. Citizens tolerated the old physical checkpoint because it was familiar, bounded, and rarely touched everyday speech. Digital checkpoints blend into the environment. They feel like part of the pathology of modern systems—an outage, a bug, an algorithmic quirk. As a result, control is obscured. The border recedes into the default settings.

This invisibility matters. When control feels like malfunction, systems of accountability weaken. A website disappears. Who is responsible? The host? The ISP? The government? A foreign regulator? A private actor halfway across the world? And who does the citizen petition for remedy? Without clarity, grievance becomes resignation. The border that hides itself governs more tightly than the border that announces itself.

To treat ports, protocols, and platforms as mere technical details is therefore to miss their political significance. They grant extraordinary power to whoever commands them. National regulators. Infrastructure monopolies. Global tech giants. Sometimes these actors cooperate; sometimes they wrestle. Their interactions decide whether an activist can livestream, whether a minority group can speak online, whether a newspaper can monetise or a university can share research. The stakes reach far beyond abstract rights. They touch livelihoods, memory, identity, truth.

And yet the story is not purely one of suppression. Borders also defend. Blocking malicious ports can shield hospitals from ransomware. Throttling traffic can preserve network stability during disasters. App store vetting can prevent malware from spreading to millions of devices. Even packet inspection, when used transparently and with oversight, can protect citizens from surveillance by hostile states. The same tools that can silence dissent can also prevent carnage. This duality complicates the narrative. Every technical choice embodies a trade-off—access versus safety, openness versus resilience, neutrality versus accountability.

The difficulty lies in who decides. The public has little visibility into the processes guiding these choices, and still less influence. Engineers draft policies, legal teams reinterpret them, regulators hint preferences, advertisers withdraw support, and somewhere inside that chain a decision is made—with consequences that cascade across millions. The border is distributed, yet centralised in outcome. One platform's action reshapes the reality of nations.

Examples multiply. A government demands removal of "extremist" content; platforms comply expansively, removing satire and education alongside propaganda. A sensitive story spreads; network operators slow the video but not the text, assuming fewer citizens will persist. Infrastructure firms redirect traffic to safer regions during geopolitical tension; service quality falters in unintended places. Each action springs from a different mix of caution, obligation, and fear. Each adjusts what flows and what stalls.

Understanding ports, protocols, and platforms requires seeing them not as static systems but as instruments of power. They govern the movement of information with the subtlety of a custom official who never raises his voice. They also reveal a philosophical shift. The old border assumed that movement was default and control was exception. The new border assumes that control is default and movement must be earned.

For many citizens, the implications are only now becoming visible. A journalist abroad discovers her favourite news site unreachable. A student finds a scholarly archive suddenly blocked. A parent trying to access medical information encounters warnings, redirects, or vanished pages. The border touches everyday life. Not through spectacle, but through inconvenience.

Ports, protocols, and platforms are the infrastructure of that inconvenience.

Control has travelled downward. It no longer sits solely in governments but in companies that own routers, undersea cables, cloud regions, app stores, and search indexes. These private power centres are not accountable in the way states are. They answer to shareholders, contracts, and national law—sometimes in that order. When a platform complies with a takedown request, is it obeying the law or anticipating the next regulatory negotiation? When an ISP blocks a site, is it executing national policy or protecting its licence? The answers are rarely public.

To grasp how fragile openness has become, consider the app store ban. A small company builds a secure communication tool. Users love it. Journalists rely on it. Activists trust it. Then the store removes it, citing policy violations. The tool still technically exists. But installation requires risky sideloading methods that most people never attempt. Overnight, a thriving civic space evaporates. No one stormed the servers. The border merely shifted a few pixels.

Or take the domain name takedown. A research archive publishes material deemed inconvenient. Authorities pressure the registry. The name is revoked. International mirrors appear, but most users do not know they exist. The opposition has not been crushed; it has been rendered obscure. Without attention, obscurity is erasure by another name.

These mechanisms are potent precisely because they operate quietly. The most effective border rarely needs enforcement. It need only create the illusion of difficulty. If a site loads unreliably, users drift away on their own. If an app works only through awkward detours, adoption withers. Control masquerades as inconvenience.

Ports, protocols, and platforms together form a coordinated architecture of permissibility. One layer closes the door. Another slows the corridor. A third removes the destination entirely. Each contributes to a system that can be calibrated, targeted, and justified in ways physical borders never could.

The deeper question is whether societies will allow such invisible governance to define the future of communication. The border of flesh and blood provoked debate and oversight. The border of packets passes largely unremarked. Its quietness grants extraordinary latitude to whoever controls it. That power deserves scrutiny, because invisible walls tend to grow thicker when no one names them.

The story does not end here. These digital gates are only the first part of the frontier. Identity systems will decide who receives passage. Inspection systems will classify content. Enforcement will become ever more automated and personal. Ports and protocols provide the skeleton; platforms and policies provide the muscle. What emerges is a border that is everywhere and nowhere, immediate and distant, infrastructural and ideological.

The reader, by now, has crossed several gates just to reach these words. Their device negotiated ports, their packets traversed protocols, a platform decided this content was fit to display. Each step required permission. Perhaps it feels seamless. Perhaps it does not.

The question that lingers is simple: if the border can be made invisible, who will notice when it shifts?

Identity, Inspection, Enforcement

A border has a simple logic, whether carved into desert sand or hidden in software: *who are you, what are you carrying, and may you pass?* The ritual is ancient. At a medieval city gate, travellers declared their names and origins, carts were searched, and guards decided entry. Today, the checkpoint has dissolved into the network. The gatehouse is an authentication prompt; the search is an algorithmic inspection; and the sentry's verdict is an automated allow or deny. Yet the questions have not changed. Only the methods have.

A teenager tries to post a video of police violence. He taps "upload", expecting it to spread instantly. Instead, the platform demands identity verification. His username was once enough; now the system wants phone numbers, facial recognition, proof of personhood. The request appears routine, a neutral safety measure. But behind it lies a profound shift. Before speaking, he must present papers. Before participating, he must prove he is eligible.

Identity is the first function of any border. Without knowing who is crossing, control becomes random. In physical space, identity once revolved around passports and stamps—scarce, slow-changing, easily inspected. Online, identity is fractional and fluid. An account may be a legal name, a pseudonym, a number, a biometric hash, or a behavioural profile. States and platforms have learned that by tightening identity requirements, they can turn anonymity into privilege rather than a default. What was once a public square becomes a gated enclave.

Real-name laws in some countries openly pursue this transformation. They argue that anonymity breeds abuse and that responsibility requires traceability. Mobile SIM cards need national IDs. Social media accounts demand verified documents. Critics fear a chilling effect: speech that cannot risk attribution will evaporate, and dissent will be silenced before it begins. Supporters reply that abuse declines and digital communities become safer. Both are partly right. Identity as control is never neutral. It redistributes power—sometimes usefully, sometimes dangerously.

Platforms quietly move in the same direction even without state coercion. In a world of bots and fraud, identity is currency. A platform under pressure to reduce misinformation tightens its authentication. A payment provider combats scams by requiring government-issued IDs. A marketplace struggles with fake sellers and therefore demands biometric verification. Each measure responds to real harms. Each also expands the surveillance surface of everyday life.

Identity in the digital border is not merely *who* you are; it is also *what* you are. Are you a citizen or a foreigner? A human or a bot? A journalist, a researcher, a political organiser? A credit risk, a security risk, a speech risk? Increasingly, identity becomes a score. Risk models evaluate users before they have done anything wrong. A low trust score can degrade a person's digital rights: slower appeals, stricter limits, less visibility. Citizenship becomes conditional and personalised. Two people in the same country receive different rights, not because of law but because of machine inference.

Once identity is acknowledged, the next function emerges: inspection. At a physical border, inspection is unmistakable. Customs officers search luggage, question travellers, examine goods. Digital inspection is silent. Machines examine packets, files, URLs, metadata, encryption signatures. They search for patterns: forbidden keywords, unlicensed software, circumventing signals. Inspection typically happens before the user realises it exists. A file upload stalls; a message is delivered but unreadable; a livestream buffers into oblivion. The inspection layer has classified the traffic and decided its fate.

Deep packet inspection illustrates the precision of this tool. In many countries, ISPs deploy systems capable of identifying encrypted tunnels used by VPNs. The ban is never advertised as censorship. It is framed as security, or anti-terrorism, or anti-fraud. But the effect is unmistakable: the citizen is corralled back inside an information perimeter. A digital checkpoint stamps passports invisibly. Those with technical knowledge slip through. Most do not.

Inspection can be crude or delicate. A simple blacklist blocks entire domains. A more refined filter targets only specific protocols or file types. The most advanced systems evaluate content semantically: machine learning classifiers decide whether an image is violent, whether a message incites protest, whether a video references forbidden history. When the classifier makes mistakes, appeals are possible—but often slow, opaque, or meaningless for those without influence. As with physical borders, the poor and marginalised are most likely to be misidentified and least able to contest the decision.

The third function—enforcement—is where power becomes visible. Enforcement determines whether the gate opens. In a traditional border, enforcement might be a stamp in a passport or a soldier waving a traveller forward. Online, enforcement is a blocklist, a takedown order, a platform suspension, a geo-fence that forbids content outside particular coordinates. Each enforcement action redraws the boundary between permitted and prohibited, safe and suspicious, citizen and exile.

Enforcement can masquerade as technical failure. A domain name vanishes from DNS records, and the site appears to have evaporated. A payment processor quietly disables payouts for an online newspaper, forcing it to cease operations. A government pressures an app store to remove a messaging tool, depriving users of updates. Platforms claim to be merely enforcing policy; governments claim to be merely following law; users suffer the silence in between.

What makes the triad of identity, inspection, and enforcement so powerful is its speed and granularity. A state need not shut down an entire platform. It can target activists during elections, journalists during crises, or foreign media during geopolitical tension. A platform need not ban everyone for a single offence. It can adjust visibility, recommendation strength, or monetisation. Enforcement becomes scalable and personalised. The border shifts for each individual.

There is also a deeper philosophical transformation under way. Physical borders create collectives: citizens on one side, foreigners on the other. Digital borders create categories of one. A teenager with a high-risk score may face harsher speech limits than his peers. A journalist who uses encryption might trigger extra inspection. A refugee with expired documents may find his digital wallet locked. A protest organiser may discover that her posts reach only a fraction of her audience, deemed unsafe by an unseen algorithm. In this world, rights are no longer universal. They are allocated by classification.

Supporters of strong digital borders point out that these tools protect societies from genuine threats: disinformation campaigns, cybercrime, terrorism, and coordinated harassment. Without identity checks, malicious actors exploit anonymity. Without inspection, platforms drown in spam, fraud, and abuse. Without enforcement, rules have no meaning. These arguments resonate, particularly in moments of crisis.

But every intervention has collateral consequences. Systems that promise safety can produce silence. A platform trained to remove extremist propaganda might erase documentation of war crimes. A government filter meant to stop child exploitation material might block educational resources, LGBTQ+ support networks, or reproductive health information. Errors do not distribute evenly. They fall hardest on the vulnerable, the dissenting, the misunderstood.

The border metaphor holds one more truth: discretion. Border guards hold exceptional power. They can make mistakes, exercise bias, or respond to political pressure. Digital guards are no different—except they operate at incomparable scale. A classification error by an algorithmic system affects millions. And unlike a human officer, a machine rarely explains itself. The citizen is left with a frozen process: account suspended, appeal in limbo, information unreachable.

What makes the modern border unsettling is not only its reach, but its invisibility. Identity checks hide inside "user safety". Inspection hides inside "network health". Enforcement hides inside "community guidelines". Each term sounds benign. Each masks coercion. Borders that cannot be seen are difficult to contest. They create a society governed by silent permissions.

Yet there is nuance here. Not every use of identity, inspection, and enforcement is oppressive. Some communities build them for self-protection. A small online forum might require identity checks to prevent trolling. A platform might inspect files to prevent malware. A cloud provider might enforce geo-restrictions to obey trade sanctions. Context matters. Motive matters. Oversight matters most.

The tension lies in the accumulation of control. When identity becomes mandatory across platforms, inspection becomes ubiquitous in the network, and enforcement becomes automatic, society enters a new political condition. Surveillance is ambient. Punishment is software. Citizenship is algorithmic.

History suggests that rights erode not with dramatic decrees but with technical adjustments. A login requirement here, a content filter there, a licence renewal quietly leveraged for compliance. Each step appears reasonable. Each step, taken together, shifts the boundary of freedom.

The border, once a line, becomes a cloud. It surrounds, evaluates, and decides. The citizen cannot see where it begins or ends. They only feel its effects: missing messages, vanished pages, muted voices.

The unanswered question is whether these systems can mature into accountable institutions or whether they will evolve into a permanent architecture of digital control. Identity, inspection, and enforcement are the grammar of the modern border. But grammar is not destiny. Someone still writes the sentences.

For now, the border watches, listens, and calculates. The citizen logs in, uploads, clicks send—hoping the gate will open.

The New Cartographers

A user wakes to find a familiar application has changed. The search bar now returns fewer results. A messaging feature has disappeared. Payments that functioned yesterday fail today. There has been no new law, no public announcement, no visible decree. Yet the shape of the digital world has shifted. Overnight, the border moved. Someone redrew the map.

Cartography once meant ink on parchment, coordinates fixed with survey poles and compasses. Empires fought over coastlines and mountain passes, and treaties were signed to etch lines permanently into human memory. But digital space does not tolerate permanence. In the modern network, cartography is fluid and dynamic. The map is rewritten not by diplomats or generals, but by cloud providers, standards bodies, and app stores whose decisions alter the terrain for billions. Their authority is technical rather than territorial, and because it is technical, it is often invisible.

Standards bodies are the most overlooked of these mapmakers. They operate quietly, buried beneath acronyms and process documents that few citizens will ever read. Yet their decisions cascade across everything built on the internet. When a standards committee deprecates a protocol or changes a security default, vast swathes of devices can become incompatible with parts of the network. A browser that once accessed a site smoothly suddenly throws a warning. An old phone cannot connect to a service it relied upon. The map has not been erased with force; it has been reconfigured through consensus. But consensus among whom? Engineers, corporate delegates, national representatives—actors whose motivations range from security to competition to nationalism. The choice of a cipher suite or routing policy becomes a geopolitical act, whether described that way or not.

Take encryption. When standards bodies decided to phase out older, weaker encryption algorithms, they did so for sound technical reasons. But the decision also created a practical border: countless low-cost devices could no longer meet the security threshold. Users in wealthier nations upgraded without notice. Users in poorer regions discovered that formerly open websites now rejected them. No parliament voted for this. No court reviewed it. Yet the lived geography of access changed. A digital wall rose, not between nations, but between hardware classes.

Cloud providers redraw maps on a grander canvas. Their data centres are positioned strategically—part asset, part shield, part bargaining tool. Entire countries depend on a handful of corporations for hosting. When a provider shifts traffic between regions for efficiency or compliance, it reroutes sovereignty. A set of servers that once sat under European jurisdiction might be quietly mirrored in Asia; a latency optimisation could move data closer to a government interested in surveillance. Suddenly the laws governing data have shifted without legislative process. The user has migrated across borders without moving an inch.

This power is amplified by the sheer scale of dependency. Start-ups, hospitals, schools, and public agencies entrust cloud providers with critical infrastructure. When a provider suspends service to satisfy sanctions, local businesses become collateral damage. When a provider enforces stricter content moderation than national law requires, domestic speech rights shrink by corporate decree. These decisions are not always ideological; sometimes they are defensive—legal risk minimisation or compliance templating. Yet their consequences are indistinguishable from state censorship. The frontier moves because a vendor updated policy.

App stores act as customs and border control for the device ecosystem. They decide which applications may enter, which may stay, and which must be ejected. Their review processes are opaque, uneven, and often driven by commercial logic that masquerades as safety. A secure communications tool can be removed for failing to meet a shifting compliance rule; a news app can be demoted in rankings during political unrest; a payment platform can be restricted to certain countries because licensing negotiations stalled. No legislation compels these outcomes. The border is enforced by policy documents and review queues, not soldiers.

Consider the case of mobile payments. A platform rolls out a popular peer-to-peer feature in selected countries. Users in excluded regions do not receive an explanation, only a greyed-out button. To them, the digital economy remains smaller and less flexible than the one advertised in global marketing. Some find workarounds; others accept the limitation as a natural inequality of technology. But inequality is not natural. It is designed. A feature that exists everywhere in principle becomes local in practice because the mapmakers have drawn it so.

Geographic restrictions are not always about law. They can be used to test features in markets deemed "safer" or less politically sensitive. They can serve as bargaining chips in negotiations with regulators. They can enforce business strategies that divide the world into tiers of priority. A social network might offer encrypted messaging only to citizens of certain regions; another might allow political advertising in one country while prohibiting it in another. The map of digital rights is dynamic, differential, and proprietary.

There is a longer history to this. Every empire required mapmakers, and mapmakers often served the interests of power. They surveyed territory, tax bases, and populations. Their craft was not neutral. Today's digital mapmakers perform a similar function. When cloud providers establish regions, they influence where data is taxed, where law applies, where privacy protection is honoured or ignored. When standards bodies choose technical defaults, they favour some actors and marginalise others. When app stores curate, they influence culture and commerce simultaneously.

These decisions are not always malicious; most are not. But they are consequential. They alter who may speak, who may compete, who may innovate. The digital frontier is not a wide-open plain. It is a landscape of pathways and dead ends, widened streets and narrowed alleys. A shift in ranking can banish an app to obscurity as effectively as a legal ban. A default path can steer overseas traffic through inspection-friendly jurisdictions. A pricing change can force local businesses to withdraw from global markets.

The practical effect is that billions live inside maps they cannot see. Their information routes are drawn by infrastructure companies; their digital citizenship is mediated by platform policies; their economic possibilities are constrained by cloud contracts and interoperability standards. The citizen's relationship with the state once passed through town halls, courts, and elections. Increasingly, it passes through sign-in screens and subscription plans.

There are defenders of this model. They argue that private cartographers maintain the internet's stability. Without centralised standards, fragmentation would explode. Without cloud providers, infrastructure would be brittle and unsafe. Without app stores, malware would flourish. These claims carry truth. The network is more usable, secure, and innovative because powerful actors coordinate it.

But power without scrutiny attracts exploitation. When a dominant cloud provider unilaterally changes prices or terms, small countries and small companies must comply. When a platform shifts ranking criteria, entire industries rise or fall. When a standards body adopts a protocol that favours one nation-state, geopolitical leverage hardens into technical inevitability.

Governments are not blind to this influence. Some nations cultivate domestic alternatives precisely to escape dependency. Others negotiate aggressively with platforms, demanding data localisation and preferential treatment. A state that cannot redraw its own digital map is a state that cannot guarantee its sovereignty. In response, cloud providers establish so-called "sovereign regions" designed to reassure regulators. Yet even these remain controlled by private entities whose loyalty is corporate, not constitutional.

The tension deepens when platform cartography intersects with national politics. During elections, platforms may adjust algorithms to reduce misinformation or foreign interference. These interventions are often invisible and unannounced, justified as civic responsibility. But responsibility is a matter of perspective. A government might applaud the suppression of extremist content until its own criticisms fall under the same filter. Opposition leaders might rely on social platforms to reach voters—until the platform, fearing legal repercussions, limits distribution without warning. Each action redraws access routes in real time, altering the democratic landscape.

The map changes again when governments react. Some demand algorithmic transparency; others impose fines or threaten bans. In response, platforms harden moderation, restrict features, or exit markets entirely. The citizen inherits the consequences. Their right to speak or transact becomes collateral in a negotiation no ballot box can influence.

It is easy to imagine a solution: more regulation, more oversight, more public accountability. But regulation itself can become a form of cartography. A requirement for data localisation creates new digital walls. A demand for content takedowns can be used to silence critics. The state can harden the border as easily as soften it. And unlike private platforms, states have police and armies. The new cartographers are powerful, but they are not the final authority. They are the negotiators of a hybrid frontier where public law and private infrastructure collide.

This hybridity creates systemic uncertainty. When a feature suddenly vanishes, no one knows whether it was removed for legal compliance, business efficiency, political appeasement, or engineering accident. When a site is blocked, responsibility could lie with the ISP, the platform, the government, or an upstream provider. Ambiguity is not merely a by-product; it is a form of control. Without clarity, citizens cannot challenge power, for they cannot locate it.

There is one more layer of mapmaking: default settings. Defaults shape most behaviour because most users never change them. When a browser chooses a particular search engine, that search engine becomes the effective gateway to knowledge for millions. When a device pre-installs certain applications, competing products struggle for survival. When encryption is optional rather than mandatory, privacy becomes a luxury. The map solidifies in muscle memory, not decrees.

Default paths also determine jurisdiction. Traffic routed through certain regions falls under specific regulatory regimes. Some governments quietly pressure companies to route domestic data through local data centres, where it can be inspected. Users seldom realise that their data has travelled through new frontiers. The map shifted while they slept.

If the map is dynamic, who advocates for its fairness? Standards bodies include public-interest representatives, but their influence varies. Cloud providers offer compliance assurances, but transparency remains selective. App stores publish guidelines, but enforcement is inconsistent and appeal processes limited. The current system distributes responsibility so widely that no single actor can be held fully accountable. That is precisely why it persists.

Yet the story is not finished. Civil society organisations audit platform decisions. Journalists expose hidden negotiations. Technologists develop decentralised tools that bypass centralised cartography entirely. In pockets of the network, communities build their own maps—messier, slower, but accountable to the people who use them. These experiments are fragile, but they prove that the digital frontier can be drawn differently.

For now, the privileged mapmakers remain those who control standards, infrastructure, and distribution. Their logic shapes what billions take for granted: which services exist, which ideas travel, which voices can be heard. They redraw the borders of the internet not with armies but with updates. And because updates feel mundane, few recognise their politics.

The old cartographers believed that maps were instruments of truth. The new cartographers understand that maps are instruments of power. They do not merely document the world; they produce it. The next time a familiar feature disappears or a new restriction appears without warning, one might remember that a map has moved—and ask who drew it, and for whom.

Algorithmic Nationalism

A traveller searches for the same phrase in two countries, moments apart. In one place, the top results are domestic newspapers, official statements, and patriotic commentary. In the other, foreign outlets dominate, critical voices appear, and conspiracy-minded forums bubble near the surface. The traveller's device has not changed. The platform has not changed. Only the territory beneath their feet has. The border is not a wall; it is a ranking system.

The early internet promised a universal feed, a flat landscape where information would circulate freely. This vision lasted just long enough to become mythology. Platforms learned that neutrality is neither profitable nor politically sustainable. States learned that platforms could be steered without visible coercion. Recommendation engines, once optimised for engagement, now carry national preferences. A government that once censored newspapers now influences algorithms. And a platform that once boasted apolitical engineering now shapes perception with silent levers.

Algorithmic nationalism is not a slogan dreamt up by activists; it is an observable pattern. Nations—democratic and authoritarian alike—have discovered that ranking, recommendation, and risk scoring are potent instruments of sovereignty. They do not block information; they organise it. They tilt visibility, reorder priorities, and make some voices louder than others. A citizen scrolling through a feed may never know that their world has been nationally curated.

Consider ranking systems. Search engines appear universal, yet their behaviour varies by location. Some of these variations are cultural: surfacing local news, prioritising local businesses, accommodating language differences. But others are political. A government might insist that certain historical events be framed in particular ways. Hostile coverage of leaders may be algorithmically downgraded to avoid diplomatic confrontation. A disputed territory may appear differently on maps depending on the user's IP address. The citizen receives a cartographic truth tailored to national sensibilities.

Platforms defend this practice as localisation—meeting user expectations, satisfying cultural norms, obeying local laws. Sometimes that explanation holds. But beneath the surface, ranking becomes a vehicle for ideology. When a platform promotes state media above independent outlets, when foreign media is quietly relegated, when criticism surfaces only after endless scrolling, the feed becomes a nationalist pamphlet disguised as a neutral interface. There is no warning label, no flag indicating editorial intervention. The platform claims to be objective. The citizen receives a curated reality.

Recommendation engines intensify this effect. A government rarely needs to demand a ban when it can request a boost. State-friendly content can be privileged through partnerships, content subsidies, or official "fact-checking" roles. In some countries, patriotic influencers enjoy algorithmic promotion; dissident creators discover their audiences shrinking. Nothing is removed; it is simply hidden behind a forest of louder voices. The platform can insist it has done nothing more than optimise for engagement. And technically, that may be true. But engagement is easily manufactured. A well-funded campaign, a state-backed bot army, or a coordinated comment strategy can push content into the metrics that define relevance. The algorithm obeys statistics, not ethics.

Risk scoring adds a sharper edge. Platforms build models to detect harmful behaviour: misinformation, extremism, coordinated manipulation. States often pressure platforms to expand these models to national interests. A peaceful protest movement may be labelled "organised unrest". Environmental activists may be classified as "high conflict" groups. Journalists reporting on corruption may be flagged for "abnormal posting patterns", triggering automated downranking. No law requires criminalisation. The algorithm has done the work.

Risk scoring also applies to users. A platform can assign trust scores, safety scores, or authenticity scores—numerical identities that travel with a person across the digital realm. When a country demands stronger identity verification, these scores tighten. A citizen with a low risk score sees seamless service. A citizen flagged as high risk, perhaps for routine political discussion, experiences subtle friction: delayed posts, slower appeals, monetisation limits. Punishment by delay. Repression by throttling. No knock on the door, no courtroom, only a silent reclassification.

The justification for algorithmic nationalism is almost always stability. Governments argue they must protect citizens from foreign disinformation, hate speech, terrorism, or external propaganda. Platforms claim they must obey the law, reduce harm, and foster trust. These arguments are not empty. Every country has the right to safeguard its information space, and every platform has the duty to minimise abuse. But the tools that defend can also dominate. And the incentives rarely align with democratic transparency.

One tension lies in the feedback loop between state pressure and private optimisation. If a government signals displeasure with certain content, platforms anticipate consequences. High-profile fines, licensing threats, tax audits, or the risk of total banishment can encourage platforms to self-censor proactively. Even in open societies, regulators may suggest "voluntary" cooperation. Platforms comply eagerly, preferring quiet accommodation to public confrontation. The government benefits without legislating; the platform protects revenue; the user loses rights.

This feedback loop becomes perverse when nationalism is profitable. Platforms know that local content fosters user loyalty and political favour. In some markets, domestic content is a revenue engine backed by advertising or state subsidy. A recommendation system that promotes local creators becomes not only politically safe but economically lucrative. The algorithm obeys market logic, not patriotism, yet the effect is indistinguishable. National interest and platform profit converge.

A subtler form of algorithmic nationalism emerges through interfaces. Interfaces are not neutral windows. Their menus, prompts, and defaults can encourage certain behaviour. A platform may ask users to follow local politicians or state journalists during registration. It can place national holidays, official events, or government initiatives at the top of feeds. It can encourage "relevant local news", silently steering users toward state-approved narratives. These design choices appear harmless—patriotic even. But they shape exposure, expectation, and consensus.

The effect on speech is uneven. A well-connected citizen with VPNs, digital literacy, and English-language proficiency can escape many filters. They see a wider world. But the average user, reliant on default settings and unaware of ranking manipulation, receives a version of reality designed to reinforce domestic viewpoints. The information sphere fragments by geography, but not openly. Instead of banning foreign ideas, the system buries them.

In democracies, this creates an uncomfortable contradiction. The state claims to value open debate, yet quietly encourages platforms to privilege national narratives. Citizens believe they are consuming free information, yet much of what they see has been algorithmically cultivated to avoid friction. Political pluralism survives, but on a diet of soft constraint. Dissent becomes possible but harder to find. International perspectives exist but feel marginal. The nation is placed at the centre of a shrinking universe.

In authoritarian systems, the mechanism becomes sharper. Ranking is not merely preferential; it becomes punitive. Dissident pages vanish from recommendations. Foreign platforms are permitted only if they agree to content partnerships with state broadcasters. Recommendation engines are weaponised to suppress organisation, making protests harder to coordinate and dissent harder to amplify. Instead of arresting every critic, the state reduces their reach to zero. The public cannot rally behind voices it never hears.

Some argue these outcomes are inevitable. Every country has media ecosystems shaped by history, language, and cultural norms. Newspapers, broadcasters, and publishers have always reflected national priorities. Why should platforms be different? There is a difference. Traditional media is explicit about its editorial perspective. It can be critiqued, mocked, or boycotted. Algorithms are hidden. Their decisions are framed as neutral optimisation. And unlike newspapers, algorithms adapt in real time. They do not merely reflect public sentiment; they sculpt it.

Platform engineers often insist they do not want to be drawn into geopolitics. They prefer to speak in terms of safety, integrity, and user experience. But engineering does not inoculate them from politics. When a platform restricts foreign media in one country, displays state propaganda in another, and complies with takedown demands in a third, it has become a geopolitical actor whether it admits it or not. The line between regulation and manipulation blurs.

National governments have noticed the leverage. Some reward platforms for ideological alignment—tax incentives, favourable licensing, streamlined approvals. Others punish disobedience: threats of exclusion, algorithm audits, forced data localisation. Platforms respond rationally, adjusting models to protect market access. The border is co-designed: public policy sets expectations; private optimisation enforces them.

The algorithm becomes a diplomatic instrument. During periods of tension, platforms may quietly reduce the spread of foreign narratives. During elections, certain topics may be algorithmically de-amplified. None of this appears in public law. Citizens learn of it only when independent researchers, whistleblowers, or investigative journalists uncover hidden parameters. By then, the political moment has passed.

There is a moral argument for resisting algorithmic nationalism: global information should not be fenced by invisible hands. But there is also a pragmatic challenge. Without some localisation, platforms risk cultural insensitivity, exploitation by foreign influence campaigns, and regulatory backlash. The question is not whether localisation is good or bad. The question is whether the nation should be encoded into the logic of visibility.

There are counter-movements. Some platforms experiment with transparency: publishing content removal reports, opening datasets to researchers, offering appeals. A few try to decentralise moderation, giving community councils or regional panels more say. But transparency is selective, appeals are inconsistent, and councils are often toothless. The invisible hand of ranking remains mostly invisible.

Citizens, too, are beginning to notice. Users compare feeds when travelling and recognise the shift in tone. Activists track downranking and shadowbanning. Scholars document differences in platform behaviour across borders. Awareness is emerging, but accountability remains weak. Algorithms learn faster than critics can interpret them.

The deeper philosophical question is unsettling: if every citizen sees a nationally tailored version of reality, what happens to shared truth? Nations have always cultivated narratives. But algorithmic nationalism turns narrative into infrastructure. It is persistent, personalised, and largely unquestioned. A citizen can reject propaganda in print. Rejecting it in a feed requires recognising it exists at all.

A future conflict might not begin with soldiers at borders, but with ranking adjustments. A government could accelerate patriotic messaging, bury dissent, and amplify friendly voices—all while maintaining plausible deniability. A platform could quietly restrict foreign news during negotiations. Manipulation becomes polite, bloodless, normal.

Or perhaps the opposite future emerges. Perhaps platforms discover that neutrality—true neutrality—is a selling point. Some may market themselves as geopolitically independent infrastructure, refusing state interference, defending universal feeds, and accepting bans as the price of integrity. A few have tried. Most cannot afford it.

The question lingers: who should draw the ideological boundaries of the digital world—governments, platforms, or citizens? Each answer carries risk. Each answer promises stability to someone and oppression to someone else. For now, the border is adaptive, learning from engagement curves and political incentives. It hides in ranking tables and risk scores. And because it hides, it is powerful.

Algorithmic nationalism shows that sovereignty can be encoded without a single new law. A nation needs only to nudge the algorithm and let the machine do the rest. The citizen scrolls, unaware that the world before them has been nationally curated.

Some borders are made of fences and flags. Some are made of code. The latter may prove harder to dismantle.

Why Borders Moved

A government minister once joked that if newspapers had arrived all at once—global, instantaneous, and unlicensed—they would never have been allowed. The room laughed, but everyone understood the truth beneath the humour. States tolerated the internet when it seemed like a toy. They asserted authority only after realising it had become the nervous system of modern life. By then, the network was already carrying money, speech, elections, and power. Borders did not vanish in this new world; they followed the centre of gravity.

For decades, the prevailing myth was that the internet would dissolve the nation-state. Cyberspace, we were told, was too fast, too open, too decentralised for governments to tame. A dissident could send an email abroad; a citizen could watch foreign news without permission; a business could scale globally from a laptop. The border looked obsolete.

Then reality arrived.

When a country noticed that its citizens preferred foreign shopping platforms, tax revenue leaked offshore. When activists circumvented domestic media by live-streaming protests to millions, narrative control weakened. When hackers breached hospitals, pipelines, and energy grids, leaders realised the stakes. Economic power, political legitimacy, and national security were flowing through systems they did not control. The state responded the only way it knows how: it built borders.

Not walls of stone, but filters, licences, and protocols. Not guards at checkpoints, but algorithms and compliance teams. The shift was not sudden. It was cumulative, path-dependent, shaped by accidents, crises, and incentives rather than a master plan. Borders moved because the network demanded governance—and where governance appears, control follows.

Begin with money. Governments fund themselves by taxing commerce and labour. Historically, both were tied to territory. You earned wages where you lived; you sold goods in nearby markets. But digital businesses do not respect geography. A ride-hailing company headquartered on another continent can extract fees from local drivers. A social network can monetise domestic audiences while declaring profits in tax-friendly havens. The state watches economic activity occur inside its borders but sees revenue flow elsewhere.

The first instinct is regulatory: require local offices, demand licences, impose value-added tax on digital services. But regulation without enforcement is theatre. To enforce, the state needs leverage, and leverage lives in the network. A platform that refuses tax compliance can find its app store listing suspended, its payment channels closed, its domain throttled. Borders are not red lines; they are points of pressure.

Revenue protection is rarely advertised in patriotic language, yet it explains a remarkable portion of digital control. When India banned dozens of foreign apps after a geopolitical clash, national security made the headlines. Less discussed was the economic vector: domestic competitors exploded in popularity overnight. When European regulators force US tech giants to host data locally or pay for news content, the justification is privacy or fairness. Beneath it lies industrial strategy. Even the most principled digital policy has a fiscal shadow.

Narrative management has deeper roots. Every government fears losing the ability to set the terms of public debate. In the twentieth century, control was straightforward: influence newspapers, broadcasters, and major publishers; shape discourse through licensing, subsidies, or pressure. The internet fractured that model. A blogger in exile could reach millions. A viral video could undermine official messaging. Foreign media, unfiltered and unlicensed, filled timelines.

Some states responded with brute censorship—blocking platforms, shutting down mobile networks, arresting influencers. These moves were loud, costly, and globally embarrassing. Others chose subtler techniques: pushing platforms to remove "illegal" posts, encouraging algorithmic promotion of state media, or flooding the information environment with patriotic content. Platforms that resisted faced fines, bans, or criminal liability for executives.

This interplay created a pragmatic bargain. Platforms, eager to avoid confrontation and protect market share, adapted. They built country-specific content policies, geo-restricted political posts, or created expedited takedown mechanisms. Governments interpreted compliance as recognition of sovereignty. Users saw less and less of the global conversation. The border had moved again—soft, quiet, effective.

Narrative control does not always look like oppression. During public health crises, governments pressured platforms to suppress misinformation and amplify official guidance. Many citizens agreed. The line between coordination and censorship blurred. When does safety become paternalism? When does filtering become silencing? Answers depend on who controls the switch.

Yet the most urgent motivation for digital borders is security. Modern infrastructure is hybrid: electricity grids depend on cloud control systems; hospitals run on networked devices; ports coordinate through digital logistics. An attack on servers can shut down cities. A single ransomware strike can paralyse healthcare. States learned this the hard way. The first major cyberattacks were dismissed as technical nuisances. The next wave disrupted elections, pipelines, and stock exchanges. Suddenly the internet looked less like a playground and more like a battlefield.

National security establishments began treating platforms as critical infrastructure. They demanded visibility into network traffic and insisted on data localisation to prevent foreign surveillance. They introduced emergency powers to throttle networks during riots or disinformation campaigns. They pressured telecom operators to remove foreign equipment deemed risky. Sometimes these fears were justified; sometimes they were excuses.

The logic of security is simple: a porous border is an invitation. If hostile actors can influence public opinion, steal intellectual property, destabilise markets, or compromise infrastructure, then sovereignty loses meaning. Digital borders emerge as defence mechanisms—firewalls, inspection gateways, compliance regimes. Civil liberties advocates warn of surveillance, mission creep, and authoritarian drift. Security officials warn of cyberwar, hybrid threats, and invisible enemies. Both speak truths. Stability and freedom tug constantly against each other.

The shift toward digital borders also reflects the limits of faith in globalisation. For years, policymakers believed that economic interdependence would produce peace. If countries depended on shared infrastructure and integrated markets, conflict would be too costly. But interdependence also creates vulnerability. A single platform breach can expose millions. A foreign payment provider can cut off merchants overnight. A dominant cloud provider can dictate compliance to entire industries.

States therefore seek autonomy: national clouds, domestic app stores, sovereign payment rails, independent routing. Each project is framed as resilience. Sometimes it is. Other times, it is economic self-protection disguised as patriotism. Citizens are promised privacy, but delivered patriotically branded isolation. Politicians warn of foreign manipulation, but neglect domestic abuse of the same controls.

Crucially, this shift was not orchestrated by conspiracy or grand strategy. It emerged from path dependency. Once a state discovers it can nudge a platform to remove content, it uses that tool again. Once a telecom operator can block apps during unrest, police forces request it during elections. Once a regulator realises licensing renewals can demand concessions, renewal becomes leverage. No single decision creates the border. The border accumulates through habit.

Path dependency also shapes private actors. If a platform self-censors to avoid fines, it will repeat the behaviour in similar markets. If cloud providers win contracts by offering sovereign environments, they will standardise those products. If app stores survive by appeasing regulators, appeasement becomes precedent. Over time, voluntary compliance becomes structural obedience.

Some defend this trend as realism. Borders, they argue, never disappeared; they merely adapted. If the internet is essential to national life, then states must govern it. Total openness, in this view, is naïve—a relic of a brief, anarchic era. But others warn that the cure can poison the patient. A state that can silence speech with a network filter may be tempted to suppress opposition, not just crime. A regulator that demands visibility into data flows may also surveil citizens. A border built to stop cyberattacks can be repurposed for political control.

The conflict is not between democracy and dictatorship. Liberal democracies have blocked websites, pressured platforms, and demanded data access. Authoritarian states have adopted similar tools with far fewer constraints. The difference is accountability. In constitutional systems, courts, journalists, and activists can challenge abuses—though not always successfully. In closed systems, digital borders harden into permanent iron.

And the citizens? Most do not notice until something breaks. A news site disappears. A transfer fails. A protest livestream lags into uselessness. The experience feels technical, not political. That is the genius of digital borders: they operate through friction, not force.

The stakes of this transformation are vast. If borders continue to multiply, the internet risks fracturing into national networks speaking different truths. Knowledge loses universality. Protest loses reach. Innovation slows. The global conversation shrinks into provincial echo chambers. Yet abandoning borders entirely would expose nations to predators—criminal, corporate, and geopolitical.

There is no simple antidote. Digital borders exist because the network became powerful. When power concentrates, law follows. When law struggles to keep pace, platforms become proxies. When platforms hesitate, governments act unilaterally.

The unanswered question is whether borders can defend without suffocating, protect without isolating, govern without dominating. That balance has not been found. Some countries veer toward centralised control. Others pursue transparency, oversight, and interoperable openness. Most drift somewhere in between, improvising as crises force their hand.

What is clear is this: borders did not move because states love control. They moved because the internet became too important to leave alone. The transition may not be reversible. But it is not inevitable either. Every border is a choice—sometimes prudent, sometimes misguided, always political.

If the twentieth century was shaped by the lines nations drew on land, the twenty-first will be shaped by the lines they draw in code. The map is still unfinished. The hand that holds the pen is still contested. And the world that emerges will depend on who gets to draw next.

Chapter 2

Sovereignty Without Geography

A small technology company once received three legal notices in a single week. One came from a judge in a country where it had no offices, no servers, and no staff. Another came from a regulator on the opposite side of the world. The third came from a city-state whose citizens used the company's messaging app so heavily that officials considered it critical infrastructure. Each notice demanded action: remove a post, hand over data, restrict a feature. The company's lawyers stared at maps that offered no guidance. Territory used to anchor authority. Now, authority travels with data.

The legal imagination was built for land. Kingdoms and empires claimed soil, rivers, and seas. Even the most modern constitutions presuppose geography: courts rule within borders, police enforce within jurisdictions, laws apply to those inside the fence. Yet digital life does not stay inside anything. A message written in Cairo might be stored in Dublin, processed in California, displayed in Nairobi, and archived in Singapore. Which court governs that message? Which nation owns the crime, the speech, or the evidence? The world never agreed.

And so, states improvised. They now assert sovereignty over whatever touches their people: a post read by their citizens, a user registered with their telecoms, a company handling their data. Territory is reimagined through connection rather than soil. Geography dissolves into jurisdictional reach.

Territoriality once meant control of land; today it means control of networks. A state may demand that data about its citizens remain on servers within its borders. The justification sounds technical—latency, security, privacy. The effect is political. Foreign platforms must build local data centres or partner with domestic vendors. What emerges are *data embassies*: physical islands of storage and computation that exist because the state insists that its laws accompany its people wherever they go online. When a social network stores user data locally, it becomes subject to domestic warrants and seizures. What looks like infrastructure is, in fact, a sovereign claim.

The consequences ripple outward. A global start-up hoping to operate in twenty markets suddenly faces twenty data regimes. Some require full localisation. Others demand "mirror copies" for law enforcement. Others request that encryption keys be held domestically. A business built on scale finds itself sliced into jurisdictional fragments. Compliance becomes more complicated than engineering. Small firms withdraw; only giants can afford the bureaucracy. The border, once a line, becomes a competitive moat.

Licences—once mundane pieces of paperwork—now serve as the sharp edge of sovereignty. Telecom operators, cloud providers, and payment firms all require government permission to function. That permission is rarely unconditional. A government may insist that a cloud provider host local data. It may require that a telecom notify authorities of suspicious traffic. It may compel a payment processor to freeze funds belonging to listed organisations. Companies comply not because they agree, but because the alternative is losing access to entire nations.

Ride-hailing apps illustrate the leverage. A city unhappy with labour practices threatens to revoke operating licences. Within days, the company promises reforms. A national regulator accuses a platform of tax evasion; suddenly, all payments must be routed through state-approved banks. App stores are instructed to remove noncompliant versions. Consumers still tap the icon, but the rules beneath the surface have changed. The border has been enforced through licensing rather than lawmaking.

The same pattern unfolds with content platforms. A video-sharing service refuses to remove political satire; regulators hint that its licence may not be renewed. Overnight, moderation becomes stricter. Officially, the platform is merely following community guidelines. Unofficially, it has received a warning: sovereignty must be respected.

These pressures collide in the strangest places: courtrooms that have no obvious jurisdiction over the servers they claim to govern. The "jurisdiction maze" has become a defining feature of digital disputes. One country demands data for a criminal investigation; another prohibits disclosure under privacy law. A company caught between them risks prosecution either way. Some nations claim authority because a server touches their infrastructure, others because a user is a citizen, others because a post is visible within their territory. Jurisdiction becomes a tug-of-war without a referee.

Lawyers call this *conflict of laws*, but for the average person it feels like absurdity. A journalist publishes an article legally in her home country; a foreign court demands its removal globally. If she refuses, the platform may comply anyway to preserve market access. The journalist learns the hardest truth of interconnected life: legality is not universal. A right recognised in one nation can be nullified by another's court order. The border has moved inside the feed itself.

In this maze, large platforms practice *forum shopping*: choosing the safest court to challenge rulings, structuring subsidiaries to limit exposure, and negotiating behind closed doors. Smaller companies cannot. They comply or vanish. Sovereignty without geography favours the powerful.

Yet not all control arrives through courts or licences. Some is baked into technology itself. Standards bodies—technical organisations that decide how encryption works, how networks authenticate, how devices interoperate—have become authors of soft law. When a standard mandates weak encryption for lawful intercept, privacy erodes for everyone. When a carrier implements a protocol that allows traffic filtering, governments can demand filtering without passing new statutes. The standard becomes the law, and the vendor becomes the enforcement arm.

Default encryption choices exemplify this soft power. One messaging app enables end-to-end encryption only in certain countries, fearing regulatory anger elsewhere. Another disables secure backups by default, making user data easier to seize. Most users never touch the settings; the default becomes destiny. A state that struggles to legislate surveillance can simply lean on carriers and developers, who quietly adjust the technical baseline. No parliamentary debate, no public outcry—just a patch, a toggle, an update.

Sometimes sovereignty is enforced through ambiguity rather than clarity. Governments announce broad speech rules but decline to define them precisely. Platforms, afraid of sanctions or shutdowns, over-comply. They remove borderline posts, silence vulnerable groups, and block content that was never illegal. The chilling effect is more effective than explicit bans. Everyone guesses the rule; no one knows the line. Ambiguity becomes a tool of control.

Platforms face a dilemma. If they demand clear rules, regulators accuse them of resisting local values. If they apply strict interpretation, users accuse them of censorship. Many choose the safest path: quietly restrict high-risk content and pray no minister calls a press conference. The public sees less, hears less, and thinks less freely—not because law required it, but because uncertainty bullied compliance.

Strategic ambiguity also serves domestic politics. A government can deny censorship while enjoying its effects. Officials claim that platforms voluntarily align with national culture. Platforms claim they are following the law. Users cannot prove otherwise. The border is everywhere and nowhere.

Behind these maneuvers is a philosophical transformation. Sovereignty is no longer a matter of fences and flags; it is a function of enforceability. If a state can compel data access, dictate platform rules, or punish noncompliance, it exercises sovereignty—even if the server sits continents away. Geography becomes a secondary consideration. Authority flows through infrastructure, markets, and legal risk.

This transformation is not entirely sinister. Without sovereign claims, criminal investigations stall, cyberattacks go unpunished, and abusive platforms operate with impunity. Countries argue that if a foreign company profits from their citizens, it must respect their laws. That logic resonates with voters who see tech giants as unaccountable monopolies. Sometimes sovereignty reins in corporate excess.

But the same tools that protect can suppress. A demand for localisation can morph into surveillance. A license condition can morph into censorship. A vague rule can silence minorities. The danger is not sovereignty itself, but sovereignty exercised without transparency or constraint.

The chapter ahead traces these fault lines. It will show how states project power across borders, how companies navigate legal minefields, and how citizens inherit the consequences. It will reveal a world where data travels faster than law, where jurisdiction is contested, and where the shape of freedom depends on invisible negotiations.

For now, it is enough to grasp the central tension: nations no longer need physical territory to assert control. They need a connection. Wherever data flows, sovereignty follows. The only question is whose jurisdiction arrives first—and whose rules shape the world the rest of us must live in.

Territoriality Reimagined

A server rack hums quietly in a warehouse outside Dublin. Most days, it is more mundane than mystical: blinking lights, cooling fans, redundant power. Yet to one government thousands of kilometres away, those drives are not Irish at all. They are part of its own sovereign domain because they contain data about its citizens. Investigators in a distant capital issue a warrant; lawyers in Dublin object; the company hosting the data is caught between two laws written for worlds that no longer exist. The physical location of the machine matters less than who touches its information. Territory has slipped its geographical anchor.

For centuries, sovereignty was defined by land and the bodies upon it. Borders were fences, rivers, and walls—visible markers of where one rule ended and another began. The internet shattered that simplicity. Data does not queue at border gates or present a passport. It travels through undersea cables, satellite relays, and cloud platforms with no regard for the shape of coastlines. A voice message can leave Lagos and reach Vancouver without a human ever noticing the invisible succession of routers and exchanges. In this frictionless world, states faced an existential problem: how to govern what they cannot physically grasp.

Their answer was astonishingly literal. If you cannot control where data goes, control what data touches. A state may claim sovereignty over any information involving its citizens, companies, or infrastructure. If a platform uses a local payment system, the state asserts jurisdiction. If an app markets to domestic users, jurisdiction. If a post is visible inside the territory, jurisdiction. The logic is seductively simple: law must follow the citizen, even if data does not.

This reimagined territoriality has consequences that ripple far beyond law courts. To enforce claims over data, states began insisting that certain kinds of information remain within their borders. They call it localisation—presented as a technical necessity, a privacy safeguard, or a national security precaution. Yet localisation creates a new kind of frontier: the *data embassy*. It is a physical enclave of servers demanded by law, bound by domestic rules even if owned by foreign companies. A messaging platform that once stored everything in a central cloud must build regional data centres or strike deals with local operators. In the public's eye, nothing changes. In reality, something profound has happened: sovereignty has been embedded in metal and fibre.

Supporters of localisation argue that it protects citizens from foreign surveillance and makes companies more accountable. A state cannot compel a firm in California to hand over evidence for a crime in Mumbai. But if the data sits in Mumbai, the legal levers are stronger. Yet the same logic can also enable repression. If a journalist criticises a minister, a server within reach makes it easier to seize records, identify contacts, or silently erase posts. Localisation is a double-edged sword—defence for some, vulnerability for others.

Tech companies that once imagined themselves borderless soon discovered the cost of this reimagined territoriality. A start-up handling customer analytics may find that storing French data in Germany violates domestic law. A cloud provider offering centralised storage must create parallel infrastructure for South Korea, Brazil, and Indonesia. Engineering teams build features; compliance teams build borders. Small firms retreat; only giants can afford the duplication. The internet, once compressing distance, begins to fracture along legal lines.

The public rarely sees the machinery. When a payment application suddenly stops working abroad, few realise it may be because regulators required all transactions to pass through domestic processors. When a ride-hailing service collapses in a foreign market, users assume business failure, not a revoked licence tied to data-access demands. The border is invisible, yet every tap on a screen is shaped by it.

States justify extraterritorial claims with metaphors of protection. They insist that their citizens deserve the same rights online as offline—privacy, due process, security. If a foreign platform profits from domestic users, why should it escape local accountability? The argument resonates. It feels perverse that a government cannot prosecute fraud because evidence sits on a server beyond reach. It feels dangerous that disinformation campaigns might be orchestrated from abroad with no legal remedy. In this light, territoriality reimagined looks like overdue sovereignty.

Yet sovereignty without geography produces friction that the old world never prepared for. When two states claim authority over the same dataset, companies face impossible demands: disclose and violate one law, or refuse and violate another. Encryption becomes a battleground. One country mandates keys for law enforcement; another prohibits key escrow entirely. Cloud providers respond by selling "sovereign clouds"—partitioned systems with local staff, local encryption, and local oversight. Functionally identical, politically divergent. Data begins to splinter into national blocs.

Beneath these pressures lies a deeper philosophical shift. The state used to govern bodies; now it governs signals. A passport once mattered at a border post. Today, a digital trace—an IP address, a phone number, a billing record—becomes the anchor of jurisdiction. The individual scarcely notices. She books a holiday, uploads photos, sends messages. Behind the screen, governments are negotiating who owns those footprints and who has the right to erase or exploit them.

Some countries push further. They argue that digital infrastructure itself is territorial. If a cloud platform sells services locally, its servers—even if hosted abroad—are conceptually part of the nation's information space. This logic underpins laws demanding that companies mirror data locally or station compliance officers inside the country. Enforcement shifts from network packets to office leases. Sovereignty becomes as much about who sits in a chair as where a server rack stands.

Critics warn of balkanisation—the fear that the internet will fracture into incompatible zones governed by mutually hostile laws. But fragmentation is not a dramatic moment of rupture; it is a slow accretion of local demands, each rooted in legitimate concerns. Protection of children. Defence of national narratives. Prevention of foreign espionage. No single decision seems catastrophic. Yet their sum reshapes the network's architecture.

A paradox emerges. The more states localise data to gain control, the more they depend on foreign firms to operate the infrastructure. Sovereign clouds are often built by the very companies they aim to constrain. Domestic data centres may run on foreign chips, foreign software, foreign engineers. Sovereignty, like territory, is never absolute. It is negotiated, layered, and occasionally illusory.

For ordinary citizens, the reality is subtler still. A teenager in Nairobi may discover her favourite app behaves differently than her cousin's in London. Certain features disappear, certain recommendations shift, certain videos fail to load. She cannot see the policy debates, lobbying pressures, or data laws beneath the surface. She only sees that her experience is smaller. The border has moved beneath her feet without crossing a single line on a map.

Territoriality once gave comfort: you knew which state governed you based on where you stood. Now sovereignty reaches through cables, protocols, and corporate policies. It governs data in flight, not just data at rest. And it raises unsettling questions. If two states claim the same data, whose rights prevail? If a citizen moves abroad, do her digital rights travel with her? And if sovereignty can be projected without territory, what restrains its reach?

These questions are no longer theoretical. They shape the design of networks, the survival of start-ups, the fate of dissent, and the texture of daily life. Each new localisation mandate redraws the invisible atlas of the internet. Every data embassy stands as a reminder that the cloud is not a cloud at all, but land reborn in code and steel. The frontier has returned, just beneath the servers, waiting to be discovered by those who still believe that geography is fixed.

Licences as Levers

A ride-hailing app once disappeared from a major city overnight. There was no court ruling, no police raid, no dramatic press conference—simply an announcement that its operating licence had lapsed pending regulatory review. Cars vanished from the streets. Drivers who depended on the service lost income. The public heard vague references to "compliance issues". Behind the euphemisms sat a message every platform understood: licences are not paperwork; they are pressure points.

In the analogue world, a licence certifies that someone may drive a car, run a shop, or build a factory. In the digital world, licences control the arteries of modern life: telecom networks, cloud services, payment rails. A platform may span continents, but if regulators cut one of these arteries, it bleeds locally and instantly. Disable payments and sellers vanish. Suspend cloud access and data freezes. Revoke a telecom interconnection and messages refuse to send. The sovereign does not need to pass a law. It needs only to decline a stamp.

Licences occupy a curious place in the imagination. They appear bureaucratic, dull, almost clerical. They rarely attract journalists or protestors. Yet they are among the most potent levers of digital power. They offer governments something legislation cannot always guarantee: discretion. A law must be debated, written, voted upon, and challenged. A licence can be quietly amended during renewal. A regulator can make a phone call. A minister can hint that cooperation would be appreciated before the next inspection. The result is not coercion, exactly, nor freedom. It is conditional compliance—companies adjusting their policies to keep the doors open.

Telecom licences are the original template. To operate a mobile network or an internet service provider, a company must secure spectrum, numbering resources, and interconnection rights. Governments add conditions to these licences: lawful interception capabilities, data retention requirements, content blocking upon notification. Most users never notice, because the rules live deep in the network. When a website goes dark, the public blames the platform. Few imagine that the underlying telecom licence required the block.

Cloud licences extend the logic. A cloud provider entering a new market needs a host of approvals related to data handling, security, and local partnerships. Regulators can insist that specific types of data remain on domestic servers or be made available to local authorities. They can demand that foreign engineers lack access to certain systems. In contentious moments—unrest, elections, investigations—a cloud provider might be ordered to suspend services to noncompliant apps or platforms. The cloud becomes an instrument of governance, not merely infrastructure.

Payment licences are sharper still. Unlike speech, which may provoke legal ambiguity, money moves through strictly regulated channels. Payments firms require permission to operate; that permission can be narrowed, frozen, or revoked. When a platform relies on digital payments—creators receiving funds, drivers collecting fares, sellers processing orders—the suspension of payment access is more devastating than content deletion. Posts can be mirrored. Servers can be relocated. But when revenue stops, participation collapses.

This is why payment switches have become a favoured tactic. If a social platform refuses to remove disinformation, a regulator might ask banks to restrict its advertising purchases. If a ride-hailing service disputes classification of its workers, a city can require all fares flow through a state-run gateway. If a donation platform hosts political groups without registration, it can lose its payments licence. No censorship statute needs to be drafted; compliance emerges from commercial necessity.

These levers are not always wielded with malicious intent. Sometimes they address real risks. A country suffering rampant financial scams might insist that foreign platforms use domestic verification systems. A regulator concerned about tax evasion may require a marketplace to process payments locally. The problem is not the licence itself, but the opacity of its enforcement. When governments are free to threaten revocation without public scrutiny, policy becomes negotiation, not law.

Ride-hailing services illustrate this dynamic in miniature. Cities everywhere have struggled to classify these companies—are they transport providers, technology intermediaries, or something in between? Without waiting for judicial clarity, regulators used licences to settle the argument. Some cities demanded real-time sharing of trip data. Others insisted on local data storage. Others required companies to collect taxes at source. Firms that complied stayed. Those that resisted found their apps disabled on local networks or their drivers fined into withdrawal. Public justification was couched in safety and fairness. Behind closed doors, it was leverage: obey, or disappear.

Cloud providers face similar pressures. To sell services in some countries, they must operate through joint ventures that include domestic firms. Officials gain oversight not by law, but by corporate structure. Certain data types must be hosted on "sovereign" servers staffed by local citizens. Encryption keys may need to be recoverable under court order. A provider that balks risks loss of its cloud licence—and with it, the livelihoods of thousands of business customers who rely on the service.

Payment gateways offer perhaps the starkest examples. A government unhappy with a news outlet's editorial stance can ask domestic banks to stop processing its subscription payments. A streaming service that declines to remove a controversial documentary may discover that app-store payments for its country have been quietly disabled. The move is always framed in administrative terms: licensing irregularities, failure to provide required documentation, violation of financial regulations. The effect is unmistakable. Content is suppressed not by banning speech, but by strangling revenue.

What makes licences so powerful is their asymmetry. A government need not win a public argument. It need not defend its decision before a constitutional court. It only needs to signal that licence renewal will be "difficult" unless compliance improves. For a multinational corporation, the calculus is straightforward: concede a little to avoid losing everything. The strategist's term for this is *regulatory risk*. The citizen's experience of it is quieter: one day the service they rely on behaves differently—more surveillance, less privacy, stricter moderation—and no one can point to the exact moment when policy changed.

Defenders of licensing power argue that platforms cannot simply enjoy profits without responsibility. Telecom carriers must allow lawful interception because crime crosses borders. Payment processors must verify identity because money laundering finances violence. Cloud providers must ensure data accessibility because crises demand rapid information retrieval. The state, they say, is not bullying but protecting. To an extent, that argument has merit. No government wants vital infrastructure governed by private whim.

Yet there is a tension between safety and sovereignty. When licences are used to negotiate policy, democratic oversight weakens. The public cannot see the terms of the threat. The platform, bound by confidentiality, rarely explains why its rules tightened or why certain content vanished. Corporations become quiet enforcers of political preference. The market becomes a proxy legal system, opaque and unaccountable.

Some governments have embraced maximalism. They renew licences in short increments, forcing companies into perpetual negotiation. They demand "voluntary" agreements that allow access to encrypted content. They require the creation of in-country legal representatives who can be personally liable. These representatives—often mid-level employees—carry the threat of arrest. The licence is no longer a commercial tool. It becomes a weapon of intimidation.

Other countries take a more measured approach. They establish transparent criteria for licence renewal, publish compliance reports, and provide independent appeal processes. Their goal is not to silence dissent but to secure critical infrastructure. In these cases, licences function as legitimate instruments of governance, not tools of coercion. The difference lies in clarity. A system with clear rules allows companies to plan. A system of whispered warnings produces fear.

For platforms, the challenge is existential. A global service cannot maintain twenty national versions of its ruleset forever. Over-compliance risks alienating users who value openness. Under-compliance risks being shut down. Some firms try localisation—hiring local moderators, creating domestic operations, partnering with regional data centres. Others withdraw entirely from hostile markets. The border, once drawn with code, is redrawn with corporate exit.

The philosophical dilemma runs deeper. A platform built to connect people now finds itself entangled in competing sovereignties, each claiming moral legitimacy. Whose norms should prevail? The country that hosts its headquarters? The country where most users live? The country that threatens to revoke its licence? There is no simple answer. Digital sovereignty is not a single contest; it is a distributed negotiation fought on the terrain of permits and approvals.

And the leverage is growing. As more services move to subscription models, micropayments, and digital wallets, control over payment licences becomes a gatekeeper for participation itself. A state that restricts payment access can silence creators, hinder activists, punish media outlets, and drive small businesses to bankruptcy without ever banning a website. Monetary infrastructure, once dull and technical, has become a political border.

The effect on citizens is subtle but profound. They may believe that platforms enforce rules neutrally, when in fact the rules are shaped by quiet state pressure. They may assume a service failed commercially, when it was removed for defying licensing conditions. They may think censorship is illegal in their country, unaware that the government does not censor—it merely threatens the licence of a company that refuses to censor itself.

This subchapter leaves an unsettled question: if sovereignty can be exercised through licences rather than laws, what becomes of democratic accountability? Who ensures that rule-making through regulatory pressure remains fair, transparent, and proportionate? If the future of digital governance is negotiated privately rather than debated publicly, citizens inherit a system they did not choose.

Licences are levers, and levers move heavy things with little force. States have discovered that in the digital age, the smallest administrative hinge can swing open—or slam shut—entire parts of the online world. The consequences stretch far beyond compliance. They shape who speaks, who earns, who travels, who organises. A licence that was once a formality has become a frontier.

The Jurisdiction Maze

A journalist publishes an investigation that embarrasses a foreign minister. The article appears on a small website hosted in Iceland, written by a reporter in Kenya, edited by a collaborator in Canada, and read by thousands across Asia. Weeks later, the platform receives legal threats from three different countries: one demanding removal, another demanding user data, and a third issuing a global injunction. None of the author's team has visited those countries. None of their servers sit within those borders. Yet each government insists it has the right to decide what should vanish from the internet. The map offers no guidance. Jurisdiction, once tethered to soil, has become a sprawling web of claims.

The modern internet turned geography into an illusion. Messages cross borders so quickly that the notion of "where" something happened loses meaning. A defamatory post written on a phone in Athens may be uploaded to a server in Amsterdam, cached in Frankfurt, and read in Delhi. Which country's law governs that post? Where, legally, did the harm occur? Is jurisdiction tied to the speaker, the platform, the data centre, or the audience? Courts answer differently, and those differences collide like tectonic plates beneath our digital conversations.

When two courts claim authority over the same piece of content or the same slice of data, the result is not a philosophical conundrum but a practical crisis. A company ordered to reveal user information in one country may be prohibited from disclosure by the privacy laws of another. To comply with one is to violate the other. This is the heart of the jurisdiction maze: a world where legal systems overlap without a mechanism to decide which one wins.

Some of the earliest jurisdiction battles involved defamation. A statement posted online in a country where it was legal might be considered criminal elsewhere. Plaintiffs realised that the internet blurred the concept of publication. If a post could be read in London, then, in theory, it had been published in London. If it could be read in Singapore, it had been published there too. Suddenly, writers found themselves vulnerable to lawsuits in places they had never set foot. The fear was justified. Courts in several jurisdictions accepted this logic: if content reached residents, the country's law applied.

From there, jurisdictional claims escalated. Privacy regulators demanded global compliance with local rules. Law enforcement agencies sought data stored abroad. Copyright offices asserted authority over files hosted on foreign servers. Each actor saw their responsibility as legitimate and urgent. But the network was never built to referee legal conflicts. It simply delivered packets, indifferent to borders.

To make sense of the chaos, lawyers refer to two old ideas: comity and conflict-of-laws. Comity, in theory, is politeness between nations—a willingness to respect each other's legal decisions to avoid chaos. Conflict-of-laws governs what to do when two legal systems contradict one another. Yet neither doctrine mapped neatly onto the internet. Politeness fails when politics intervene, and conflict rules assume a world in which location is knowable. The internet makes location slippery.

Take the seemingly simple question: where is a server? Physically, it sits in a data hall. Legally, it may have multiple domiciles. A server owned by a US company but managed by a Singaporean subsidiary, hosting data for European citizens, becomes a stack of overlapping sovereignties. Each layer implies a legal hook. A regulator connects to whichever hook offers leverage.

Platform operators have responded with a quiet form of cartography. If a government demands data sitting outside its jurisdiction, a company might contest the order in a more favourable court abroad, seeking a precedent that limits extraterritorial reach. If another government demands global removal of content, a platform might restrict access only within that country and argue proportionality. These tactics resemble trade negotiations more than legal procedure. Victory is rarely permanent. As soon as one government secures a concession, others demand the same.

The realists in this story are the corporate lawyers who practice what technologists euphemistically call "forum shopping". They choose the most advantageous venue—courts known for strong free-expression protections, regulators more comfortable with nuanced interpretations, or jurisdictions that require warrants rather than political letters. A platform may structure its subsidiaries in countries with robust privacy law to shield user data from weaker regimes. It may maintain separate corporate entities for each region, each with distinct accountability. The public sees a single app; in reality, that app is stitched together from a patchwork of legal persons designed to survive the jurisdiction maze.

Forum shopping is not merely a defensive tactic. Governments do it too. A prosecutor denied access to data in one jurisdiction may seek the same data through diplomatic channels in another. Intelligence agencies establish partnerships that bypass domestic restrictions by sharing information gathered abroad. The maze is not just legal—it is geopolitical.

To appreciate how far this has progressed, consider financial crimes. A fraudster in one country scams victims in another through a social platform headquartered in a third, using payment processors in a fourth. Each state claims jurisdiction. Each seeks evidence. Each applies different privacy, surveillance, and disclosure laws. The platform faces a barrage of conflicting demands. One court orders data release. Another forbids it. The platform can be punished for obeying or punished for resisting. The law, built on the assumption of territorial clarity, becomes self-contradiction.

Even nations that prize due process sometimes bend the map. A court might insist that if content is illegal domestically, it must be removed globally to prevent circumvention. Critics argue that this sets a dangerous precedent: the most restrictive jurisdictions end up setting rules for everyone. A film banned in one country might disappear everywhere rather than risk violating local law. A journalist's investigation, legal where it was written, may become inaccessible worldwide because a distant government disapproved. The border expands outward.

Faced with global injunctions, platforms are trapped between accusation and acquiescence. Some comply without complaint. Others resist to avoid setting a precedent. The most dramatic response is withdrawal: simply refusing to operate in a jurisdiction that imposes intolerable demands. But withdrawal is rare. Markets are too valuable. Instead, companies carve out tailored versions of their platforms—one set of rules in Germany, another in India, another in the United States. The dream of a universal platform dissolves into a federation of local variants.

For users, the jurisdiction maze is invisible until it is personal. A researcher requesting access to public government records discovers that foreign laws restrict publication. A dissident's anonymous blog is unmasked because authorities leveraged a third-country subpoena. A court's effort to protect a child's privacy accidentally removes crucial evidence for journalists abroad. Freedom and constraint flicker unpredictably because no one knows which rule applies until someone with power decides.

Occasionally, comity works. Courts acknowledge each other's interests, negotiate limits, and avoid escalation. A judge may decline jurisdiction if another forum is more appropriate. Regulators may coordinate investigations to avoid duplication. But comity relies on trust between nations. In a world of rising geopolitical tension, that trust is fragile. When governments see data as strategic resource, cooperation becomes the exception, not the rule.

The deeper trouble is conceptual. Law assumed a world of stable borders. The internet created a world of distributed actions. Posting a video is not a single act in a single place—it is a cascade of processing, caching, and replication across dozens of nodes. Trying to say "where" something happened is like trying to say where a conversation occurs during a phone call. In law, location matters. On networks, location is an illusion.

To navigate this, companies build internal maps—not geographic maps, but maps of legal risk. They classify jurisdictions by aggressiveness, transparency, corruption risk, judicial independence, and diplomatic leverage. When a removal order arrives, they consult the map: comply automatically in one country, seek clarification in another, push back quietly in a third, escalate to courts in a fourth. The public rarely sees this choreography. Users simply observe that content appears or disappears, not the diplomacy behind it.

This legal choreography produces strange asymmetries. A tiny jurisdiction with a strict legal regime can exert disproportionate influence over global platforms because ignoring it risks cascading consequences. A company may worry that defying a small country today will embolden a larger one tomorrow. So platforms comply even when objections seem trivial. Compliance becomes precedent. Precedent becomes policy.

Governments are not blind to this leverage. Some deliberately file cases in friendly courts known for broad jurisdictional theories, hoping to obtain orders that platforms treat as globally binding. Others pass laws asserting extraterritorial reach, betting that corporations will capitulate rather than fight. The arrogance of sovereignty collides with the architecture of networks, and users inherit the confusion.

There is a haunting irony in this maze. The internet promised to dissolve borders, giving everyone equal access to knowledge and voice. Instead, borders have multiplied. They now exist in moderation policies, licensing agreements, data localisation statutes, and court injunctions. They shift without warning. They are enforced by platforms themselves, fearful of legal reprisal.

Where does this end? Some imagine a world in which international treaties harmonise digital law, reducing conflict. Others believe platforms will fragment into national clones, each obeying its local sovereign. More pessimistic observers fear a race to the bottom: the harshest jurisdictions dictating global standards because companies choose the path of least resistance. There is no obvious resolution.

What is certain is that the jurisdiction maze is not a technical glitch; it is a feature of a world in which information flows ignore borders but law does not. Every post, every upload, every private message moves through a landscape of competing sovereignties. The illusion of simplicity hides the truth: when you speak online, you speak everywhere—and you speak under laws you have never read, written in countries you have never visited, enforced by courts that will never hear your voice.

A future chapter will ask whether this maze can ever be made fair, transparent, or predictable. For now, the question lingers: if speech belongs to everyone and everywhere, who has the right to silence it?

Standards as Soft Law

In 2014, a messaging app flipped a single setting: end-to-end encryption became the default for every user. No parliament debated it. No minister signed a decree. Yet overnight, hundreds of millions of conversations slipped beyond the reach of policemen, intelligence agencies, and opportunistic criminals. A few lines of code had the practical effect of a sweeping civil liberties reform. The app had not passed a law. It had written a standard.

Technical standards sit in an odd twilight. They lack the ceremony of statute or treaty, but they govern behaviour with equal force. When engineers decide how browsers trust websites, how phones verify SIM cards, or how payment systems authenticate a transaction, they create rules that billions obey without reading a word. Those rules do not appear in law books. They appear in source code and configuration files. And while parliaments argue about technology, vendors quietly rewrite reality.

Encryption is the most famous example, but far from the only one. When the default setting on a device is *secure*, security becomes normal. When the default is *open*, surveillance and interception become effortless. Governments may demand access, but if the underlying protocol keeps keys on user devices, the state cannot seize what does not exist. What looks like a design decision is, in effect, a legal position: a refusal to create the capacity for intrusion. Some states applaud it. Others rage at it. Yet the protocol remains indifferent. Once adopted, the standard stands between citizen and authority like a silent charter.

Consider the seemingly mundane world of Wi-Fi. In its earliest years, networks relied on a flimsy form of encryption that could be cracked in minutes. Criminals took advantage. Law enforcement demanded better tracing, and user groups demanded privacy. The response was not a law but a specification: WPA, then WPA2, now WPA3. Today, home routers enforce authentication, rotate keys, and encrypt traffic by default. Millions now enjoy a level of protection that would once have required expert configuration. Legislation barely noticed the transition. Standards did the work.

This is the quiet power of soft law: it shapes what is possible before anyone argues about what is permissible. Carriers choose routing protocols that prioritise one kind of traffic over another, implicitly deciding whose data arrives smoothly and whose does not. Browser vendors set certificate rules that dictate which websites appear safe and which load with a warning. These choices govern commerce, communication, and trust. They often matter more to everyday life than the laws printed on paper.

Soft law is not always benign. At times, a standard can undermine public expectations. In some countries, carriers quietly configure network equipment to allow government interception by design. No statute orders it. The capability sits in the technical baseline, documented only in vendor manuals and closed-door procurement contracts. What looks like neutral engineering is, in fact, a policy: the assumption that communications should be accessible to power.

Critics argue that this undermines democratic accountability. If parliament has not voted for surveillance, why should it exist by default? The answer lies in incentives. Governments value access. Vendors value contracts. The easiest compromise is for a feature to appear technically necessary, rather than politically imposed. Once the feature exists, law enforcement presents it as a fact of nature: "the system already supports this; we are merely requesting use of it." The citizen has no idea the hit was arranged in advance.

Even when standards are designed to protect rights, the politics remain fierce. When Apple introduced secure enclave chips to protect biometric data, some governments protested that criminals would hide behind them. When Signal refused to implement weaker protocols for certain countries, those countries threatened to ban the app altogether. Each conflict followed the same pattern: a technical choice becomes a political battlefield.

The reason is simple: standards resolve disputes without public argument. When a platform adopts default encryption, users gain privacy without having to demand it. When a browser enforces strict certificate rules, scammers lose tools without a parliamentary vote. Conversely, when a payment network adds a requirement that merchants share identity metadata, anonymity evaporates quietly. Policy happens without the shouting.

Sometimes, soft law arises not from power but from cooperation. After major data breaches rocked global retailers a decade ago, payment processors imposed rigorous security standards on anyone handling card details. Merchants suddenly faced mandatory encryption, monitoring, and audit controls. Those who failed were cut off—not by police, but by banks and vendors enforcing a technical charter. Consumers gained protection because engineers and merchants agreed to a standard that regulators struggled to mandate.

Cloud providers are now the most prolific soft-law actors. Their infrastructure underpins commerce, media, and public services. When a provider deprecates an insecure protocol, millions of systems must upgrade or fall offline. When it changes authentication rules, entire sectors scramble to comply. Cloud policies become de facto regulation: hospitals, schools, fintech start-ups, and charities must adopt newer encryption suites, logging requirements, and data-handling safeguards whether or not domestic law requires them. The cloud's default becomes the nation's rule.

This shift unsettles traditionalists. Should unelected engineers at standards bodies or platform companies wield so much influence? Should a developer's design choice determine the privacy rights of hundreds of millions? Yet the alternative—waiting for governments to legislate technical detail—is often worse. Legislators lack expertise. Political cycles move slowly. Markets outrun committees. By the time law catches up with technology, the harms are already entrenched.

Standards, by contrast, evolve continuously. They respond to new attacks, new research, and new social expectations. They offer agility that law, bound by process, cannot match. The paradox is that their legitimacy lies not in democratic endorsement, but in practical consensus. If browsers, carriers, and device makers adopt a specification, it becomes reality. Dissenters may grumble, but they cannot change the tide.

Still, consensus is not neutral. When a handful of corporations dominate implementation, their values shape the global default. If a vendor believes that children's safety requires scanning private messages for harmful content, it may build that capability into an operating system update. Governments cheering greater enforcement will applaud. Privacy advocates will call it a backdoor. The law remains silent, but the standard has spoken.

This concentration of influence leads to uneasy alliances. Activists petition standards bodies to adopt privacy-friendly architectures. Security agencies lobby quietly for features that allow lawful interception. Industry groups insist on performance and reliability. The result is a tug-of-war waged in technical language. The public rarely notices until the consequences surface in daily life: messages that cannot be read by authorities; uploads that refuse to send without identity verification; websites that fail to load unless they adopt newer cryptographic suites.

Default encryption settings are the emblematic battleground. When WhatsApp encrypted its messages by default, governments in several regions demanded special access. They were refused. The standards behind the encryption—public-key cryptography, forward secrecy, key rotation—made compromise technically risky. To weaken protection for a few was to endanger everyone. In effect, maths became a political veto. Lawmakers could rage, but the code held its ground.

Yet the same mechanism can be used in the opposite direction. In some countries, carriers and social platforms are pressured to use filtering standards that detect banned content. These filters are dressed in neutral language—"content safety," "harm detection"—but the implementation varies. A classifier tuned to block terrorist propaganda in one place may be used to suppress dissent in another. Once the filter lies inside the standard, re-purposing is easy. No auditor can see the black box.

Soft law also shapes economic power. App stores enforce technical requirements that double as regulatory controls. A store may require apps to use government-approved payment systems or to store data in local servers. Developers face a choice: comply or disappear. No election authorised this power. It emerges from a mix of market dominance and platform policy. The app store becomes legislature, regulator, and judge—through code.

For businesses, navigating soft law is now as important as complying with formal statute. A fintech operating across borders must follow data localisation requirements in one country, privacy defaults in another, and payment tokenisation rules in a third. When standards conflict, firms choose the more restrictive path to avoid being cut off from key platforms or carriers. Risk-averseness becomes regulation by stealth.

The philosophical tension is profound. In democratic theory, authority flows from consent. In digital practice, authority flows from adoption. No one votes on a protocol. No one reads the terms of a cryptographic suite. Users accept standards because their devices do. Sovereignty sits not only in parliaments, but in specifications maintained by technical committees few citizens could name.

Some legal scholars argue that soft law is beneficial, even necessary. They see it as a safety net: technology forces a baseline of protection that politics often fails to guarantee. Others worry that private regulation lacks transparency and public accountability. If power is exercised through code, how can the public challenge it? How does one appeal an algorithmic veto?

Engineers will protest that their standards arise from good intentions: security, interoperability, efficiency. But every choice has a shadow. A secure default frustrates police. A weak default endangers journalists. A filtering standard protects children, yet risks silencing whistle-blowers. Law traditionally mediated these conflicts through debate and appeal. When standards decide, the conflicts remain, but the forum vanishes.

And the stakes will only grow. As devices proliferate—from smart speakers to connected cars—the standards that govern them become silent governors. A vehicle may refuse to operate without updated security keys. A medical implant may require cloud authentication to deliver treatment. If those systems adopt policies that favour one jurisdiction's rules, others are displaced without a word of legislation.

The question, then, is simple and unsettling: if code behaves like law, should we treat its authors as lawmakers? If a consortium of vendors can set the privacy rights of billions by adopting a new protocol, should it be bound by duties akin to public office? If a platform's default settings can rewrite the balance between liberty and security, should those decisions be debated in daylight rather than on Git repositories and conference calls?

No one has a definitive answer. Some countries push back by drafting laws that mandate or forbid certain technical choices. India and the United Kingdom have sought access mechanisms inside encrypted communications. The European Union legislates standards into regulation. China requires vendors to build interception interfaces. Yet each such law competes with the physics of mathematics and the reality of global markets.

Soft law remains potent precisely because technology is borderless and politics is not. Standards leap across jurisdictions faster than legislatures can respond. Carriers enable or disable features at scale. Browser updates arrive silently in the night. By morning, a billion people follow a new rule, unaware it exists.

There is power in such invisibility. It can shield citizens from surveillance. It can protect credit card holders from fraud. It can enforce safety and interoperability. But invisibility also obscures accountability. When a rule is written in code rather than statute, who watches the watchmakers?

The future of digital sovereignty may hinge not on parliamentary votes, but on which standards the world decides to adopt—and who gets to decide. In that struggle, the most consequential battles will not be fought in grand chambers but in technical working groups and vendor boardrooms. The law is no longer the only source of authority. Soft law has taken its seat at the table, backed by the power of implementation.

And as the world becomes more connected—and more contested—the quiet question grows louder: when a line of code governs lives, who governs the code?

Strategic Ambiguity

A minister stands at a podium and announces that the government "will not tolerate harmful content" online. Reporters ask what counts as harmful. The minister smiles briskly: "Platforms know what we mean." The statement seems straightforward, even responsible. Yet it contains no definitions, no thresholds, no due process. The ambiguity is not accidental. It is a feature, not a flaw.

Strategic ambiguity is an old tool dressed in new code. States have long preserved vagueness in speech laws, assembly permits, and national security doctrines because uncertainty is a form of power. If rules are clear, they constrain the rule-maker. If rules are vague, their meaning can stretch and contract at will. In the digital sphere, this tactic scales beautifully. A single, woolly phrase—*harmful, extremist, destabilising, fake*—can govern millions of posts without ever explaining what the terms entail. Platforms, terrified of penalties or shutdown, read between the lines and act far more harshly than the government explicitly demands.

The dynamic is simple: governments hint; platforms over-comply. Citizens feel the chill, even if no one announced winter. When a law threatens "swift action" against "dangerous misinformation", major platforms do not wait for an official blacklist. They pre-emptively remove borderline material, throttle controversial keywords, or close accounts that might attract scrutiny. Moderators err on the side of caution. Algorithms lean towards suppression. In the absence of clarity, risk aversion becomes policy.

Every platform manager understands the stakes. Losing a licence, failing to renew a spectrum allocation, or being placed under an audit regime can cripple business overnight. Governments need not send armies of censors. They use uncertainty as leverage. A letter from a regulator, a phone call from a ministry, a public reprimand—each can signal the need to tighten content controls. The words are polite. The implications are unmistakable.

Ambiguity is powerful precisely because it is deniable. If civil society complains that satire or dissent has been suppressed, officials shrug and blame the platforms. "We never asked for that," they insist. "They acted on their own." The state retains the chilling effect without the reputational cost of overt censorship. Platforms shoulder the backlash. Users believe the rules are formal, when in fact they are the shadows of threats that never needed to be spoken aloud.

In some cases, ambiguity arises from haste rather than strategy. Legislators rush to respond to moral panics—terrorist attacks, child exploitation scandals, riots—and produce broad mandates without technical specificity. Platforms, fearful of being accused of negligence, interpret these mandates aggressively. Lawyers advise caution. Engineers harden classifiers. Vast swathes of speech narrow without a single prosecution. The chilling effect is not merely top-down; it is internalised.

Yet to dismiss all ambiguity as authoritarian would be misleading. Some ambiguity is productive. Technology evolves faster than statutes. Legislators who try to define every potential harm in advance may lock society into outdated categories. A flexible rule can allow room for interpretation as new threats emerge. It can give regulators time to learn, and platforms time to innovate. Productive ambiguity is purposeful and transparent: the government acknowledges the uncertainty, creates public mechanisms for interpretation, and offers guidance that evolves openly.

Performative ambiguity is different. It treasures the absence of definition because the vacuum grants maximum discretion. In countries where speech is officially protected, but unofficially constrained, ambiguity allows selective enforcement. A journalist is prosecuted for "promoting unrest", while loyal media outlets spout inflammatory rhetoric with impunity. The line never appears in writing. Everyone is expected to know it—and to know that its position may change tomorrow.

Platforms, caught in this fog, often resort to blunt tools. They remove content that mentions keywords associated with trouble. They disable features in certain regions. They restrict livestreaming for minority groups inaccurately flagged as "high risk". Engineers, lacking clear instructions, err towards prohibition. The result is fragile speech: unpredictable, inconsistent, and easily manipulated.

To see the consequences, look at health information during pandemics. Officials urged platforms to curb "harmful misinformation". The definition of "harmful" shifted week by week. In some countries, citizens were punished for criticising shortages; in others, activists found their posts about official negligence algorithmically buried. Platforms could not trust that yesterday's permissible topic would remain safe today. Users learnt to avoid taboo subjects. Honest discussion suffocated under the weight of silence.

Financial platforms face similar dilemmas. Anti-terror rules forbid transactions linked to illicit groups. But when the rules are vague, banks and processors blacklist entire regions or charities rather than risk penalties. Innocent users find accounts frozen without explanation. Customer support staff, themselves in the dark, cite "security concerns". Ambiguity spreads like a stain: undefined threats justify sweeping restrictions.

This chilling effect ripples outward. Journalists self-censor to avoid takedown. Researchers mute sensitive keywords to keep channels open. Citizens assume surveillance where none may exist. The mere possibility of punishment shapes behaviour more effectively than punishment itself. This is the psychology of control: fear of the undefined.

Yet clarity is not always kindness. A brutally specific law can be oppressive. Ambiguity, when wielded with good faith, can protect. Consider data protection regimes that mandate "reasonable security measures". The phrase is deliberately open because technology changes. What counted as reasonable last year is inadequate today. The vagueness compels continuous improvement. Here, ambiguity encourages innovation rather than suppression.

The difference between productive and performative ambiguity lies in process. Productive ambiguity comes with guardrails: published guidance, transparent enforcement statistics, independent oversight, clear appeals. Performative ambiguity arrives with none. It speaks loudly about principles and softly about specifics. It keeps definitions fluid, enforcement opaque, and appeals futile.

A diagnostic test is straightforward. If platforms can ask regulators specific questions and receive documented answers, ambiguity may be productive. If platforms receive smiles, nods, or warnings without records, ambiguity is performative. If civil society can challenge decisions in court, ambiguity can evolve into clarity. If the only court is a back-channel meeting between officials and platform executives, democracy is merely theatre.

States learn that ambiguity is efficient. It requires little bureaucracy, no parliamentary vote, and minimal public scrutiny. The threat of withdrawal—licence, spectrum, payment permissions—is enough to discipline. Platforms, driven by revenue and reputation, tend to out-perform the state's expectations. They do not merely comply; they anticipate. The shadow grows longer.

In some regimes, ambiguity becomes doctrine. Laws reference "state security" or "social harmony" without elaboration. Courts inherit the vagueness and interpret at will. A mural criticising corruption becomes "disruption of civic order". A meme mocking a politician becomes "propaganda for destabilisation". The vagueness is contagious: citizens internalise the message that the boundaries are invisible but dangerous.

Paradoxically, ambiguity also creates markets. Companies sell compliance dashboards, automated filters, classifier tuning, and legal risk assessments. Start-ups promise "harm detection" services that flag content based on murky criteria. Private firms monetise uncertainty by turning fear into features. The line between safety and censorship blurs.

And what of users? Some take comfort in platforms scrubbing away hatred and fraud. Others see political speech vanish under the same algorithms. Communities at the margins—activists, dissidents, minority groups—feel the chill first. When their words are flagged as "risky", they learn to speak in coded language. The digital public square becomes a pantomime of euphemisms.

Strategic ambiguity will not disappear. Humans have always governed partly through uncertainty. But digital ambiguity is sharper. Its reach is instantaneous. Its enforcers are algorithms tuned to err on the side of silence. Its victims rarely know which rule they violated—and often, there is no rule at all.

The question is not whether ambiguity exists, but how societies keep it accountable. Could transparency dashboards force governments to clarify requests? Could independent auditors review takedown orders and publish reports? Could courts demand that regulators issue written guidance rather than whisper threats? Could platforms resist the impulse to over-comply by insisting on due process?

If ambiguity is a weapon, clarity is a shield. But clarity carries its own risks: ossification, loopholes, procedural capture. Democracies must decide how much uncertainty they can tolerate without eroding public trust. Authoritarians already know the answer: they will keep ambiguity as long as it chills more than it reveals.

As digital borders harden, strategic ambiguity becomes a quiet currency of control. It thrives in the gaps between law and practice, between policy and implementation, between what is said and what is meant. And as long as platforms fear the worst interpretation, they will behave accordingly.

Perhaps the final question is the most unsettling: when silence becomes safer than speech, how long before citizens forget what genuine freedom sounds like?

Chapter 3

Firewalls, Filters, and Fragmentation

One evening, a journalist in a major capital opens a video stream from across the border. The protest is live. People are chanting; sirens cut through the noise; a citizen lifts a camera to the sky to show helicopters circling. Then, without warning, the stream turns into a mosaic of frozen pixels. A buffering wheel spins. The chat disconnects. Minutes later, the app insists the video "may be unavailable in your region." Hours after that, the stream remains intact for viewers elsewhere—but in this particular country, only an error message appears. Nothing dramatic has happened on the surface. Streets look the same. Borders remain where they were yesterday. Yet something quiet and decisive has shifted. A wall has risen without a single brick.

This is the world of digital perimeters: not the iron curtain or the guarded checkpoint, but the invisible infrastructure that decides which signals pass and which suffocate. To the untrained eye, a network seems borderless, a fluid mesh indifferent to geography. In reality, the digital world is patched and partitioned with a precision that would make nineteenth-century mapmakers envy its subtlety. Nations can throttle, reroute, intercept, or drown traffic with clinical finesse. They do not always need to ban a platform; it is often enough to make it useless.

And yet, the most striking twist is that these controls rarely appear as monolithic blocks, despite headlines that speak of "national firewalls" as if they were massive concrete dams. Some are policy stacks layered in software, hardware, contractual terms, and commercial incentives. Some are surgical—slowing a specific protocol during elections, degrading video quality around sensitive anniversaries, keeping images grainy while text remains crisp. Others are blunt and brutal, cutting entire networks from the global web in one sweep. The architecture varies, but the effect is uniformly clear: power has migrated from border guards with guns to routers with rules.

The modern firewall is not merely a technical artefact. It is a policy instrument, a diplomatic bargaining chip, a domestic tool of narrative control. Its existence raises uncomfortable questions. Where exactly is the border? At the undersea cable landing? At a state-owned telecom? At the terms of service written by an American company complying with a foreign demand? Does a teenager in one country have the same internet as a teenager in a neighbouring state? The map suggests yes; the network answers no.

These contradictions are not abstract. They dictate how citizens learn about public crises, how diasporas communicate with family, how businesses operate across borders, and how governments preserve authority. The internet once promised frictionless flows; now friction is a dial that states can turn up or down depending on circumstance. To understand this world, one must set aside the fantasy of a single global network and see instead a patchwork of sovereignties layered atop the same cables.

National perimeters are the most visible manifestation of this shift. Some countries build centralised filtering gateways; others distribute control across regional carriers. Some target specific platforms, while others treat protocols themselves as suspicious. A protest may trigger a slowdown of livestreaming traffic, even as ordinary browsing continues. The goal is plausible deniability: officials can claim that "technical difficulties" are to blame while everyone understands the message. Unlike an outright ban, a throttle leaves less evidence and invites fewer headlines.

Platform-layer borders are subtler still. Companies deploy geo-fencing to customise content region by region. A feature appears in one country but remains locked in another; a news feed that promotes local sources in one market sidelines them elsewhere. Sometimes this reflects legal requirements. Sometimes it reflects commercial strategy. A livestreaming tool might be restricted in a region with strict speech laws; monetisation might be disabled for creators outside approved jurisdictions. To the user, these distinctions feel like technical quirks. In truth, they are borders drawn by code.

To grasp their significance, consider the diaspora member trying to send money home. One app works in London but not in Lagos. Another works in Lagos but cannot receive transfers from Berlin. On maps, the distance is measured in kilometres. On networks, the distance is measured in licences, partnerships, and compliance checklists. Geography is not abolished; it has migrated into configuration files.

Inspection at scale turns the internet's openness into something conditional. Traffic classification began as a benign engineering practice—optimising congestion, prioritising essential services—but it has become a lever of control. An IP address can be blocked; a keyword can trigger review; a waveform can be analysed to recognise a particular type of video. Machine learning promises efficiency, yet it also codifies bias and error. False positives creep in. Activists find their channels flagged as "spam." Journalists see uploads vanish because an automated system misreads context. Users appeal, but the decisions feel opaque and arbitrary, as though the border guards are made of protocol rather than policy.

When blocking looks too harsh, slowing does the job. The throttle is the quiet instrument of digital governance. It works because frustration, not censorship, does the silencing. A video that refuses to load may as well not exist. A call that constantly drops becomes impossible. A livestream that lags is a livestream no one watches. Governments can deny responsibility. Platforms can blame congestion or maintenance. Meanwhile, a nation's information environment becomes calmer, tidier, more predictable. The invisible hand is not invisible at all. It simply leaves no fingerprints.

Where borders tighten, citizens search for cracks. VPNs, mirrors, proxies, and diaspora relays form counter-perimeters. They are not romantic acts of digital rebellion. They are often tedious, fragile, and risky. VPNs slow traffic and require technical literacy. Mirrors are taken down quickly. Relays rely on volunteers or sympathetic organisations abroad. The cat-and-mouse dynamic is relentless: each workaround spawns a countermeasure, and users are whiplashed between fleeting access and abrupt denial.

What matters is not merely the technology, but the experience of living with these constraints. People learn to mistrust the feed. They double-save documents. They exchange instructions in coded language. The public sphere becomes a nervous space in which nothing is guaranteed: not speed, not accuracy, not reach. Citizens internalise the possibility that the network may fail at the moment it matters. The psychological border is as powerful as the technical one.

This fragmentation has geopolitical consequences. When states carve their own perimeters, global platforms splinter into regional variants. A creator who earns a living from online audiences finds that monetisation is barred in certain countries. A scientist trying to share data discovers that file transfers stall across borders. A software developer realises that an open-source library is blocked because a classifier labelled it dangerous. These are not dramatic events, but chronic irritations—death by a thousand throttles.

And yet, the picture is not purely grim. In some contexts, controlled access serves legitimate aims: shielding critical infrastructure from attack, protecting citizens from mass scams, defending hospitals from ransomware. Firewalls can be instruments of resilience as well as repression. The trouble begins when states refuse transparency. Citizens have no way to distinguish between protection and suppression. Platforms guess. Rumours fill the void. Trust erodes.

The central tension of this chapter is simple: the internet's architecture enables freedom, yet the same architecture enables control. Firewalls can protect a nation's hospitals or silence its protestors. Geo-fencing can localise services or cage dissent. Traffic inspection can filter malware or muzzle journalists. Every tool is dual-use. What changes is intention—and intentions are not encoded in protocols, but in politics.

As networks fragment, the language of sovereignty returns with unexpected force. The border officer now sits in a data centre. The checkpoint is a software rule. Instead of stamping passports, the system checks certificates. Instead of inspecting luggage, it inspects packets. Instead of denying entry to people, it denies entry to ideas. The metaphor is not metaphorical. It is structural.

The reader should not leave this introduction believing that all borders are malicious, nor that all workarounds are noble. The truth is uneven. States are wrestling with real security threats. Platforms are struggling with real incentives. Citizens are caught in the middle, improvising futures that depend on flickering connections.

What matters is that we abandon the myth of a singular, open internet and confront the one we have: a network in which access is conditional; a commons routinely fenced and unfenced; a public square that can be throttled into quiet compliance. The story of firewalls and filters is not merely technical. It is social, political, psychological. It is the story of how power relocates into ducts and packets without announcing itself.

The next pages will move from the abstract to the concrete: why perimeters rarely look like the caricatures we imagine; how platforms draw invisible customs lines through feeds and features; how modern inspection operates at planetary scale; why slowing traffic can reshape perception more effectively than banning; and how citizens build their own escape routes, however fragile, in response.

Some readers may find the details unsettling. Others may consider them overdue adaptations to a dangerous world. Both perspectives are valid. What unites them is a recognition that the internet is no longer a place where borders disappeared. Instead, borders have multiplied—and they are learning to whisper.

National Perimeters

Late one night, residents of a coastal city notice that live video streams have turned to sludge. Messages still send, but voice calls crackle, and anything with motion refuses to load. Foreign news sites are sluggish. Domestic portals are fine. There is no announcement, no warning, no law to point to. The network still exists, yet the world beyond its borders feels impossibly far away. Most citizens shrug and blame congestion. A smaller group knows the timing is no coincidence: a protest has begun to spread, and somewhere deep in the country's internet backbone, a dial has been turned.

This is the texture of a national perimeter in the twenty-first century—subtle, layered, and engineered to avoid spectacle. Forget the caricature of a single "Great Firewall" guarded by dour technicians. Modern states build borders like palimpsests. Some layers are legal, some contractual, some buried in fibre routers or in quiet agreements with foreign platforms. A citizen sees inconvenience, not censorship. A politician sees stability without headlines. A telecom engineer sees a routing policy that can be switched off as quietly as it was enabled.

The idea of a digital border once seemed absurd. The internet was conceived as a network of networks—messy, decentralised, impossible to seize in one grip. That mythology lingers in popular imagination, as though connectivity floats in the sky, impervious to politics. But state power has followed the cables, the data centres, the exchange points. What was once a borderless frontier has become a landscape of pressure points and policy levers. The nation-state, long predicted to fade, has instead learned to govern the network with astonishing finesse.

The first misconception worth dismantling is that a national firewall resembles a concrete wall. In reality, it is a stack: routing rules at telecom gateways, DNS manipulation, deep packet inspection, contractual restrictions on foreign platforms, and sometimes simple intimidation of local carriers. The sophistication varies, but the logic is consistent. Instead of banning a platform outright, a government may order all major carriers to block a handful of DNS entries. Websites vanish without ceremony. Users assume the sites are broken. The state remains politely invisible.

Other interventions are almost surgical. A protocol used by secure messaging apps can be throttled until it times out. The service becomes unreliable, even though no formal ban is in place. During periods of unrest, livestreaming may stutter into uselessness while other content loads just fine. The message is indirect: protest will be tolerated as long as nobody can see it.

Routing controls, once the domain of engineers optimising traffic, have become instruments of sovereignty. Domestic internet exchange points can be engineered to route local traffic internally, ensuring that most communication never leaves the country. It is efficient, but it also means that authorities can isolate the domestic network if necessary. A crisis arrives; an order is issued; the international gateway tightens. Banks continue operating. Government websites stay up. But foreign media, cloud services, and messaging apps flicker and fail. Citizens experience something rare in the digital age: informational isolation in real time.

Some countries prefer precision. Rather than shutting down the network, they block specific services: social platforms during elections, encrypted messengers during protests, or even cloud hosts associated with dissident organising. Others prefer broad strokes: the wholesale removal of foreign news sites, VPN providers, or privacy tools. Each choice reflects a political calculus. Blanket bans provoke backlash. Targeted throttling is quieter, harder to document, easier to deny.

Every national perimeter contains this delicate balance: suppress enough to shape narratives, but not so much that commerce or daily life grinds to a halt. Most governments do not want total isolation. They want control. And control is easier to maintain when the boundaries are blurry. A protest movement believes the world is watching, until the signal degrades. Activists encourage citizens to tune in, only to discover that video quality has dropped to a slideshow. The protest is still happening; only the audience has been dispersed.

Consider the irony: in many places, the most oppressive borders are not the ones that block. They are the ones that slow. A website that takes sixty seconds to load might as well be down. A messaging app that delays photos makes coordination clumsy. A livestream that freezes every few seconds deters viewers. Citizens cannot easily tell whether the problem is deliberate interference or bad infrastructure. That ambiguity protects the state. A regime can insist it would never censor its people, while quietly murdering bandwidth in the background.

These borders are policy disguised as accidents. A misconfigured route here, a "maintenance window" there, a cloud provider facing "technical difficulties" just as police prepare to clear a square. In some countries, journalists collect these events like meteorologists tracking storms: timestamps, traceroutes, packet loss. The evidence rarely satisfies legal thresholds, but the pattern becomes unmistakable. Politics spills into the network not with a roar, but with a whisper.

Even countries that champion open internet norms have built digital perimeters. Some do it to defend critical infrastructure; others to block foreign propaganda; others because a foreign platform refuses to comply with tax, privacy, or data localisation laws. States that once scoffed at network control find themselves nudging traffic through domestic gateways, building regulatory checkpoints, demanding the ability to "lawfully intercept" certain communications. The narrative rarely invokes censorship. It speaks instead of security, sovereignty, and public interest.

There is a danger in assuming that national perimeters represent a single ideological project. They vary dramatically. One country uses them to silence dissent. Another uses them to filter spam and malware. A third uses them to pressure global platforms into paying fair taxes. Citizens experience the symptoms—sites unavailable, services restricted—but rarely see the cause. And because explanations are sparse, users speculate. Some blame foreign hackers; others blame government censors; still others blame corporate greed. The opacity corrodes trust.

Beneath the politics lies a practical truth: the physical internet has choke-points. Undersea cable landings, exchange points, state-owned carriers, licensing regimes for ISPs—each is a hinge where policy can become force. A country may have thousands of ISPs, but if all international traffic passes through a handful of gateways, those gateways become de facto border crossings. A single command can turn a bustling digital city into a quiet provincial town.

What makes these borders newly potent is their integration with commercial platforms. A social network may be asked to remove content in one jurisdiction. If it refuses, the state can threaten to restrict connectivity, throttle mobile data, or suspend the platform's local operations licence.

Most companies capitulate. A request becomes policy; policy becomes a filter; the filter becomes a fact on the ground. Citizens assume the silence is organic.

Of course, national perimeters generate counter-perimeters. VPNs flourish. Proxies proliferate. Diaspora communities set up mirror sites. For every government tightening the net, there are thousands of citizens learning to slip through it. But the cat-and-mouse game is not symmetrical. States can devote entire ministries to blocking tools; ordinary people have jobs, children, limited patience. Circumvention becomes a hobby for the technically confident, while most citizens retreat to whatever remains accessible.

The socioeconomic consequences are stark. When governments block key cloud services, small businesses suffer. When messaging apps fail, families abroad lose contact. When video platforms degrade, creators lose income. National perimeters reshape the digital economy in ways that rarely appear in policy debates. A freelancer in Cairo or Karachi may find that clients in Europe cannot access her portfolio. A developer in Nairobi may discover that an essential coding library is blocked because it sits on a domain flagged for unrelated content. A medical researcher in Buenos Aires may lose access to datasets hosted on servers caught in a geopolitical dispute.

The emotional toll is quieter but no less real. People raised on an open network feel the constriction in their daily routines. News becomes fragmented. Conversations become cautious. The internet no longer feels like a window to the world, but a window with bars. Some adapt. Others lose faith in the idea of a shared digital commons.

What happens next depends on choices that are rarely made in public. Some democracies are tempted by the efficiency of control—why bother with messy public debate when throttling a protocol is quicker? Some authoritarian states experiment with partial openness, allowing just enough global access to fuel entrepreneurship while choking off dissent. The perimeters expand, contract, and adjust according to threat perception, economic need, and political mood.

The most unsettling question is not whether national perimeters exist—they do—but how many of them are mislabelled as "technical issues." Citizens cannot challenge what they cannot see. Oversight collapses when policies are invisible. The line between resilience and repression becomes dangerously thin.

Yet there are sparks of accountability. Network measurement groups monitor outages and throttling with forensic precision. Journalists document patterns. Activists create decentralised backup channels. A growing number of courts insist that if a service is to be blocked, the order must be written and justified. These efforts do not dismantle borders, but they demand honesty about them.

What is clear is that the idea of an unbroken global internet is fading. In its place, we see a mosaic of national networks—interconnected but conditional, open but only on certain terms. The borders of the digital world are not drawn on maps. They sit in routers, licences, legal demands, and throttled streams.

And somewhere, on another night of unrest, a family opens a livestream and sees the world freeze into pixels again. The city outside their window has not changed. But the border has shifted—with a keystroke, a policy, a momentary twist of the dial. The only question left is how many citizens will notice that the horizon has moved, and how many will quietly acclimate to the narrowing view.

Platform-Layer Borders

A young filmmaker in Lagos uploads a short political documentary to a global video platform. Her analytics show viewers in London, Toronto, and Johannesburg—but not in the very city where she filmed. Locals searching for the title see only music videos and cooking clips. The documentary is not removed; it is simply unshown. No government claims responsibility, and the platform never offers an explanation. The border is invisible, yet absolute. A geo-fence, placed silently in an algorithmic corridor, has done what customs agents once did at airports: decide who may see what, and where.

The average user assumes that their "feed" is the same as everyone else's—a shared window into a global commons. The truth is more fragmented. Platforms carve the world into thousands of micro-jurisdictions, shaping experience by geography without ever invoking the word censorship. A creator in Berlin earns revenue from a video viewed in Paris but not from views in Doha. A song is available in Madrid but muted in Mexico City. Two users set their phones side-by-side and scroll, yet watch entirely different realities unfurl. The border is not at the base of a fibre cable but inside the software that curates, ranks, and pays.

Geo-fencing is often sold as a mundane engineering feature: compliance with licensing deals, protection of local advertisers, or tailored cultural relevance. These explanations are not false, but they are incomplete. Behind every location check sits a decision—whether by legislators, regulators, or companies—to draw lines through digital space. Those lines determine commerce, art, public speech, and sometimes democratic contestation. A creator who depends on viewer revenue may discover that her own region has been quietly excluded from monetisation. The platform makes no grand announcement; a toggle in an internal dashboard is enough to redraw the map of her livelihood.

What makes platform-layer borders so powerful is their dual nature. Sometimes they are acts of compulsion: a government demands that certain content be hidden from domestic viewers, and the platform obliges rather than lose its operating licence. Other times they are acts of business segmentation: a platform may launch new features only in wealthy markets, or restrict payout systems to countries with robust financial infrastructure. To the citizen, the reasons are opaque. All they see is whether a button exists or does not exist; whether the feature is "coming soon" or permanently absent.

Consider the way streaming services handle catalogues. A film available in Stockholm may vanish when a traveller lands in Cairo, not because Egypt has banned it, but because rights were negotiated country by country. The border is contractual, not ideological. Yet the effect is the same: geography dictates access. When politics, culture, and commerce collide, the line between compliance and choice blurs. A government insists on removal of satirical cartoons; the platform evaluates the business risk; the cartoons disappear—locally at first, then globally to avoid ambiguity. The company insists it is following the law. Critics accuse it of submission. Somewhere in between lies the quiet truth: the border moved because it was cheaper to move it than to fight.

Platforms learned an uncomfortable lesson during the last decade: operating everywhere means obeying everywhere—or at least appearing to. Local regulators demand that companies appoint in-country representatives empowered to receive takedown requests. Some demand that user data be stored domestically. Others require that content decisions be handled by staff subject to national laws. When faced with these pressures, platforms do not simply comply; they re-architect their services. They separate databases. They introduce country-specific terms of service. They build region-tuned algorithms engineered to show less of what might provoke local scrutiny. The code itself becomes diplomatic.

This shift from one global service to many quasi-national services is rarely acknowledged publicly, because it clashes with the mythology of the borderless web. Companies still promote a narrative of universal connection: a single community, a shared digital town square. But engineers know better. Under the hood, the town square is zoned, fenced, and subdivided. A user in Delhi sees a recommendation feed weighted toward domestic content by policy and profit. A user in Dublin sees something entirely different. In theory, this respects local culture. In practice, it can quarantine creativity, isolate dissent, and reinforce national silos.

Feature flags make this even more granular. A platform can activate a tool for 0.5% of users in Seoul, restrict live-video sharing in Jakarta, or roll out encrypted messaging only in countries where regulation permits. These changes are reversible with a keystroke. A journalist investigating election interference finds she cannot livestream from protests. A civil rights group realises that visibility has dropped precisely when it matters most. The platform swears no content was removed. *Technically*, that might be true; the feature controlling dissemination has simply been disabled. The border has shifted from a blunt ban to a silent toggle.

The philosophical challenge is that platform-layer borders can be justified in ways that sound entirely reasonable. A country has legitimate interests in protecting children from exploitation. A platform has legitimate interests in avoiding criminal liability. A publisher may choose to licence music only in specific regions. Each individual justification is defensible. The aggregate result is a world where access to knowledge, art, and politics depends not on citizenship, but on IP addresses and device settings.

The most striking cases emerge when platforms redraw borders overnight. A messaging service that once allowed secure channels across the Middle East suddenly blocks cross-border group creation. Officially, this is to prevent spam. Unofficially, it disrupts diaspora activism that relied on cross-border organisation. A video platform introduces monetisation for short clips but restricts payouts in countries deemed "high-risk" for fraud. Millions of creators discover that their work is encouraged but not rewarded. A social network facing a legal threat from a foreign regulator begins auto-blocking posts about a domestic court case—but only for users in that regulator's jurisdiction. Everyone else sees the story unfold. Citizens inside the border do not.

None of this requires government censorship. Platforms build borders because the world has handed them incentives to do so. A company threatened with fines complies to protect shareholders. A company seeking expansion in a new market pre-emptively hides controversial content. A company facing payment fraud disables monetisation in entire regions rather than refine detection systems. The result is a kind of algorithmic triage: some populations are profitable; others are tolerated; a few are quietly walled off.

At the same time, there are genuine benefits to localisation. Language support, cultural relevance, and regionally appropriate safety policies are essential for a diverse digital world. A blanket global feed dominated by wealthy English-speaking markets would not be liberation; it would be colonialism in another form. The tension lies in distinguishing cultural adaptation from political containment. A platform offering Hindi-language tools empowers creators. A platform suppressing political cartoons in Hindi to avoid scrutiny disempowers them. The surface behaviour—different feeds, different features—looks identical. Only intent distinguishes one from the other, and intent is rarely disclosed.

Users respond in creative ways. VPNs help bypass geo-fences. Creators upload content through foreign proxies. Diaspora communities mirror banned videos on global platforms. But these tactics remain fragile. Platforms can detect and limit VPN traffic. Governments can threaten local employees, forcing companies to harden compliance. The user must decide whether the risk of evasion is worth the reward of access. Most choose the safer path: silence, or self-censorship.

Platform-layer borders are especially potent because they intervene at the level of suggestion. A state firewall tells you something is forbidden. A platform geo-fence hides the forbidden thing so effectively that you might never know it exists. Borderless ambition becomes bordered reality, without a single visible checkpoint.

Even commercial segmentation has civic consequences. When monetisation is enabled only for creators in certain markets, inequalities deepen. A YouTuber in Manila may produce work as exceptional as one in Munich, yet struggle to earn a living. The barrier is not creativity; it is eligibility. A writer in Nairobi builds an audience of millions, yet cannot access the same subscription tools as a peer in New York. Global platforms speak of "community," but their business models distribute privileges unevenly across the map.

Could platforms resist? Occasionally they do. A company may refuse takedown orders and accept temporary blocking. Another may withdraw from a market entirely. But withdrawal punishes citizens who relied on the service. The moral victory is cold comfort to those who lose a lifeline to news, income, and connection. In most cases, platforms negotiate. They geo-block a handful of posts. They restrict a feature. They comply with data localisation in exchange for market access. Incremental concessions accumulate. A platform that once championed openness becomes a patchwork of regional compromises.

Citizens are left in a landscape where borders are mobile, conditional, and often invisible. The freedom once promised by the early internet has not vanished; it has been partitioned. In one country, a digital artist sells prints through platform-integrated payment tools. Across a nearby border, the same tools are disabled, and the artist resorts to informal channels. In one city, activists organise livestreamed debates. In another, live video flickers off, replaced by grainy clips that cannot mobilise momentum.

The uncomfortable reality is that platform-layer borders often feel less oppressive than state firewalls, yet their effects are just as profound. They turn global platforms into quasi-state actors, with diplomatic responsibilities they never sought and cultural consequences they rarely acknowledge. Their borders are drawn not on maps but in code.

What remains unanswered is whether these borders will ever be made transparent. If a feature is disabled in Nairobi, should citizens know why? If a video is invisible in Riyadh but watchable in Rome, should the platform disclose the order that caused it? At present, opacity prevails. Users are not told; regulators are not challenged; the status quo drifts toward fragmentation by default.

Some imagine that decentralised technologies will dissolve these barriers—content stored across peer-to-peer networks, uncensorable by design. Yet even decentralisation confronts practical realities: app stores can block clients, mobile networks can restrict protocols, and payment systems can choke the economic lifelines of creators. The border simply relocates: from platform to app store, from app store to payment processor, from payment processor to bank.

And so the paradox stands: the digital world that promised global connection has instead produced borders of exquisite granularity. A platform can permit a protest video in Bangkok but hide it in Phnom Penh. It can pay a podcaster in Oslo but not in Harare. It can enable women's rights campaigns in Paris and disable them in Riyadh. The borders are drawn automatically, algorithmically, and often in silence.

The question is not whether platform-layer borders exist—they do. The question is what happens when citizens realise that the borders shaping their digital lives are not written in law, debated in parliament, or voted upon in public. They are written in recommendation models, payment policies, and quiet geo-fences. If sovereignty has shifted from territory to network, then power has shifted from states to platforms—unless states intervene to reclaim it.

Somewhere in Lagos, the filmmaker checks her analytics again. Exports thrive; domestic views remain frozen. Her film travels everywhere except home. She knows now that borders did not disappear in the digital age. They multiplied, learned to hide, and set up residence in the code she must pass through to speak.

Inspection at Scale

On a winter evening, a university student in Minsk tries to load a livestream of a peaceful rally. The page hangs, then fails. His friend in Warsaw watches the same stream without difficulty and wonders why he switched it off. The student did not. Something in the network recognised the traffic, classified it, and quietly dropped the packets. Nothing so crass as a public blocklist banner appeared. No law was invoked. The gateway simply decided this flow belonged to a category it did not intend to carry. Borders, once visible as fences and gates, now operate as classifiers.

Traffic inspection began as a practical engineering task. A network needed to distinguish video from voice, spam from mail, malware from routine downloads. To keep a system running, one must know what is flowing through it. Yet classification has crept from maintenance into governance. Once a network can tell which packets are video calls and which are encrypted messages, it can prioritise, delay, or discard with surgical precision. The crude sledgehammer of nationwide blocking—shutting off entire platforms—has given way to scalpels that slice through specific protocols, domains, or file signatures, often without users ever knowing what was cut.

The simplest border is an IP block. A government demands that a particular address be unreachable; routers obey. From the user's perspective, the site "just doesn't work today." It feels like a glitch. It might be temporary. The ambiguity is a feature, not a bug. IP blocks are cheap, fast, and blunt.

They are also easy to bypass: services rotate addresses, users install VPNs, engineers tunnel through other ports. Like customs agents who learn that smugglers have built new paths through the hills, network operators escalate. They move from blocking the door to watching the crowd.

Thus came packet inspection: looking not only at where traffic is going, but what it seems to contain. A packet's header shows origin and destination; its payload reveals hints of purpose. Is this a video stream? A torrent? A secure call? In the early days, "deep packet inspection" sounded sinister, but to engineers it was largely mundane—spam filtering, intrusion detection, quality-of-service tuning. Over time, however, the tools matured. They learned to recognise encrypted protocols, to infer meaning from patterns rather than visible text, to segment users by behaviour.

Imagine a customs office where officers no longer open every suitcase. Instead, they run them through scanners that detect density, shapes, anomalies—automated suspicion. Most bags pass through untouched. A few are diverted to inspection. The travellers never know what triggered the intervention: size, weight, a faint outline of something that resembled contraband. At network scale, the same logic prevails. Most packets fly; a small percentage is delayed, dropped, or reshaped. The public sees only that some services feel slow or unreliable, especially at sensitive moments.

Inspections become especially powerful when paired with machine learning. Rather than static rules ("block this domain"), algorithms classify traffic by patterns: how quickly packets arrive, how often they retransmit, how the encrypted handshake looks. Encrypted messaging platforms once boasted that their traffic was indistinguishable from ordinary HTTPS. Then classifiers learned to recognise the characteristic fingerprints—subtle timing, packet size distributions, connection bursts. The border moved again: from content to behaviour.

False positives are an unavoidable by-product. A teenager gaming late at night discovers her connection collapses every time she joins a voice channel; the classifier mistakes her app for a banned VoIP service. A hospital's telemedicine software buffers endlessly during a political crisis because it shares network characteristics with livestream tools that authorities are throttling. The network does not hate hospitals or teenagers. It simply cannot tell the difference.

False positives expose the deeper truth: classification is guesswork at scale. The more sensitive the policy, the more likely innocent traffic will be caught in the net. Operators face an uncomfortable trade-off. Too strict, and ordinary life breaks—business meetings, online schooling, medical consultations. Too lenient, and targeted content slips through. Some countries err on the side of aggression, especially during unrest. The collateral damage becomes part of the deterrent. If using a messaging platform is unreliable, fewer people will try.

Adversaries respond with their own tactics. Activists disguise livestream traffic as innocuous file downloads. VPN operators pad packet sizes to mimic web browsing. Some messaging apps fragment packets into unpredictable patterns or shuffle ports ceaselessly, forcing classifiers to work harder. The dynamic resembles cryptography: defenders build systems, attackers probe weaknesses, defenders patch, attackers innovate. Every upgrade in inspection triggers an upgrade in evasion.

This arms race is not always political. Commercial platforms also inspect traffic to enforce terms; streaming services block VPNs to honour regional licences. A user pays for a subscription in one country, travels to another, and finds content inaccessible. The classifier senses a VPN and rejects the request. The user blames the platform, but the platform is often obeying a contract. In this sense, inspection enforces both law and commerce. The border becomes multi-tenant—shared by governments, corporations, and intellectual property holders.

The paradox is that nobody admits to running a border. Regulators talk of "network security." Platforms talk of "protecting rights." Operators talk of "quality of service." Yet each classification decision is implicitly distributive: who gets full speed, who gets narrowed pipes, who gets blocked outright. In authoritarian contexts, classification is a tool of control. In democracies, it is sometimes justified as harm prevention—slowing disinformation, restricting illegal material, filtering scams. The tension lies in opacity. Without transparency, citizens cannot distinguish protection from suppression.

To grasp the scale, imagine moderating speech not at the post level but at the packet level. A social network may remove harmful videos after review. A state firewall may never let those videos arrive. The social network apologises if it makes a mistake; the firewall never speaks. Machine learning models decide, silently, that certain flows look suspicious. The citizen is left with a spinning wheel, a broken image, or a vague error message. Borders that speak are easier to contest. Borders that fail silently are harder to map.

Some governments defend inspection as a necessary security measure. They argue that criminals exploit encryption; that hostile states spread disinformation; that unrest can spiral into violence if live coordination tools go unchecked. But the same mechanisms that throttle rumours can throttle dissent. A system calibrated for stability drifts toward managed speech. A classifier designed to catch dangerous propaganda might flag satire or critical journalism. After all, satire and propaganda share certain shapes: rapid sharing, sharp spikes in traffic, strong emotional reactions. The algorithm does not know motives.

One of the most revealing episodes came when a popular video platform experienced "technical difficulties" during a wave of protests in South Asia. Videos uploaded from the affected region encoded normally but failed to distribute. Creators suspected censorship. The company blamed "capacity issues." Independent researchers analysed traceroutes and detected selective slowdown of traffic with signatures matching certain file formats. The block was not total; it was just slow enough to make high-quality video pointless. For viewers, the experience was simply: it doesn't play. For the state, it was plausible deniability.

Throttling rather than banning introduces a new genre of control. If users cannot prove intentional interference, authorities escape scrutiny. Network operators can claim congestion, maintenance, or malicious traffic spikes. During elections or crises, such explanations become politically convenient. A border that murmurs technical excuses is safer for its architects than a border that declares intention.

Machine learning models add another layer of indirection. Once classification is outsourced to an adaptive system, accountability blurs. A minister may not have ordered suppression; a network engineer may not have written a blocking rule. The model simply "learned" to treat politically volatile content as risky because prior data suggested such content triggered scrutiny. In this way, power diffuses into infrastructure. Censorship ceases to feel like an act of will. It becomes statistical.

Yet inspection is not omnipotent. Determined communities find seams. Diaspora groups host mirror sites abroad. Technologists route files through decentralised storage. Messaging apps implement "domain fronting," hiding traffic within cloud providers that governments dare not block. For a time, such techniques succeed. But classifiers evolve. They learn new fingerprints. The cat catches up to the mouse.

The most intriguing conflicts occur when classifiers collide: platform moderation models versus state firewalls. A government might block encrypted traffic; the platform might encrypt more aggressively. A government might throttle video; activists might compress streams. Each iteration nudges the balance. Citizens become infrastructural tacticians, experimenting with proxies, browsers, and alternate DNS resolvers. Ordinary people gain the instincts of smugglers.

Not all inspection is malign. Spam filters, malware scanners, and child protection systems are indispensable. A world without them would be chaotic and dangerous. But the same systems that protect can also suppress. The difference lies in governance. Do citizens know what is blocked, why, and by whom? Can they appeal? Can independent auditors inspect the inspectors? In many countries, the answer is no. The inspection system is treated as a security asset, beyond public scrutiny.

Even well-intentioned systems face dilemmas. Social networks deploy machine learning moderation to detect hate speech, violence, extremism. They must act quickly: millions of posts per hour, thousands of languages, countless cultural nuances. The models make mistakes. Sarcasm becomes hate; activism becomes extremism; minority languages are misclassified as noise. The border between harm prevention and silencing marginalised voices becomes thin. For users, errors feel personal, not statistical.

What makes inspection at scale so influential is its invisibility. Borders used to be theatrical—stamped passports, armed guards, great steel fences. Now the checkpoint is a classifier buried in a data centre. It never raises its voice. It never explains itself. One click loads, another stalls. Some countries receive information unfiltered, others receive it delayed, and others receive only fragments. People adapt to the silent seams without realising they have adapted.

If there is a lesson, it is that digital borders do not announce themselves. They are inferred from experience: a broken stream, a muted video, a missing message. Citizens learn to sense the border the way villagers once sensed changing winds. But a digital wind is harder to chart.

Can transparency fix this? Possibly. Platforms could disclose when content is throttled or geo-blocked. Governments could publish technical orders. Carriers could log interventions. Some democracies have begun to consider these rules, worried about invisible constraints on speech. But technical transparency is complex. If censors reveal their signals, adversaries will evade them. If auditors demand full access, operators will resist. The border thrives on opacity.

Some engineers argue for encryption everywhere, padding everywhere, traffic shaped to look uniformly bland. If all packets appear identical, classifiers lose their leverage. But ubiquitous encryption also shields criminals and creates tensions with law enforcement. The debate mirrors a centuries-old struggle: privacy versus security, liberty versus order. Technology merely accelerates it.

Meanwhile, inspection grows more sophisticated. Machine learning models learn to anticipate evasion. They spot anomalies in timing, jitter, and packet bursts. They suspect flows that zigzag across proxies or bounce through VPNs. The classifier becomes a hunter. Users become prey. Until users become hunters again.

If physical borders once defined where power began and ended, digital inspection defines who may speak, organise, and participate. It decides whether a protest can gather momentum or whether it dissolves in lag and buffering. It decides whether a journalist's file uploads in seconds or hours. It decides whether a diaspora can share news back home or whether the link arrives broken.

None of this looks like censorship in the cinematic sense. There are no bonfires of banned books, no screens filled with ominous warnings. There is only the quiet choreography of packets—some prioritised, some delayed, some never delivered.

And so a final question lingers: if a border operates silently, is it any less a border? If an algorithm, not a guard, decides who crosses, does accountability evaporate? As inspection systems deepen, citizens may find that the frontier of digital freedom is not where lines are drawn on maps, but where patterns are decoded in traffic. The next battles over speech and sovereignty will be waged not in courts or parliaments, but in classifiers whose logic is hidden from public view.

Who, then, inspects the inspectors?

The Throttle as Policy

The livestream never stops. It merely shrinks. One moment the protesters' chants sound crisp and close; the next, the image softens into a pixelated smear and the sound dissolves into static. The comments beneath the video fill with confusion—why has the feed dropped to sludge? Viewers blame the uploader, the platform, the weather, anything but the state. Yet the slowdown is not an accident. It is a choice, and a very deliberate one:

keep the service nominally available, but make it effectively useless. A ban shouts; a throttle whispers. Its power lies in the whisper.

Over the past decade, governments and network operators have learned that outright blocking is crude, conspicuous, and often counterproductive. Shut down a platform, and headlines scream censorship; protesters gain new momentum; international observers take notice. Throttling, however, inhabits the grey zone. Speeds fall, videos buffer, calls drop. Nothing is technically "banned." The infrastructure remains online; only the experience is dulled. The state presents clean hands. Perhaps there is congestion. Perhaps a fibre cut. Perhaps malicious traffic. Who can say?

Throttling is a dark art of signal management. Instead of building walls, authorities slow the road. They target specific protocols—video streaming, secure calls, messaging apps—or particular destinations. They dial back throughput, introduce jitter, or downgrade video quality. For the user, frustration replaces outrage. Instead of the galvanising clarity of a ban, there is only the grinding fatigue of an unreliable network.

Political optics explain part of the appeal. A government that blocks a platform must defend that decision publicly. Parliamentarians ask questions; journalists investigate; watchdogs analyse logs. But if a service simply becomes sluggish, officials can express sympathy. "We are aware of intermittent issues and are working with our telecom partners to address them." For a public not versed in network diagnostics, the explanation suffices.

The other advantage is deniability. When speed tests degrade, the state can blame cyberattacks or infrastructural strain. When encrypted messaging fails, officials can claim the platform is at fault. The ambiguity distributes responsibility across many shoulders. Users complain to platforms; platforms blame carriers; carriers blame attacks. Meanwhile, the intended effect is achieved: political coordination becomes painful.

During a wave of unrest in parts of the Middle East, activists reported that encrypted video calls worked in the morning but collapsed by evening. Social networks loaded quickly, but images and videos lagged. Researchers measured packet loss rates that spiked only for traffic matching specific signatures. The throttle was not uniform; it was targeted. Most internet activity remained smooth. Only coordination-heavy tools suffered. By keeping the disruption narrow, operators minimised the collateral damage that would have provoked public anger.

Throttling also exploits a psychological feature of digital life: users blame themselves. A dropped call could be Wi-Fi, hardware, or bad signal. A blurry livestream could be the broadcaster's connection. Only dedicated network analysts see the pattern. In this way, throttling turns censorship into personal inconvenience rather than political grievance. It fragments collective experience into isolated irritations.

At its core, a throttle is a manipulation of time. Every additional second of buffering dissuades the casual viewer. A stream that loads in five seconds may hold an audience; a stream that loads in thirty seconds may lose it. In politics, attention is currency. Drift away, and the moment dissolves. The throttle ensures that by the time a video plays, its urgency has evaporated.

States favour throttling over blocking for another reason: global platforms often resist bans. They lobby, negotiate, and sometimes refuse compliance. Throttling sidesteps confrontation. Platforms cannot easily protest a slowdown because they cannot easily prove intentional interference. They may suspect, but suspicion is not evidence. Governments know that platforms, wary of losing entire markets, will often remain silent.

Measurement is the Achilles' heel of throttling, and governments know it. Rigorous proof requires controlled experiments, distributed sensors, and comparative baselines. Researchers deploy probes across cities, simulate traffic, record metrics. But perfect attribution is rare. A clever throttle masks itself as everyday congestion. It degrades speeds during high-traffic events when users already expect delays. It targets specific ports or protocols that can be written off as technical faults. Even when evidence emerges, the state can claim coincidence.

Carriers participate for their own reasons. Telecom licences are valuable and revocable. When instructed to throttle, many comply to protect their business. Some rebrand throttling as "quality of service optimisation." Others simply obey quietly. The border shifts from political order to infrastructure policy. Engineers adjust parameters; executives sign compliance papers; the public remains unaware.

Throttling can also be selective across geography. In capital cities, where media scrutiny is high, networks may run at full speed. In rural or minority regions, the clamps tighten. Protests in peripheral areas become invisible. The centre sees no chaos, because video never reaches it. A national narrative of peace is preserved not by propaganda alone, but by bandwidth.

Ironically, throttling also becomes a tool of central banks and finance ministries. When capital flight is feared, online banking slows. Crypto exchanges time out. Money moves less freely. Again, nothing is banned. The pipes are merely narrower. Citizens feel friction, but the state has plausible justification: fraud prevention, system load, security checks. The political and economic border converge.

There is a moral danger in throttling: because it is invisible, it does not provoke the outrage necessary for reform. Democracies that would never ban speech outright may quietly degrade it. Platforms that pride themselves on connectivity may quietly permit slowing to retain market access. Journalists face audiences that cannot view their reports in real time. Activists find that livestreams fail at the very moments visibility is most crucial. Repression disguised as inconvenience evades accountability.

Yet throttling, for all its sophistication, has limits. Savvy users detect abnormal lag. VPNs reroute traffic. Diaspora communities re-upload videos on foreign platforms. Distributed sensors record anomalies. Civil society groups publish reports correlating slowdowns with political events. In this cat-and-mouse contest, transparency efforts have begun to emerge. NGOs maintain open measurement dashboards. Journalists learn the language of latency and packet loss. Public understanding grows.

Still, most citizens will never run a traceroute. They will never inspect packet logs or compare throughput graphs. They will simply experience the internet as sluggish when dissent peaks. Authoritarian states exploit that asymmetry. But even democratic states flirt with throttling in moments of crisis. The temptation is universal: a softer form of control, insulated from scrutiny.

The dilemma extends beyond politics. Platforms themselves throttle to enforce business rules. Music services degrade quality for non-paying users. Video sites adjust bitrates based on region. Ride-hailing apps slow refresh rates to manage demand. Each case shows the same logic: throttling shapes behaviour without prohibiting it. In commerce, the tactic is accepted. In governance, it becomes perilous.

A subtler risk is normalisation. If citizens grow accustomed to faltering livestreams during elections or protests, they may stop expecting real-time information. If platforms adjust by compressing resolution or limiting livestream lengths "due to technical constraints," a new baseline emerges. A society can slip from free expression to managed expression without ever seeing a ban.

Measurement is the antidote. When independent researchers expose throttling, they strip away deniability. When courts receive credible data, they can demand explanations. When international observers correlate slowdowns with unrest, they rewrite the narrative. The state's whisper becomes audible.

Yet even measurement has a ceiling. As machine learning spreads into network management, throttling becomes dynamic. Algorithms detect "abnormal" use patterns and apply pressure automatically. When classifiers act, no single human orders suppression. Responsibility vanishes into code. Regulators seeking accountability face ghostly decision-making systems optimised for profit, security, or both.

What happens when a democracy adopts such systems? Imagine an election in which disinformation spreads rapidly. Officials ask carriers to "mitigate harmful activity." Carriers fine-tune their networks. Messaging apps slow. Video uploads buffer. The public largely supports the intervention, believing it protects the democratic process. Yet the mechanism outlives the crisis. Next time, it may be used not to shield democracy, but to shape it.

The throttle, unlike the ban, has no ceremony. There is no day zero when speech vanishes. There is only a gradual dulling. The frontier of expression becomes viscous. Creativity shrugs and adapts. Citizens shorten videos, avoid livestreams, rely on text. The space of possibility shrinks.

The final irony is that throttling may not even be effective in the long term. Movements find other channels. Diaspora media amplify suppressed stories. Encrypted apps adopt obfuscation. In some cases, throttling fuels suspicion and anger, particularly among those who recognise the pattern. The tactic is powerful when invisible; once exposed, it erodes trust.

The throttle reveals a profound shift in the philosophy of control. Bans are authoritarian theatre—spectacles with clear villains and victims. Throttling is managerial—soft power expressed through infrastructure. It treats speech like traffic, not like a right. It measures dissent in megabits per second.

What, then, counts as censorship: the absence of service or the collapse of usability? If a protest video exists but plays at a trickle, does the world truly see it? And if the border presents itself as a technical glitch, who—if anyone—will hold it to account?

Seams and Workarounds

In cities where the internet never quite stops but never fully flows, a strange ritual unfolds at nightfall. Young people huddle in cafés, swapping configuration files like sheet music for an improvised symphony. A VPN server in Prague works for a weekend, then dies. A new proxy in Singapore flickers to life. Social feeds open, then stall. Messages slip through in bursts. Nothing resembling freedom—only breathing spaces stitched together by code and luck. These are not the dramatic breaches celebrated in films. They are the quiet seams through which reality leaks.

Every border creates two imaginations: one for the authority that builds it, and one for the citizens who attempt to slip past. National firewalls, content filters, and throttles are engineered to shape behaviour inside a territory. But the internet, architected for resilience, leaves cracks. Those cracks become seams: VPN tunnels, mirrored websites, diaspora-run relays, peer-to-peer overlays. They are not glamorous. They are fragile, unpredictable, and often clumsy. Yet millions depend on them.

The mythology of circumvention paints it as a technical duel—hackers versus censors. The truth is duller, more human. Most people do not relish fighting their own internet. They simply want a reliable news feed, a functioning bank app, a stable call to friends abroad. When a government blocks a platform, citizens seldom switch to command-line tools; they download the simplest VPN recommended by a friend. Convenience beats ideology. But convenience is also the censor's ally. A VPN that requires frequent reconfiguration soon becomes unusable. The cat-and-mouse game is fought in the terrain of friction.

VPNs represent the easiest seam to imagine: one tap and a user's traffic appears to originate from another country. Yet even this simple picture is degrading. Governments pressure app stores to remove popular VPN clients. Payment processors are nudged to cancel subscriptions. ISPs identify VPN signatures and drop packets. Some states go further, using deep packet inspection to detect encrypted tunnels even when they mimic benign traffic. The response from VPN developers is constant mutation—new protocols, obfuscation, stealth modes. It is evolution accelerated by pressure.

Mirrors form the second major seam: exact replicas of blocked websites hosted on new domains or IP addresses. Activists launch them; diaspora groups maintain them; volunteers pass the links by word of mouth. Mirrors work until they do not. Once discovered, they are blacklisted. The process repeats. The cost of maintenance rises. Platform owners sometimes assist, sometimes demur, wary of provoking regulators. A mirror is a stopgap, not a foundation. In authoritarian contexts, they may survive hours or days—not because they are undetectable, but because enforcement lags.

Diaspora relays are more personal: relatives abroad capture videos, repost them on foreign platforms, and amplify voices silenced at home. This pattern was visible during uprisings from North Africa to South Asia. An activist records footage locally but cannot upload it; she sends it to a cousin overseas via an encrypted messenger when the network flickers back to life at dawn. The cousin uploads it, and the world sees what was meant to be hidden. States know this route exists. They tolerate it until it becomes too visible, then disrupt encrypted messaging or throttle uploads. The relay survives only because it is decentralised.

All these workarounds share a trait: fragility. A VPN server can be blocked. A mirror can disappear. An encrypted message can lag. The seams are not stable channels of resistance; they are pockets of temporary relief. And temporary relief is often enough. Information flows like water, not like a parade. It seeps under the door when the door is locked.

There is a temptation to celebrate these workarounds as triumphs of human ingenuity. And to some extent, they are. But heroism is not the central story. The central story is usability. A VPN that crashes is useless. A mirror that demands technical skill will stay empty. A relay that requires luck and timing may fail when it matters most. The real barrier is not encryption, but ergonomics.

Governments understand this. That is why many pursue deterrence by inconvenience. They do not need to destroy VPNs; they need to make them unreliable enough that only the most motivated persist. A population forced to refresh feeds for ten minutes will often stop trying. When the average citizen gives up, control is achieved without spectacle.

In this landscape, design choices become political. Mobile VPN clients that auto-rotate servers, use domain fronting, or mimic video traffic are valuable not because they are clever, but because they reduce effort. Messaging apps that queue content for delayed burst uploads help citizens slip past throttles without actively monitoring bandwidth. Diaspora networks that script automated mirroring systems reduce the need for manual intervention. The best tools are invisible, because the user should barely know they are using them.

And yet every advance generates a countermeasure. When VPNs mimic HTTPS, states throttle all HTTPS. When mirrors proliferate, states automate domain blocks using machine learning. When encrypted chat becomes too effective, states demand client-side scanning or key escrow. The border adjusts. So do the seams. The cycle is endless.

Proxy infrastructure is now a global political actor. Cloud providers unwittingly shield traffic because blocking them would break the services governments rely on. If a censor blocks a handful of popular CDNs, half the country's infrastructure collapses. Activists exploit this dependency: by routing dissident traffic through globally essential platforms, they force governments to choose between silencing speech and damaging their own digital economy. Sometimes it works; sometimes governments bite the bullet and block anyway.

The economics matter. Many states lack the deep technical expertise required for precision filtering. They outsource censorship technology to foreign vendors. Those vendors innovate, and the seams shrink. But innovation is patchy. Some regions enforce strict blocks; others exhibit inconsistent or poorly configured filters. In those cracks, circumvention flourishes. A single misconfigured router can open a tunnel for thousands.

Usability constraints do not only affect citizens; they burden authorities. States must avoid over-blocking, which would anger businesses and elites. They must avoid obvious disruptions that damage foreign investment. The art of censorship is surgical, not blunt. But surgical systems are expensive and fallible. Every dollar spent closing a seam is a dollar not spent elsewhere. Activists know this. They multiply seams, forcing censors to chase many small flames rather than extinguish one inferno.

Amid these dynamics, there is a sobering truth: most people do not circumvent at all. They adapt to a smaller internet. They migrate to state-approved platforms, self-censor, or retreat to private spaces. Workarounds are used by minorities—urban, educated, motivated. The digital divide widens. Those with technical literacy enjoy illicit windows onto the world; those without remain inside the border. The seam becomes a class privilege.

New technologies offer fresh hope and fresh risk. Peer-to-peer networks help content propagate even when platforms are blocked. DNS-over-HTTPS hides queries from ISPs. Mesh networks operate even when the internet is down. But for every innovation, there is pressure. States demand backdoors, block DNS resolvers, and restrict hardware imports. The cat learns fast.

Still, when the stakes climb, people find ways. During natural disasters and political crackdowns, communities set up offline file-sharing nodes using Bluetooth or local Wi-Fi. Universities distribute banned literature on USB sticks. Journalists burn data onto discs. This is not nostalgia; it is resilience. The seams extend beyond the internet into the physical world. When digital channels shrink, analogue ones revive.

The geopolitical layer adds complexity. Some governments tolerate circumvention quietly as a safety valve. Others crush it ruthlessly. Alliances form: one state's enemy becomes another state's hosting provider. A platform banned domestically reappears through servers funded abroad. Information sovereignty becomes entangled with diplomacy.

Platforms, too, walk a tightrope. They want to serve users inside restricted markets, but cannot publicly support circumvention without risking expulsion. Some quietly assist by designing resilient protocols. Others capitulate entirely. Citizens are left decoding corporate silence: is the outage technical, political, or self-censorship?

Over time, a culture of workaround emerges. Ordinary users acquire an instinct for switching servers, choosing mirror links, rotating messaging apps. The border teaches digital agility. But agility is tiring. Most citizens want stability, not an arms race. When instability becomes normal, a society grows accustomed to uncertainty—the erosion of trust becomes the censorship.

The cat-and-mouse metaphor is incomplete. In truth, it is a race between friction and motivation. The more friction a state introduces, the more motivation a user requires to persevere. Many fall away. Some push harder. A few pioneer breakthroughs. The state does not need to catch every mouse; it only needs to slow them enough.

But borders leak. Not because citizens are heroes, but because perfect control is expensive, technically impossible, and socially destructive. Every time a video escapes, a report circulates, or a censored idea reappears in translation, the border is shown to be porous. That porosity shapes politics. It prevents total isolation. It keeps reality within reach.

The question is not whether seams will exist—they always do. The question is who will control them, who will access them, and at what cost. When friction becomes the primary tool of governance, citizenship becomes an exercise in workarounds. And in that world, the very definition of a border changes. If freedom arrives only through a VPN that may die tomorrow, is it freedom—or just a borrowed signal waiting to be cut?

Chapter 4

Identity: Passports, Logins, and Real Names

On a humid afternoon in Manila, a group of teenagers found their social lives abruptly amputated. Overnight, their government required mobile SIM cards to be registered with valid IDs. The policy was presented as a crime-prevention measure, a blow against fraud and harassment. Shops sold out of cheap feature phones as citizens scrambled to register multiple numbers. Months later, the fraudsters were still active, but anonymous satire pages, LGBT support groups, and migrant worker forums had begun to disappear. The people most visible to the state were not the criminals; they were everyone else.

Identity on the internet once felt like a costume party. You chose a username, picked an avatar, and wandered through endless rooms of strangers. A crude freedom, but a real one. Today, governments and platforms increasingly demand the equivalent of a digital passport at every door. Name, phone, passport number, facial scan—credentials traded for access. For many, the bargain feels natural: fraud is rampant, children need protection, and the online world has grown too dangerous to stay anonymous. Yet for others, this same bargain feels like a velvet-gloved restraint. The same systems that keep scammers out can keep dissenters in.

The chapter that follows asks a disquieting question: when identity becomes the gatekeeper of digital life, who designs the gates?

Real-name regimes are spreading because they appear sensible. It seems obvious that trolling is easier when no one knows who you are; that scams thrive when criminals cannot be traced; that hate speech might soften if the speaker feared consequences. But policy is more than intuition. South Korea once tried a national real-name requirement for major platforms. Abuse fell slightly; misinformation did not. Meanwhile, political critics vanished, overseas users were locked out, and privacy breaches soared. Eventually the law was struck down as unconstitutional. Yet the logic survived and resurfaced elsewhere.

In many places, the real gatekeeper is not a government office but the mobile operator. A phone number increasingly functions as a universal login: messaging apps, banking apps, gaming accounts, ride-hailing, food delivery. When a SIM card becomes a speech licence, terminating that number becomes a form of quiet punishment. No jail, no trial—just silence.

Identity is also becoming infrastructural. Some governments now offer—or mandate—single sign-on using national ID systems. At first glance, this is convenience made elegant. Citizens can access tax records, healthcare, banking, and school portals through one secure credential. The integration seems obvious and modern. Yet integration always asks a second question: who holds the logs? When platforms authenticate via a national identity backbone, the state becomes a silent observer of login patterns. A sudden spike in sign-ins from a particular VPN? A wave of withdrawals from an online wallet? A pseudonymous account linked to a controversial activist suddenly tied back to a verified national ID? The architecture invites temptation.

Platforms rarely resist. Being authorised by the state grants legitimacy, eases regulatory burdens, and attracts local advertisers. The result is federation: government identity systems stitched into corporate logins until the two are nearly inseparable. Once that stitching is complete, account suspension becomes a matter of administrative procedure. A single credential lost—and the citizen is digitally homeless.

But what happens when governments are not the ones assigning identity? Platforms have built their own passports, based not on names but on patterns. Device fingerprints track the unique constellation of sensors, fonts, network quirks, and browser settings on a phone or laptop. Behavioural profiles watch typing rhythms, scroll speeds, and click habits. Algorithms can often identify a user even if they switch accounts, clear cookies, or mask their IP address. These *shadow IDs* are invisible and unchallengeable. If the system mistakenly flags an innocent user as a scammer or bot, the appeals process feels like shouting into fog.

Shadow IDs do not replace real-name requirements; they supplement them. A government can outlaw pseudonyms, but a platform can recognise you even when you follow the rules. The shift is subtle and profound: identity becomes probabilistic, not declarative. You are not who you say you are—you are who the system thinks you are.

Age gates illustrate how identity determines access even when names are not at stake. Platforms claim to protect children by requiring age verification.

Politicians demand it to block adult content or restrict addictive features. But age is rarely a simple fact. Identification systems exclude millions who possess no documents: refugees, undocumented workers, teenagers estranged from parents, adults in countries without robust civil registry systems. When age verification becomes a precondition for speech or commerce, entire populations fall through the cracks. Risk tiers produce similar effects. Users classified as "high-risk"—sometimes by opaque behavioural scores—find features disabled, limits imposed, or entire services withdrawn. Identity becomes not a label, but a verdict.

Every identity policy—whether imposed by governments or designed by platforms—carries politics. Real-name rules make speech traceable; shadow IDs make users predictable; age gates and risk scores make rights conditional. The philosophical stakes are old: Who deserves to speak? Who deserves to transact? Who deserves to be trusted? Yet the implementation is startlingly new: machine-readable verdicts that trigger instantly and automatically, invisibly to the person judged.

Anonymity is often portrayed as a moral hazard, a cloak for misbehaviour. But anonymity can be infrastructure. It can be a design choice that protects whistle-blowers, journalists, vulnerable minorities, and those whose personal safety depends on silence. The challenge is not whether anonymity should exist, but how. Many systems already blend accountability with pseudonymity: anonymous medical helplines, protected-journalist platforms, whistle-blowing channels with provable audit trails. The internet could adopt similar structures—spaces where identity is shielded from the public but provable to a trusted intermediary. Instead of all-or-nothing, anonymity could be governed.

The politics of identity are rarely explicit. A government might justify real-name registration as child protection; a company might claim behavioural scoring is spam prevention. Sometimes the stated rationale is sincere. Sometimes it is cover. But once an identity system exists—once every account is tied to a phone, a tax number, a device fingerprint—it becomes a lever. Levers get pulled.

Critics warn of surveillance. Defenders cite safety. Both are partly right. A verified identity makes harassment prosecutions easier. It also makes political policing easier. A single sign-on system makes bureaucracy smoother. It also makes de-platforming devastating. Shadow IDs reduce fraud. They also entrench automated discrimination. Policy arguments swap slogans, but the deeper question remains unsettled: What is the minimum identity a citizen should be forced to offer in order to exist online?

This chapter follows that thread across five dimensions. It begins with real-name regimes: why governments impose them, how platforms implement them, and what happens to those caught at the edges. It then examines state-platform federation, where national IDs become the master keys to online life. From there, it turns to shadow IDs and the unsettling world of invisible profiling. It traces the rise of age gates and risk tiers—administrative identities that decide who may join, buy, post, or earn. And it closes with the politics of anonymity, reframing the debate not as a moral choice but an architectural one.

Identity has always been political. But as national borders move into networks, identity becomes the new border control. Passports, logins, and real names are no longer mere credentials; they are instruments of power. They decide who gets a voice, who gets a livelihood, who gets a platform—and who disappears into silence.

The systems shaping those decisions are being built now, often quietly, sometimes accidentally. They will determine the character of digital citizenship for decades. Whether they yield safety or submission will not depend on ideology alone, but on architecture—on the choices buried deep in sign-up screens, authentication flows, and probability scores.

If the internet is becoming a governed territory, then identity is the customs desk. And the person holding the stamp has changed. Governments, platforms, payment networks, cloud providers, analytics teams—all compete to decide who is *someone* online, and who is nobody.

Somewhere in Manila, those teenagers are still online. Their phones registered, their accounts compliant, their identities verified. They can message friends, play games, watch videos. On good days, nothing feels different. On bad days, everything does. A joke too sharp, a post too bold, a group too political—and the same system that verified them can erase them.

Identity was supposed to make the internet safer. It might. It might also make the internet smaller, quieter, and easier to control.

The question is not whether identity will govern the digital world. It already does. The question is whether that governance will reflect trust, autonomy, and dignity—or convenience, caution, and power. The gates have moved. Now we must learn to see who is building them.

Real-Name Regimes

On a grey morning in Nairobi, a university student walked into a mobile shop to replace a SIM card stolen the night before. The process, she expected, would be routine. Instead, the clerk handed her a stack of forms. She needed a national ID, proof of address, a photograph, and a biometric scan. Her number—once a simple tool of convenience—had become a licence. Without it, she could not receive mobile payments from her part-time tutoring work, could not log into her bank account, could not reset her password on social media. Her voice, her income, and her civic presence had been locked behind a bureaucratic gate. Losing a SIM card had become the digital equivalent of losing her passport.

This is the quiet revolution of real-name rules. What began as a crime-fighting strategy—keep fraudsters off the networks—has evolved into a global push to verify identity before people speak, transact, or even browse. The promise is safety. The reality is more complicated.

Real-name regimes offer a seductive logic. If trolls, scammers, and extremists hide behind anonymity, make anonymity impossible. If online spaces are toxic because people can reinvent themselves with every login, tether them to a government ID. Citizens must present identity offline to board a plane or transfer large sums of money; why should digital life be any different? From this perspective, anonymity is not a right but a loophole.

Governments rarely sell these policies as censorship. They promise protection: fewer fake accounts, fewer fraudulent transfers, fewer threats. The language is familiar—"accountability", "responsibility", "safety"—and who can disagree with safety? In societies battered by scams, disinformation, and predatory marketing, mandatory verification feels like common sense.

Yet a SIM registration database can do more than curb fraud. It creates a perfect map of communication. A protest organiser's phone becomes a beacon; a satirical blog post becomes a traceable act. In some countries, critical journalists have found their phone numbers mysteriously disabled after publishing uncomfortable investigations. No arrest, no court order, no official accusation—only silence. The line between safety and suppression narrows in the hands of power.

Real-name requirements do not even guarantee their stated goals. South Korea's experiment with mandatory real-name posting on major platforms is a textbook example. The policy reduced abuse marginally but pushed it to foreign platforms outside national jurisdiction. Disinformation continued;

harassment adapted; fraudsters learned to rent identities. Meanwhile, ordinary users—particularly political commentators and critics—simply stopped speaking. It was not the criminals who were deterred. It was everyone else.

The design of these systems matters. In some countries, verified identity is linked to mobile operators. In others, it is tied to payment networks, national ID databases, passport systems, or special digital certificates. The more centralised the identity infrastructure, the more sweeping its leverage. A telecom company can cut a phone number. A payments provider can freeze an account. A government ID authority can revoke a certificate. Each dependency becomes a point of pressure.

Businesses often support real-name systems because verified users are easier to monetise and cheaper to moderate. Platforms want stable advertising identities, predictable customers, and low fraud rates. They do not need coercion; incentives are enough. Regulation amplifies the trend by threatening fines or licence suspension for failure to curb illegal content. Faced with legal risk, platforms adopt real-name verification as the safest path—better to demand identification than risk being held responsible for anonymous users.

The practical effects are uneven. In cities with high documentation rates, the change feels administrative. In rural areas and among low-income populations, real-name laws can function as exclusion. Millions of people lack formal ID: migrant workers without paperwork, refugees without recognised documents, rural residents without birth certificates, women whose legal identities are entangled with patriarchal systems. When access to communication, commerce, and civic discourse requires identity, the undocumented are erased from digital life.

For dissenters, the trade-off is sharper. A satirist in Hanoi might think twice before mocking local officials from a traceable account. A women's rights group in Lagos might fear that verified accounts expose them to harassment or political retaliation. Encryption protects the content of messages; real-name rules expose the sender. A government does not need to read what you say if it can see *who* is speaking.

Even outside authoritarian contexts, real-name rules reshape behaviour. People self-censor when they know their employer, neighbour, or future partner could search their posts. Survivors of domestic violence sometimes avoid social media entirely because verified identities make them locatable.

Whistle-blowers struggle to find safe channels. Sometimes the policy does not silence speech outright—it dilutes it into blandness.

Yet it is too simple to frame real-name regimes as oppressive and anonymity as pure. Anonymous harassment is real. Anonymous threats are terrifying. Anonymous financial scams destroy livelihoods. Supporters of real-name rules are not wrong to seek safety. The difficulty lies in the binary. Either everyone must be identifiable at all times, or no one is accountable. That framing is false, but it dominates public debate.

There are alternatives. Professional moderators can investigate abuse patterns without stripping anonymity from everyone. Courts can subpoena identities *after* misconduct, rather than collecting them pre-emptively. Platforms can adopt pseudonymous identities backed by trusted intermediaries—spaces where users are anonymous to the public but traceable in cases of serious harm. These models preserve speech while limiting impunity. Yet they require investment, nuance, and political will. Real-name laws are simpler for lawmakers to announce and easier for platforms to enforce.

Perhaps the most revealing feature of real-name regimes is not the demand for identity, but the presumption that identity equals truth. A verified name does not guarantee sincerity. A government ID does not prevent hate speech or propaganda. Harassment can be coordinated under real names just as easily as under pseudonyms. The belief that identity solves behaviour is comforting—and naïve.

Then there is the data. Real-name systems generate enormous databases linking devices, payments, communications, and social behaviour to legal identities. These systems are irresistible targets for hackers, extortionists, foreign intelligence services, and corrupt insiders. Breaches of voter rolls, national ID registries, and telecom databases demonstrate how fragile such infrastructures can be. The safety gained from accountability can be erased by the insecurity of exposure.

Yet the spread continues. From Berlin to Buenos Aires, from Manila to Mumbai, digital identity is becoming mandatory for participation. Critics warn of chilling effects; supporters cheer reductions in abuse. Both are partly right, yet neither captures the deeper transformation. Real-name regimes shift the burden of trust. Instead of designing systems that resist abuse regardless of who uses them, we build systems that assume safety comes from knowing *who* every user is. It is a philosophical move: from resilience to identification, from rights to permissions.

And the shift rarely reverses. Once a society normalises identity checkpoints, undoing them feels risky. Politicians fear blame if crime rises. Platforms rely on verified data for advertising and analytics. Citizens grow accustomed to the trade. The infrastructure becomes permanent long before the debate is settled.

Imagine a public square where everyone must wear a badge with their legal name, home address, and national ID number. Imagine that entering the square requires a scan of your face or fingerprint. Imagine that officials can deny entry without explanation, and that no one can see who was turned away. This, in effect, is what some digital spaces have become. Not dramatically, not overnight, but through steady layers of policy, compliance, and design.

The tension remains unresolved. Should the right to speak require the courage to be identified? Or should the right to dissent include the protection of anonymity? Real-name regimes claim to balance these interests. In practice, they tip the scales toward order, sometimes at the expense of freedom.

Safety matters. But safety purchased through universal identification risks becoming a safety for the powerful. The world's loudest voices will remain loud. The quiet ones—those who need anonymity for protection rather than mischief—will fall silent.

And so the question lingers: if every citizen must carry a digital passport to speak, who stamps it—and who decides when it expires?

State-Platform Federation

A traveller in Tallinn logs into her bank, renews her prescriptions, and signs a rental contract without once typing a password. Her national ID card sits on the desk, its digital certificate silently authorising every transaction. The state vouches for her identity; private platforms trust the state; and the citizen glides effortlessly through a bureaucracy that once relied on ink, stamps, and queues. It feels modern, elegant, even liberating. The state and the platform have merged at the point of login.

A thousand kilometres away, a student in Manila tries to register for a messaging account. The platform asks for his national ID number, and the telecom operator requires the same. Later, when he joins a Facebook group criticising a local official, his account is suspended without explanation. He cannot restore access without a selfie and an ID revalidation. Convenient authentication has become an invisible leash.

State-platform federation is sold as a simple improvement: instead of juggling passwords, people sign in with their legal identity. It removes friction, reduces fraud, and centralises trust. Banks prefer a government-certified login to an email address and a guessable password. Health-care platforms want verified citizens, not pseudonyms. Businesses appreciate a reliable identity feed that filters bots and scammers. For the average user, it can feel like progress—until they need to escape it.

At first glance, federation looks like technical plumbing: the state stores identity, platforms consume it. In practice, it reshapes the power structure of digital society. When a login becomes a national credential, every interaction sits beneath a political ceiling. That ceiling may be benign in quiet times, but in moments of protest, dissent, or instability, it becomes a point of leverage. To silence a critic, authorities need not arrest or prosecute; they can simply disable the account that allows the critic to speak.

Supporters of federation insist it is merely a tool for convenience, not control. Estonia's eID system is applauded for its transparency and robust protections. India's Aadhaar provides single sign-on for millions who lacked formal identity. Nordic BankID systems make financial authentication smoother and safer. But these systems also centralise risk. When a single credential unlocks banking, medicine, taxation, messaging, and travel, revoking it becomes the digital equivalent of social exile.

The centralisation of identity data creates irresistible incentives. Telecom firms, banks, and social platforms learn to rely on the same state-backed verification. Once dependencies form, opting out is costly and sometimes impossible. A citizen may refuse to use Facebook, but refusing to use the national login? That can mean losing access to government benefits, education portals, or tax filings. Convenience slowly transforms into compulsion.

Federation also alters the flow of public and private data. When platforms piggyback on national credentials, governments gain visibility into where citizens log in, and platforms may gain access to government-verified personal information. Even if the law forbids direct data exchange, metadata alone reveals patterns: when someone logs in, from where, how often, and across which services. Identity becomes a beacon, visible across marketplaces and messaging networks alike.

Some systems promise "privacy by design". They claim anonymity except in cases of court order. But every identity architecture embeds assumptions about trust. If political winds shift, those assumptions shift too. Tomorrow's authorities may not share yesterday's restraint. Democracies are not static; neither are their uses of data.

Lock-in emerges quietly. A national login is often required to access welfare benefits, then medical records, then school enrolment, then tax refunds. Gradually, private platforms adopt it for payments and messaging. Users internalise the logic: if your identity is not state-certified, you are not a full participant. Alternative logins become second-class. Independent platforms struggle to compete. The state becomes the identity monopoly, and monopoly powers are rarely abandoned voluntarily.

Technical design choices influence the balance of power. A system that supports multiple third-party identity providers diffuses control; a system anchored to a single state gateway concentrates it. A structure that allows pseudonymous tokens for low-risk activities preserves speech; a structure requiring hard identification for everything smothers it. These are political decisions disguised as technical standards.

In countries with weak rule of law, the dangers are immediate. National logins can be cut off for activists, journalists, minority groups, or whistle-blowers. When a platform depends on government authentication, it inherits government censorship by default. Revocation becomes effortless, unreviewable, and silent. A person may discover they can no longer log in, and no one needs to explain why.

Even in mature democracies, the philosophical trade-off is real. The right to speak, transact, and learn increasingly flows through a single authentication channel. If that channel is compromised—by hackers, insiders, or policy change—millions lose access in a stroke. Complexity is replaced by a single point of failure.

Businesses, however, love federation. It reduces fraud and eliminates the cost of trust. Instead of building verification systems, they rent the state's identity infrastructure. They can tell shareholders that customer security is strong, while shifting responsibility upwards. Federation stabilises the advertising economy, too: verified identities are more profitable, yielding richer behavioural profiles and more targeted marketing.

Citizens are caught between incentives. It feels irrational to refuse a login that makes life easier, especially when everyone else has one. But each adoption tightens the loop: the more people use it, the more platforms require it; the more platforms require it, the more citizens must comply. Lock-in is an emergent property, not a declared policy.

There are benefits. Fraud drops. Bureaucracy shrinks. Services improve. But the cost is flexibility. An ecosystem that once allowed multiple providers and self-managed identities becomes dependent on a single spine. If that spine bends toward surveillance, platforms cannot resist. If the spine breaks, services collapse together.

In federated identity, leverage flows both ways. Governments can pressure platforms by threatening access to identity systems. Platforms can pressure citizens by demanding state-backed credentials. The user stands in the middle, authenticated but vulnerable.

There is an alternative path: federated identity without centralisation. Systems can support pseudonymous tokens, rotating identifiers, and selective disclosure—revealing age or residency without revealing name or address. Some cryptographic models allow verification without visibility, accountability without exposure. But these require political ambition and cultural imagination. They are harder to explain than "log in with your national ID".

The deeper question is what kind of citizenship digital life demands. Should the right to speak and transact be mediated by the state, or should identity be plural, flexible, and contestable? Should a citizen's digital self be portable across platforms, or should each space allow reinvention? Federation answers these questions silently, through code and infrastructure rather than public debate.

The results are uneven, and the trajectory is not fixed. Estonia demonstrates that robust safeguards can coexist with convenience. Other countries reveal how easily these systems become levers of control. The same architecture that empowers can erase, depending on who holds the keys.

As more nations build digital identity networks, and more platforms adopt them as mandatory logins, the world drifts toward a future where a single credential unlocks—or locks—everything. We are trading friction for fragility, passwords for dependence, and decentralisation for centralised leverage.

The bargain is comfortable today. It may not be tomorrow. When authentication becomes governance, and convenience becomes compulsion, one question eclipses all others: who controls the gate, and who can be quietly turned away?

Shadow IDs

A woman in London buys a used phone and creates a new email address under a fresh pseudonym. She believes she has reset her digital life. Yet the first advertisements that appear in her browser reference products she viewed months earlier. Before she typed her new name, the system recognised her as the same person. Identity survived the deletion of identity.

Shadow IDs are not official credentials. They are device fingerprints, behavioural traces, and statistical guesses—patterns distilled into identifiers no human ever sees. They do not ask for consent. They do not need names. They work because, in the aggregate, we are more predictable than we imagine.

A single phone contains dozens of unique traits: screen resolution, chipset, language settings, installed fonts, time zone, battery profile, accelerometer signature. Alone, each detail is mundane. Together, they form a fingerprint. When combined with browsing habits, typing rhythm, app usage, and location patterns, the fingerprint becomes a biography. Platforms do not need to know who you are; they can simply infer that you are the same person who was here yesterday.

This shadow identity is not held in a single file. It lives in vast, distributed models built by advertisers, data brokers, mobile analytics firms, and fraud detection engines. When you open a webpage, scripts quietly test your browser to see which features it supports, which fonts render correctly, how your device responds to tiny graphical probes. Each answer shrinks the anonymity set. Eventually, the system says: "I recognise you".

For most people, this machinery is invisible. They interact with the internet as if anonymity were simply a matter of using a different username or clearing cookies. But clearing cookies is like wiping fingerprints from a table while leaving footprints in the carpet. The system knows how you scroll, how fast you type, which corners of the screen you tap first. Your identity leaks through motion.

To security teams, shadow IDs are a shield. Banks use device fingerprints to block fraud. Messaging platforms use behavioural profiles to detect botnets. Spam filters rely on the minute differences between genuine human typing and synthetic keystrokes. These tools protect users in ways that older systems never could. If a criminal steals your password but logs in from a device whose fingerprint is wildly different from yours, the system rejects them. In that sense, shadow IDs are a quiet gift.

Yet every gift has a cost. Because these identifiers are opaque, they cannot be inspected or challenged. If a behavioural model decides that you resemble a spammer, your account may be throttled or banned. No one explains how the conclusion was reached. You cannot see the profile, correct it, or appeal the logic. The identity that governs your access is invisible to you.

Opacity breeds asymmetry. Platforms know exactly how to connect activity across devices; citizens do not know how they are being tracked. Regulators attempt to discipline the advertising industry, but enforcement lags behind innovation. Companies claim they have anonymised data, yet re-identification is often trivial. A handful of behavioural signals tie back to a single person. Privacy becomes a statistical possibility, not a guarantee.

The problem deepens when governments enter the picture. Some states require platforms to fingerprint devices as part of "public safety" mandates. Others encourage behavioural profiling to identify dissidents or activists. In those environments, deleting an account does nothing; the system simply links the next account to the same device, the same patterns, the same person. Pseudonymity becomes a costume that fools only the wearer.

There is also a structural irony: shadow IDs undermine the very purpose they are often used to defend. Fraud detection seeks to prevent account takeover, yet the more accurate a shadow profile becomes, the easier it is for a well-resourced adversary to clone. Malware can mimic device signals. Bots can imitate human scrolling. Attackers learn that to pass the test they must behave like *you*, and sometimes they can. Security becomes a contest of imitation.

For ordinary users, the most troubling aspect is how normal this tracking feels. People accept personalised recommendations without questioning how personalisation is achieved. They expect targeted adverts without asking who assembled the target. The infrastructure of behavioural identity embeds itself into everyday life: airline websites adjust prices based on device history; retailers offer discounts that follow you from site to site; political campaigns micro-segment voters by profile, not by name.

Shadow IDs also reconfigure power within platforms. Customer support teams lean on automated risk assessments. Moderation systems flag "suspicious" patterns without understanding their cultural context. An activist using Tor may be flagged as a fraudster; a traveller using hotel Wi-

Fi may be denied access to banking. Systems treat deviation as danger. The world shrinks to what the model recognises.

Some technologists defend shadow IDs as necessary for survival. Without them, fraud would overwhelm e-commerce, bots would dominate social platforms, and advertising would revert to guesswork. But this argument accepts surveillance as the default business model. There are alternative paths: identity minimisation, local decision-making, privacy-preserving authentication, and transparent risk scoring that citizens can inspect and challenge. These are harder to design, slower to deploy, and less profitable to sell—yet they preserve something essential: agency.

Even where laws insist on user consent, the choice is illusory. Most people click "agree" to convoluted terms because the service is unusable otherwise. Consent becomes a ritual, not a safeguard. Shadow IDs flourish because resistance is impractical. Few users will modify browser settings, rotate devices, or employ privacy networks daily. The system counts on exhaustion.

Shadow identity also erodes accountability. When a human moderator bans a user, there is someone to question. When an opaque model quietly blocks access, there is no one to argue with. The boundary of citizenship in digital spaces is enforced by statistical inference, not by written rule. And because these systems are proprietary, even regulators cannot fully see them.

Yet the story is not entirely bleak. Some jurisdictions now require platforms to disclose the existence of behavioural tracking. Browsers introduce anti-fingerprinting features. Privacy researchers expose hidden profiling practices. Civil society pushes for audits and appeals. In these pockets, shadow IDs meet sunlight.

But the logic runs deeper than law. The architecture of today's internet rewards persistent recognition. Advertising demands targeting. Security demands consistency. Platforms demand coherence across sessions. In such an environment, anonymity is not the absence of a name; it is the improbable state of being unrecognised in a world designed to remember.

Shadow IDs force us to confront a hard question: in a digital society, who controls the right to be forgotten, and what does forgetting even mean? Deleting an account may hide the symptoms, but the profile remains. You can switch devices, change browsers, alter habits, but the system is patient.

As long as identity is a pattern and patterns are profitable, the shadows will watch.

And if identity can be inferred rather than declared, what becomes of privacy as a principle? Do we protect names, or do we protect the freedom not to be categorised at all?

The old belief was that anonymity died when we surrendered our names. The unsettling truth of the digital age is that anonymity may die even when we keep our mouths shut.

Age, Risk, and Eligibility

A teenager in Sao Paulo tries to join an online study group for advanced mathematics. The platform rejects him: his government-issued ID shows he is fifteen, and the service is only available to users sixteen and above. No exceptions, no appeals. Meanwhile, a twelve-year-old in another city bypasses age checks entirely by borrowing her brother's login, gaining access to content far more adult than she can safely navigate. The paradox is obvious: those who play by the rules are excluded, and those who break them slip through.

Digital systems love clean numbers. They prefer thresholds that are firm, automated, and easily audited: under thirteen, no account; under eighteen, no payments; under twenty-one, no encrypted messaging without parental consent. But human maturity has never obeyed calendar boundaries. A child one day shy of a birthday is not meaningfully different from the child one day past it. The internet, however, draws lines like border guards stamping passports.

Age gates emerged in response to pressure. Lawmakers demanded that platforms protect minors from predatory content, predatory advertisers, and predatory strangers. Companies responded with drop-down menus and verification services. At first, age checks were cosmetic—simple tick-boxes that children learned to click past before they learned to tie their shoes. Then came national identity checks, passport scans, and credit bureau lookups. Safety gained teeth.

With teeth came collateral damage. Millions of adults without formal identification found themselves locked out of basic communication platforms. Refugees, undocumented migrants, older users without passports, and citizens of countries with weak civil registries suddenly failed verification. The rule intended to protect children also excluded the marginalised. In digital governance, intention rarely predicts outcome.

Risk tiers added nuance. Instead of banning entire age groups, platforms began to restrict features: minors could browse videos but not message strangers; they could post content but not monetise it; they could create accounts but needed parental approval for certain actions. Some systems employed machine learning to estimate maturity: linguistic patterns, browsing histories, and social graphs acted as proxies for age. Yet every proxy carries bias. If your online behaviour resembles that of adults, the system may treat you as one; if it resembles children, you may be confined to a sandbox.

At their best, risk tiers protect the vulnerable without silencing them. A child in a crisis hotline should be able to seek help without parental oversight. A fifteen-year-old climate activist should not need a parent's permission to organise a protest. But blunt rules can suffocate agency. When policy assumes that all minors are fragile and all adults are safe, reality bends to software rather than the other way around.

The pressure to "do something" about online harm pushes platforms towards uniformity. Politicians demand certainty; headlines condemn ambiguity. A company that blocks too much appears cautious. A company that blocks too little appears reckless. Most choose over-compliance. Better to frustrate millions of legitimate users than risk a scandal involving one child. Safety becomes a shield against scrutiny.

The irony is that blunt age controls can make young people less safe. When restrictions are tight, youth migrate to unregulated spaces—anonymous forums, encrypted networks, or offshore services that ignore local law. Parents and educators lose visibility. Moderators lose context. The system encourages rule-breaking, then punishes those who comply.

Verification introduces a deeper tension: to prove age, one must surrender identity. Uploading a passport or driver's licence to a social network creates new privacy risks. Data leaks are common; forged IDs circulate; criminals harvest personal information under the guise of compliance. In the name of protecting minors, society asks them to create permanent digital records—records that may follow them for life.

Some countries attempt elegant solutions. Estonia allows age verification through cryptographic proofs that reveal nothing beyond the relevant fact: "I am over thirteen". But such systems require robust digital infrastructure, political will, and public trust. Few nations have all three. Most default to the simplest mechanism: centralised databases and photo IDs. Convenience for administrators; vulnerability for users.

The problem expands beyond minors. Platforms increasingly route adult rights through eligibility scores: payment risk models, misinformation flags, and automated trust ratings. A person with an unverified age or scant history may find themselves unable to sell goods, stream content, or access job platforms. Eligibility becomes the new currency of citizenship online.

Consider streaming services that require age verification to view "mature" content. An adult without documents is treated like a child. Consider gaming platforms that ban chat for users below a certain threshold. A deaf teenager who relies on text communication loses access to his social world. The harms are quiet but cumulative.

The conversation often turns moralistic. Critics argue that age gates are weak and children will lie. Proponents argue that some barrier is better than none. Both sides miss the structural point: the architecture of age verification shapes who participates in public life. If the price of speaking online is government-approved identification, dissenters, whistle-blowers, and vulnerable groups lose their voice.

Risk assessment is as much about power as safety. Platforms design systems that protect their legal exposure, not necessarily their users. A risk tier that limits messaging for minors also limits labour rights for young gig workers. An automated block on "new users" posting links can silence citizen journalists covering protests in real time. The line between harm reduction and civic restriction is thin.

Some policymakers propose "age-appropriate design", tailoring platforms to the developmental needs of children. On paper, it sounds humane. In practice, companies adopt conservative defaults to avoid controversy. The result is infantilisation by software: teenagers treated as toddlers, adults treated as children, everyone treated as a liability. The internet shrinks to its safest, dullest form.

And yet, the status quo is not sustainable. Children are not disappearing from the internet; they are simply learning to circumvent rules. VPNs, borrowed accounts, identity forgery—these become teenage literacy. The more rigid the gate, the more inventive the workaround. Safety achieved through brittle defences rarely holds.

Where does this leave us? A more equitable system would treat age as one dimension of risk, not the sole determinant. It would account for context: intent, behaviour, vulnerability, and support. It would allow appeal and transparency, rather than silent rejection. It would protect without erasing autonomy.

That future is technologically possible. Cryptographic age proofs. Privacy-preserving verification. Graduated permissions. Responsive oversight. But it requires a shift in philosophy: from shielding at all costs to empowering with care. Children deserve protection, but they also deserve voice. Adults deserve rights, even when they lack paperwork.

The digital age gate is a mirror of analogue governance. We legislate childhood with numbers because nuance is expensive. Systems struggle to recognise the messy world between categories. Yet citizenship—online or off—is more than a date of birth.

So the question remains: if the internet is the public square of our century, who decides who may enter, speak, learn, and earn? And what happens when the gatekeepers are neither educators nor judges, but silent rules hard-coded into software?

The next generation will not wait for an answer. They are already climbing over the fences. The challenge is not to build taller walls, but smarter ones—barriers that protect without erasing the people they are meant to serve.

The Politics of Anonymity

A woman in Istanbul posts a message beneath a pseudonym, offering evidence of local corruption. Within hours, her account disappears, her IP address is traced, and police arrive at her door. In another city, an anonymous support group for LGBTQ+ teenagers allows young people to speak openly for the first time in their lives, shielded from the judgement of families and the threat of persecution. Same internet, same anonymity—two radically different readings of its purpose. To some, anonymity is a cloak for abuse. To others, it is a lifeline.

The public argument has ossified into caricature. Governments portray anonymity as the refuge of criminals, extremists, and cowards. Tech libertarians cast it as an unqualified good, the bedrock of free expression. Each side reduces a complex architectural choice into a moral statement about character: honest people use real names; dangerous people hide. The reality is neither so simple nor so moralistic. Anonymity is not a personality trait. It is infrastructure.

Online identity is designed, not inherited. A platform can allow pseudonyms, forbid them, or require verified credentials. It can decide whether moderators know a user's real identity even if the public does not. It can store identifying data in a secure vault or discard it entirely. These choices are not ethical abstractions—they are engineering decisions that produce political consequences.

For years, major platforms insisted that real names would civilise discourse. The theory was intuitive: if people were accountable for what they said, they would behave. Facebook's "real-name" policy became emblematic. It lasted until countless users—activists, survivors of abuse, drag performers, whistle-blowers—pointed out the obvious. A name can be a threat. Women fleeing violent partners do not want their faces on searchable timelines. Journalists in authoritarian states cannot afford to broadcast their identities to security agencies. The real-name rule turned platforms into maps of the vulnerable.

Yet anonymity has its darker face. Anonymous mobs coordinate harassment campaigns that overwhelm political opponents. Trolls weaponise distance to inflict cruelty they would not show in person. Disinformation operations thrive when attribution is impossible. The harm is real, and critics are right to demand accountability. What is missing is imagination. The choice between total anonymity and full identification is a false binary. Between them lies a vast design space.

Consider pseudonymity: stable identities that are not directly tied to legal names. A pseudonym means that a user can build reputation, relationships, and responsibility without exposing their offline identity. Forums like Stack Exchange and Reddit rely heavily on this model. Users who misbehave can be sanctioned or banned; those who contribute positively earn trust and influence. The system functions because pseudonyms are persistent. They are masks, but not disposable ones.

Another variation is tiered anonymity. Under this model, a platform knows a user's identity, but the public does not. Whistle-blowers can speak without revealing themselves. Survivors of violence can seek help without risking exposure. Meanwhile, law enforcement—under legal process—can request information when serious harm is alleged. Rights and protections coexist. It is not utopia, but it is workable.

The problem is that many governments do not want nuance. They want leverage. Anonymous speech is difficult to control, so states attempt to eliminate it. Some introduce mandatory SIM-card registration, linking every phone number to a national ID. When messaging apps require a phone number to register, anonymity collapses. A protester sending encrypted texts may feel safe, unaware that the phone number they used acts as a tracking beacon. The encryption is strong; the metadata is weak.

The infrastructure, not the user, determines vulnerability. A citizen can meticulously protect their identity in public posts and still be exposed because the network logs reveal where their messages came from and when. Data trails become the real identity, even when names are absent.

There is also the phenomenon of *platform fingerprints*. Even if a service allows pseudonyms, advertisers and governments can infer identity through device analytics, writing style, and behavioural patterns. A user may believe they are anonymous when, in reality, their signature is legible to those with the tools to read it. The line between anonymity and traceability becomes invisible, opaque, and entirely outside the individual's control.

This is why the debate must shift. The question is no longer, "Should anonymity be permitted?" The question is, "Who gets to design the boundaries, and for whose benefit?" When platforms quietly erode anonymity while proclaiming it intact, accountability collapses. When governments demand identity under the guise of safety, dissent evaporates. When companies treat identity data as a commodity, privacy becomes a transactional luxury.

Still, anonymity need not be synonymous with impunity. Governance models exist that separate accountability from exposure. Some messaging apps use escrow identity systems: a trusted party verifies that a user is legitimate but does not reveal the identity unless ordered by a court. Others rely on zero-knowledge proofs, allowing a user to demonstrate attributes—adult, resident, paid subscriber—without revealing who they are. The state's interest in security is met. The individual's right to privacy is preserved.

These solutions rarely become mainstream because the incentives point the other way. Platforms like identifiable users: they are easier to monetise. States like identifiable citizens: they are easier to watch. Anonymity survives not because it is loved, but because it is hard to kill. People route around restrictions the way water finds cracks in a wall. VPNs, burner numbers, alt accounts—hardware and software become acts of self-defence.

The politics of anonymity bend with circumstance. In one country, encrypted messaging is a civil right. In another, it is treated as a sign of guilt. During protests in Hong Kong, citizens wore masks to protect themselves from surveillance. During the COVID-19 pandemic, governments banned masks at demonstrations to preserve "public order". Identity itself becomes a battlefield.

Critics argue that anonymity corrodes trust. They are not wrong. An anonymous speaker demands faith from the audience without offering reciprocity. But identity does not guarantee truth. Real-name policies did not eliminate misinformation or hate; they simply made the targets easier to locate. If the goal is trust, design systems that reward credibility—peer moderation, transparent audit logs, appeals—rather than demanding exposure.

The most sophisticated online communities understand this. Wikipedia allows editors to remain pseudonymous while maintaining rigorous accountability. Edits are tracked. Behaviour is reviewed. Sanctions are applied. The mask is permitted, but the actions behind it are visible. Trust emerges from structure, not from knowing the editor's passport number.

Crucially, anonymity is not evenly distributed. Powerful actors rarely need it. Governments, corporations, and celebrities possess legal teams and public platforms. Ordinary citizens rely on anonymity as armour. When a factory worker exposes unsafe conditions, anonymity keeps her employed. When a citizen criticises a ruling party, anonymity keeps him free. Remove anonymity and you do not create civility—you create silence.

There is a deeper philosophical point: anonymity creates space for the self to experiment. Young people try identities like clothes. Artists test provocative ideas without risking reputational collapse. Marginalised groups gather without being outed. The early internet was fertile precisely because it tolerated uncertainty about who was speaking.

Today's infrastructure is less forgiving. A single misstep—an ill-advised joke, a protest photo, a controversial opinion—can be retrieved years later and tied to a real identity. The digital memory is permanent. Without some cloak of anonymity, human fallibility becomes a permanent mark. The choice is between a society that expects perfection and one that allows growth.

What then is the path forward? A well-governed system would protect pseudonyms by default, require identity disclosure only under due process, and ensure that private data is not silently harvested. It would give users visibility into how their identity is inferred and allow them to challenge mistakes. It would treat anonymity as a protected mode, not an aberration.

But that requires political courage. Governments want control; companies want data; many citizens, frightened by online harms, demand easy fixes. Anonymity becomes the scapegoat because it is easier to attack than the structural causes of abuse: lax moderation, exploitative platforms, broken policing, and social inequality. Banning masks does not eliminate crime; it merely criminalises masks.

And so the debate continues: safety versus freedom, security versus privacy, order versus dissent. It is tempting to search for a final answer, a perfect policy that eliminates harm without silencing the vulnerable. No such policy exists. The politics of anonymity will always reveal deeper fault lines—between state and citizen, between platform and user, between collective safety and individual dignity.

Perhaps the clearest test is this: when a society demands real names, who disappears first? Journalists. Queer youth. Political dissidents. Survivors of domestic violence. The people for whom anonymity is not convenience but protection.

The real question is not what anonymity hides, but what identity exposes. If governments and platforms cannot guarantee that exposure will not lead to punishment, discrimination, or violence, then anonymity is not a vice. It is a necessary shelter.

And if the future of public life is online, then the rules of anonymity will shape who is allowed to participate. Will the digital square welcome only those safe enough to stand unmasked? Or will it recognise that democracy needs voices without fear, even when those voices cannot attach a name?

The internet was built to connect strangers. Strangers do not always speak kindly. But a world that forbids anonymity may become quieter—not because it is safer, but because the people who most need to speak have learned to stay silent.

Chapter 5

Speech at the Border

A journalist uploads a photograph of a war-torn street: shattered buildings, fleeing civilians, a mother shielding her child. Within minutes, the image vanishes. Not because a government censored it, nor because the newsroom erased it, but because a nudity classifier—built to detect pornography—flagged the visible skin of an injured child. Appeal requests disappear into a digital void. No explanation. No human review. In the world's largest public squares, speech lives or dies not by debate or law, but by an opaque rulebook written in code.

For centuries, censorship had a familiar architecture. Governments issued bans, police seized printing presses, courts ruled on sedition and obscenity. Power was visible. Decisions had names attached. Today, borders of speech are drawn by platforms that claim neutrality, even as their policies govern billions. Their rules sit in a strange constitutional space: more detailed than many national laws, more arbitrary than any democratic statute, and enforced by systems that nobody elected.

The paradox is sharp. The internet once promised a world where ideas flowed freely across nations, unburdened by geography. Instead, it has created new territories—vast, borderless domains where speech is managed by terms of service. These policies are not suggestions. They are quasi-laws, enforced not by courts but by classifiers, moderators, and ranking systems. They apply instantly, globally, and often without appeal. If the public square is digital, the constitution is a PDF, and constitutional court is an email inbox that rarely writes back.

Nothing symbolises the shift more clearly than the moment platforms began removing political content—not because a government demanded it, but because automated systems misunderstood context. Human rights documentation flagged as "graphic violence". Breastfeeding photographs labelled "nudity". Indigenous ceremonial art mistaken for "hate symbols". Speech becomes collateral damage in a system that prizes speed over understanding.

And yet, governments remain present—just in new form. When a state demands that a post be restricted, the platform must decide where. A takedown order might apply only to users in the country that issued it. Increasingly, it is applied globally, erasing speech for everyone. Jurisdiction, once geographic, becomes contagious. A single court order in one nation can remove content from all, because compliance is easier than resistance. The logic is administrative: it is simpler to delete a post everywhere than to engineer boundaries. So a local rule becomes a global one, without public debate or global consent.

The border moves silently. A demand issued at 3 a.m. in one capital reshapes what is visible in another. Citizens in democracies lose access to material because officials half a world away decided it was unfit. Scope creep is not a bug; it is a consequence of platforms built for convenience rather than principle. Speech is not adjudicated—just removed.

This power is not limited to deletion. Ranking systems—the machinery that decides what rises and what drowns—are editorial choices masquerading as neutrality. When a platform amplifies certain voices, demotes others, and buries some entirely, it is acting as a publisher in all but legal name. Trending lists, recommendation feeds, and personalised suggestions are forms of narrative construction. They do not merely reflect public sentiment; they shape it.

A political movement can surge or stall depending on whether the algorithm shows it to millions or hides it behind the clutter of daily trivia. A health rumour can spread faster than facts because the system optimises for engagement, not accuracy. Platforms deny editorial intent, yet their engineering choices perform the same function as news editors selecting front-page stories. The difference is transparency. Editors are accountable; algorithms are inscrutable.

Crucial moments expose this most starkly: pandemics, protests, elections, terror attacks. At such times, platforms activate "crisis protocols", emergency modes in which ordinary rules are suspended. Speed takes priority. Content is removed in bulk. Labels are attached. Accounts are down-ranked. Entire categories of speech—rumours, satire, criticism—may be throttled because the system cannot distinguish malice from panic.

These measures are often defensible; misinformation during crises can kill. But the governance is fragile. Who decides what counts as harmful? Who audits mistakes? In several countries, civil society groups documented the disappearance of protest videos that recorded state violence. In others, fact-check labels were applied to legitimate reporting because automated tools struggled with sarcasm or local languages. Once removed in crisis mode, content rarely reappears, even after the emergency ends.

The irony is that platforms promise transparency while obscuring everything that matters. They publish statements about "community standards" but reveal nothing about error rates, training data, or the humans who make borderline calls. Appeals systems are buried, inaccessible, or simply ignored. For most users, challenging a content decision feels like shouting into a locked room. Those with influence—governments, corporations, celebrities—can escalate through private channels. Ordinary citizens cannot.

Meaningful transparency looks different. It requires admitting that systems fail, disclosing how often and why, and providing clear routes to remedy. It requires publishing dataset lineage—where models learned, whose perspectives were included, which biases remain. It requires oversight bodies with real authority, not public relations councils. Transparency without consequence is theatre.

Speech at the border is about more than censorship. It is about power without visibility. Platforms draw lines every day—what counts as misinformation, which political slogans are allowed, which historical images are too violent, which cultural expressions break the rules. These decisions are deeply political, yet framed as technical enforcement.

And the stakes are enormous. A student documenting a protest wants the world to see. A mother searching for health advice needs accuracy, not fear and clickbait. A journalist relying on global reach cannot afford to be silenced by a misfiring classifier. A dissident cannot endure a world where a foreign court order erases their words before anyone reads them.

The chapter ahead explores these systems as borders: shifting, powerful, often invisible. It examines platform rules as law, algorithms as editorial forces, governments as silent partners, and transparency as the thin line between authority and abuse. It shows how speech can be throttled without being banned, how mistakes become policy, and how appeals vanish in deserts of automation.

Most importantly, it confronts a question that defines our time: when the digital public square is governed by private infrastructure, who protects the citizen? Courts can act only where jurisdiction reaches. Platforms answer to shareholders more than voters. Governments exploit the ambiguity for leverage.

Some imagine this as a temporary problem. The systems will mature, the models will improve, appeals will become fairer. Perhaps. Or perhaps the architecture itself guarantees a world in which speech is sorted, filtered, and ranked by systems that no one elected and few understand.

What does citizenship mean if your voice can vanish without explanation? What does free expression become when borders shift invisibly and enforcement is probabilistic? These are not abstract puzzles. They determine whether public discourse remains a right or becomes a privilege managed by corporate protocol.

The borders of speech are being redrawn every day. Not at the edges of nations, but in unseen layers of code, servers, and moderation queues. And the first step to defending the public square is recognising that those borders exist at all.

Terms as Territory

A photojournalist documents a moment of history: protesters fleeing a cloud of tear gas, police in formation, a wounded teenager carried by strangers towards safety. The newspaper publishes the image; social media shares it widely. Then, without warning, the photograph disappears. A nudity classifier—designed to detect sexual imagery—flags the exposed torso of the injured boy. The platform removes the image instantly, sends a generic notice about "safety," and offers a link to an appeal path that leads nowhere. In the public square of the digital age, a machine has made a legal decision. No judge. No jury. No meaningful possibility of review.

This is the paradox of modern speech governance: platforms insist they are not arbiters of truth or morality, yet they enforce vast rulebooks that function like law. Their terms and conditions—those sprawling documents users pretend to read—construct a legal order that governs billions. They define what counts as violence, hate, harassment, misinformation, and obscenity. They determine which political expression is permissible and which cultural imagery is forbidden. They can silence a movement or elevate it. They can erase satire, criticism, or dissent without ever invoking a statute.

To call these documents *policies* understates their power. They are constitutions written by corporations, interpreted by algorithms, and enforced by outsourced contractors working under immense pressure.

Unlike national laws, they do not require democratic consent. Unlike court rulings, they rarely include reasoning. Enforcement may be arbitrary, inconsistent, or simply mistaken. Yet for most people, they determine what the world sees.

A central myth underpins this system: that terms of service are neutral and technical. The reality is political. Platforms ban misinformation, yet decide what counts as misinformation. They remove "extremist content," yet decide which ideologies fall under that label. They prohibit hate speech, yet define it unevenly across languages, regions, and contexts. In the hands of a corporation, these definitional powers become instruments of governance.

Consider the difference between "graphic violence" and "documentary evidence." The former is removed to protect viewers; the latter is critical for accountability. Yet automated moderation systems struggle to distinguish art, satire, journalism, and advocacy from cruelty or abuse. A video recording war crimes may be essential evidence, but the classifier sees only blood, weapons, and screams. Entire human rights archives have disappeared because they triggered violence filters designed for entertainment media.

Even when humans review borderline cases, the system offers little clarity. Moderators interpret vague rules under conditions that reward speed, not nuance. They handle thousands of items per shift, with seconds to decide whether a piece of content violates a policy that may be dozens of pages long. Errors are inevitable. But the system does not record them, and victims of those mistakes have almost no remedy. The appeals mechanisms that platforms advertise are thin facades. Users submit forms and receive automated replies. The vast majority of cases are never seen by a human being again.

These are not glitches in an otherwise coherent system; they are structural features. Mass moderation at the scale of billions requires simplification: rigid categories, automated enforcement, and limited avenues for appeal. But simplification turns speech into data. Context evaporates. Irony, historical reference, cultural nuance, and linguistic ambiguity become liabilities. A classifier trained on American English will fail in Swahili, Hindi, Arabic, or Tagalog. A moderation team familiar with Western iconography may misinterpret political symbols in Myanmar or Ethiopia. The more diverse the world becomes, the more brittle the rules appear.

Advocates often argue that platforms should be held accountable like publishers. But publishers curate intentionally; platforms curate by accident. Their systems promote content that generates engagement, not civic value. Their enforcement tools remove content that triggers alarms, not content that causes harm. At their worst, they combine the power of a newspaper with the discretion of a postal sorting machine. They are authoritative, opaque, and structurally careless.

Yet there is another layer of territory: private variation. The same platform enforces different rules in different countries. A political slogan permitted in one jurisdiction is banned elsewhere. An LGBTQ+ support group survives in a liberal democracy but is quietly removed in a conservative monarchy. A feminist activist's account stays up in one nation and vanishes in another. These are not public decisions. They are private adjudications shaped by regulatory pressure, political pragmatism, and risk tolerance.

The borders of speech become invisible. Users assume they are participating in a global conversation, when in fact they are inside a country-sized pocket of permission. One region sees the full discourse; another sees a filtered version; a third receives only the state-sanctioned remainder. Platforms rarely acknowledge these differences. Their public messaging speaks of universal values, safety, and community standards. The lived experience is fractal and highly segmented.

Where citizens disagree with these rules, they have almost no constitutional recourse. There is no court of appeal for a mistaken removal of satire. There is no ombudsman for a community silenced by automated systems. A government can sue or regulate; an ordinary person is simply out of luck. Even journalists and public figures, who sometimes succeed in escalating a complaint through back channels, know the deeper truth: justice in this system depends on visibility, not rights. Those who are seen are heard; those who are not are lost.

The most disquieting question is not whether platforms enforce poorly, but whether they *prefer* ambiguity. Vague rules give companies flexibility to remove content that threatens business, politics, or reputation, without leaving fingerprints. A clear policy can be challenged; a fuzzy one can be defended indefinitely. When an image disappears, the user receives a message explaining that it violated "community guidelines" without saying which one. The opacity is a feature, not a bug. It maximises discretion and minimises accountability.

Citizens sense this. They learn to self-censor, not because the rules are known, but because they are unknowable. Activists avoid certain words; artists sanitise their imagery; journalists rewrite headlines to avoid automated suspicion. Speech shrinks, not from coercion, but from uncertainty.

Yet it would be too simple to treat platforms as villains. They face genuine pressures: governments demanding removals, advertisers fearful of scandal, users demanding protection from abuse. At scale, moderation without automation is impossible. No democratic institution could process millions of decisions per hour. But acknowledging difficulty does not excuse the abdication of responsibility. If platforms govern speech, they inherit the duties of governors.

The most promising reforms are not grand gestures but practical changes: policies written in plain language; human review for critical errors; transparent appeals processes with deadlines and explanations; public reporting on accuracy, bias, and training data; independent bodies with authority to audit enforcement. The infrastructure of speech needs due process. Without it, platforms behave like private police, issuing sentences without trial.

There is a deeper philosophical tension beneath all of this. Law aspires to reason: it explains itself, it invites challenge, it recognises rights. Machine enforcement aspires to efficiency: it scales, it simplifies, it silences. When platforms choose efficiency over reason, they create a domain where speech is permitted until a classifier makes a mistake. And when mistakes erase truth, democracy suffers.

The true measure of a society's commitment to free expression is not how it handles popular speech, but how it treats speech that is inconvenient, unfamiliar, or uncomfortable. In the digital public square, that test is being failed quietly. Posts vanish. Accounts disappear. Archives evaporate. History itself becomes fragile.

What happens when our record of the present is governed by private rulebooks shaped by commercial incentive and geopolitical pressure? What happens when the stories that matter most—abuses of power, moments of bravery, evidence of wrongdoing—are algorithmically mistaken for something else and buried before anyone can see them?

The internet once promised a world beyond borders. Instead, we received new ones: invisible lines encoded in terms and enforced by machines. If speech is a right, it cannot remain hostage to a system that treats its rules as secrets and its mistakes as irrelevant. The borders of the digital public square are not fixed. They are choices. And choices can change.

Local Laws, Global Feeds

A judge in one city signs an injunction. The order concerns a single post on a social network: a photo, a slogan, a political rumour. It should be visible everywhere except within her country's borders. Yet when the platform's compliance team finally implements the request, the image vanishes from the entire service. Millions of people, in dozens of countries, lose access to speech because one court found it uncomfortable. A local dispute becomes a global silence.

This is the quiet transformation of censorship in the digital age. Borders still exist, but they are porous in ways that benefit governments far more than citizens. A state that once had to intercept books at the frontier can now intercept ideas inside a server farm thousands of miles away. A national court can demand the disappearance of content hosted in California, Dublin, or Singapore. And while the initial target may be domestic, the effect radiates outward, reshaping what billions can see.

The difference between a local takedown and a global removal sounds technical. In practice, it is constitutional. When a government orders a platform to hide a message only from users inside its territory, the rest of the world retains access. Debate continues. Journalists, academics, and watchdogs can monitor what was said. But when platforms remove content worldwide, the decision becomes invisible. No one can see what was lost, or why. History shrinks without evidence of its erasure.

Platforms, anxious to avoid legal conflict, often err on the side of global removal. It is more convenient to delete once than to maintain a patchwork. Their engineers must detect the nationality of every user, route traffic accordingly, and defend the system against circumvention. A single universal deletion is faster. It is also safer for the company: a court cannot accuse it of insufficient compliance if the offending content no longer exists at all.

This is jurisdictional scope creep: the slow expansion of national speech rules beyond national borders. It happens subtly. A court orders the takedown of a defamatory post about a politician. Instead of restricting access within that country, the platform removes the post worldwide. Other governments notice. They ask for the same treatment. Soon, the most restrictive jurisdiction sets global norms.

The chilling effect does not require force; it requires precedent. Once a platform demonstrates it will erase content everywhere in response to a local ruling, every state understands it holds the same leverage. Authoritarian regimes do not need to persuade other nations; they only need to persuade the platforms. A handful of takedown orders can reshape discourse on an entire continent.

In the physical world, this would be absurd. A book banned in one nation remains on shelves elsewhere. A newspaper article prohibited in one jurisdiction can be quoted, critiqued, or archived abroad. But the infrastructure of global platforms makes the absurd possible. Speech is stored centrally, delivered globally, and erased silently.

Even democratic countries struggle with the implications. Some pursue aggressive defamation or privacy rulings that treat global removal as a reasonable remedy. Others pursue copyright cases that collateralise legitimate expression to remove pirated material. Courts often fail to distinguish between information that is illegal domestically and information that should be inaccessible to the world. The law imagines fixed borders; the network moves fast and everywhere.

Platforms, in turn, hold enormous discretion. They decide whether a takedown request is valid. They decide whether to comply narrowly or broadly. They decide whether to report the removal publicly or hide it in silence. Users rarely know that a post was removed due to government pressure. Transparency reports list aggregate numbers, but not the specific speech lost.

This ambiguity benefits both sides. A government that wishes to hide its influence avoids public scrutiny. A platform that wishes to appease regulators avoids political backlash. Citizens become bystanders to an unexamined bargain, where sovereignty is negotiated privately and implemented through code.

When the decision is wrong—or manipulated—there is little recourse. Suppose a dissident posts evidence of corruption. The ruling party seeks removal and claims that the content violates local law. If the platform removes it globally, watchdogs in other countries cannot review the evidence. International media cannot verify it. Foreign courts cannot grant asylum based on claims no longer visible. A local erasure becomes a global blindfold.

There are cases where global removal is warranted: child abuse material, terrorist propaganda, explicit calls for violence. Most societies agree such content should not be visible anywhere. But the vast majority of government takedown requests concern politics, religion, reputation, and public debate. Labelling these disputes as "safety issues" obscures the stakes. Democracy requires that some speech be seen, even when uncomfortable.

The international legal system has not caught up. There is no universal rule defining when a domestic court can demand a global removal. There is no treaty establishing due process for cross-border censorship. In the vacuum, platforms improvise policy. Some hire legal teams to scrutinise orders; others comply reflexively. Some maintain region-specific blocks; others erase content entirely. The outcome depends not on principle, but on politics.

Meanwhile, states learn to exploit the gaps. If one court can compel a global deletion, why not another? If one politician can scrub criticism worldwide, why not all? The incentives push in one direction: broader power, weaker scrutiny, deeper silence.

Citizens feel the effects without seeing the causes. A post disappears. A search result vanishes. A Wikipedia paragraph is edited. The missing piece might be benign—or essential. Without transparency, no one knows. The architecture of speech becomes a patchwork of invisible holes.

There is a philosophical cost. The internet once promised global conversation: South African activists learning from South American organisers, European journalists learning from Asian academics, and vice versa. Local erasures fracture that promise. The digital cosmopolis becomes a mosaic of national silences.

Fixing this problem requires more than technical finesse. It requires norms. Platforms should commit to the narrowest compliance possible: restrict locally, preserve globally. They should publish every takedown request, with reasoning and scope. They should warn when a post is hidden in one country but visible elsewhere. Users should be able to see the border they have run up against.

Democracies must also examine themselves. If they demand global erasures, they legitimise authoritarian demands. If they treat speech as a domestic matter in a global system, they distort the very marketplace of ideas they claim to defend. The true measure of a nation's commitment to freedom is how it behaves when speech is inconvenient—not only within its borders, but beyond them.

The stakes will only grow. As platforms consolidate, the number of choke points shrinks. A small set of companies decides what the world sees.

Their incentives align more closely with powerful states than with ordinary citizens. The question is not whether they *can* enforce local laws globally—they clearly can. The question is whether the world will let them.

When speech flows through centralised pipes, every valve becomes a tool of power. Local laws were designed for borders made of land and customs agents, not routers and cloud servers. Yet here we are: a world where a single legal order can scrub a memory that belonged to everyone. And if that power becomes normal, who will notice the next silence?

Editorial by Algorithm

A teenager opens a video app to follow the news of a protest. The feed shows cooking clips, celebrity gossip, and comedy sketches. Nothing about demonstrations, nothing about police, nothing about politics at all. In the streets outside, tens of thousands are marching; online, it looks like nothing is happening. No official ban, no explicit censorship, no takedown notice—just a ranking system quietly deciding what counts as "relevant".

That is how modern editorial power hides in plain sight. Platforms insist they are neutral conduits: they do not write articles, commission reporting, or choose headlines. Yet every feed is a front page. Every trending list is an editorial judgement. Recommendation algorithms decide which stories travel far and which stories never find an audience. They shape what users think the world is paying attention to. They decide what counts as reality.

The public seldom sees the choices being made. Platforms speak of "personalisation" and "engagement", as though the feed is a mirror reflecting the user's interests. But the mirror is angled. If the system elevates certain messages and buries others, that is not reflection—it is curation. An algorithm that suppresses uncomfortable news is performing censorship; an algorithm that amplifies it is performing journalism. Either way, the outcome is editorial.

The pretence of neutrality is a useful shield. Newspapers admit they choose stories, prioritise some voices, and ignore others—that is what an editor does. Platforms, by contrast, insist the system merely responds to user signals. In practice, those signals are engineered: infinite scroll, autoplay, push notifications, and "suggested for you" prompts all manipulate what users see. Recommendation is intervention.

Consider the ranking of political speech. When platforms promote sensational, emotional, or polarising content because it increases engagement, they are shaping political culture. When they downgrade independent journalism because it lacks virality, they are shaping public knowledge. And when they quietly demote material that governments consider sensitive, they are enforcing state narratives without firing a shot.

This matters because recommendation governs scale. A post without recommendation remains a whisper; the same post, algorithmically boosted, becomes a movement. Entire protest campaigns rise or fall depending on whether a trending system deems them worthy. A government need not ban dissent if the feed ensures no one sees it.

Some platforms publicly deny that they adjust rankings based on political pressure. Yet internal documents, leaked moderation guidelines, and whistle-blower testimony tell a more complicated story. It is common for governments to request the downranking of hashtags, the removal of trending topics, or the intentional delay of political information. The requests are framed as stability measures, disinformation responses, or public safety precautions. The effect is silence with plausible deniability.

The mechanics are subtle. A platform does not need to hide every critical post; it only needs to ensure those posts do not reach large audiences. A protest can be digitally shrunk to irrelevance. A social movement can be algorithmically confined to a small circle of already sympathetic followers, reducing its political danger. Nothing is explicitly censored; everything is quietly sidelined.

Because feeds are personal, suppression feels natural. If you never see evidence of controversy, you assume there is none. If no one seems to be discussing an issue, you conclude it lacks importance. Public attention becomes a managed commodity. The boundary between reality and perception blurs.

Even trend lists—seemingly raw reflections of popular activity—are curated. Platforms routinely exclude topics that are "sensitive", "violating", or "politically risky". A government preparing for an election might request the removal of a trending story that makes it look weak. A platform facing regulatory threats might pre-emptively avoid political heat. Users assume trends reflect the public mood; often, they reflect risk analysis inside a boardroom.

This dynamic is not confined to authoritarian states. Democratic governments also push for algorithmic shaping—sometimes openly, sometimes not. During emergencies, health crises, or security events, platforms accelerate official guidance and demote scepticism. Some of that may be justified. But decisions taken in haste can ossify into permanent policy: entire categories of speech become disfavoured because a platform no longer wants the liability.

There is a deeper philosophical tension. Traditional media has editors who can be named, questioned, and held accountable. Platforms outsource that responsibility to code. If a newspaper buries a story, journalists can demand explanation. If a feed buries a story, the platform can shrug: "The algorithm did it." Responsibility becomes abstracted until no one can be blamed.

The opacity compounds the harm. Users rarely know why a post was amplified or suppressed. Creators cannot challenge ranking decisions. Even governments struggle to understand how their citizens' attention is being shaped. Without transparency, platforms wield power that democracies have never previously allocated to private actors.

The effects reach beyond politics. Recommendation shapes culture, identity, and memory. A generation raised on algorithmic feeds learns to understand the world through statistical significance: what is "trending", what is "recommended", what is "popular among people like you". Narratives that fit the model rise; narratives that do not disappear. Entire histories can be lost if they fail to perform.

In multicultural societies, this shapes national conversation. Different groups receive different worlds. Minorities may see issues ignored by the majority; the majority may never realise what minorities are experiencing. In the past, a front page united readers around shared facts; today, feeds fracture them. The algorithm, not the editor, decides what a nation talks about.

Governments recognise the power and want a share of it. Some seek access to recommendation logic, demanding preferential treatment for state-approved sources. Others require platforms to ensure official narratives receive priority visibility. Some lobby to push dissenting links further down search results. These interventions are marketed as "information quality" measures, but they are indistinguishable from propaganda in digital clothing.

Platforms, meanwhile, claim that revealing ranking details would enable manipulation. But secrecy also enables manipulation—just by the platforms themselves. They hold the keys to national discourse, without meaningful oversight. Citizens experience a mediated public sphere, curated by entities that owe them no democratic duty.

Solutions are emerging, but imperfect. Some scholars propose *ranking transparency*: publishing metrics that show which sources were boosted, which were demoted, and why. Others advocate *user-controlled feeds*, where recommendations can be switched to chronological or community-driven modes. Some regulators push for "must-carry" rules, requiring platforms to preserve political neutrality during elections.

Yet these efforts face resistance. Platforms benefit from control. Governments benefit from influence. Citizens lack the time or power to demand change. And the global nature of feeds means local reforms may not travel well: a transparency rule in one jurisdiction may not apply elsewhere. Speech flows across borders even when regulation does not.

There is an ethical dilemma, too. Algorithmic curation is not inherently sinister. It can elevate under-represented voices, amplify marginalised communities, and expose people to perspectives they would never seek out. A feed can fight prejudice as easily as it can fuel it. The question is not whether recommendation should exist, but who shapes it, and with what accountability.

Some countries attempt to legislate neutrality, mandating platforms to treat political content equally. But perfect neutrality is impossible: ranking is always a choice. Even a chronological feed advantages the largest accounts. Even a random feed is a decision. The fantasy of impartiality distracts from the real task: governance.

A better approach is proportionality and clarity. Platforms should state when they manipulate political visibility. They should publish the criteria used to up-rank or down-rank civic information. Citizens should know when they are being steered. Only then can society decide whether the steering is legitimate.

A public sphere mediated by algorithms raises deeper questions about sovereignty. When a multinational company determines what speech is heard in a country, who holds power? When government influence crosses borders through platform decisions, whose laws apply? These are not abstract problems; they shape elections, protests, and public trust.

As feeds become the primary source of news for many people, editorial by algorithm becomes the primary form of governance. It is faster than legislation, less visible than censorship, and more pervasive than propaganda. It blurs the boundary between private product design and public political authority.

Perhaps the most unsettling truth is this: the system does not need to lie to distort reality. It only needs to choose which truths to show first.

The next time a protest seems small, a scandal seems trivial, or a debate seems settled, the question should not be "What do people think?" but "Who decided what we see?"

Crisis Protocols

A rumour flares online: a poisoned water supply, a failing bank, an armed convoy heading for the capital. The claim is false, but its spread is real. Panic unfolds not through sirens or broadcasts, but through retweets, forwards, and frantic screenshots. Within minutes, a platform must decide what to do. Remove the posts and risk suppressing truth? Leave them up and risk chaos? Downgrade them quietly and hope the fire dies out? There is no law book for this moment, only improvised rules written at full speed.

Crisis concentrates power. In emergencies, platforms that normally insist they are neutral conduits become de facto public authorities. Health scares, election narratives, military clashes: every one demands decisions about which information is trustworthy, which accounts can be believed, and which messages must be contained. Governments turn to platforms as information infrastructure; platforms turn to governments for guidance or legitimacy. The result is a hurried fusion of technical systems and political judgement.

The hallmark of these moments is centralisation. Regular moderation involves sprawling processes—contractors in multiple countries, automated filters, appeals, and community guidelines. Crisis strips all that away. Decisions move to war rooms, escalation channels, and executive suites. A handful of people determine what the world will see. The public seldom learns who they are, what evidence they reviewed, or what trade-offs they accepted. The complexity is hidden behind statements about "protecting users" or "maintaining the integrity of the platform".

Speed forces simplification. Platforms adopt sweeping rules: remove specific keywords, block certain hashtags, demote whole categories of content. The principles are broad, sometimes crude, because nuance is expensive under time pressure. When a rumour spreads faster than staff can investigate, algorithms step in as blunt armour. Entire regions may see throttled sharing; fact-checking labels proliferate even on harmless posts. Error rates spike. Some truthful voices vanish alongside the malicious ones.

Governments treat these systems as tools of stability. In high-risk moments, officials demand accelerated takedowns, wider filters, and rapid demotions. Few platforms refuse. Regulatory threats, licence pressure, and national security rhetoric make cooperation seem prudent. Yet the effect is subtle concentration of power: emergency rules blur into everyday governance. What begins as crisis response becomes a default posture of caution.

Public health offers a vivid illustration. When inaccurate medical claims spread, platforms cooperate with health authorities, elevating official sources and suppressing rumours. The intentions may be admirable. But authority is not infallible. Experts disagree, advice changes, and uncertainty is the rule rather than the exception. In these conditions, platforms still act as if certainty exists. The feed becomes a controlled channel for approved knowledge. Alternative hypotheses—some reckless, others merely inconvenient—are pushed down or pulled out.

Elections produce similar tensions. Platforms remove posts that could mislead voters, demote disputed claims, or limit resharing on sensitive topics. These interventions arguably protect democracy. They also constitute editorial choices about what kinds of persuasion are acceptable. If a platform quietly suppresses a scandal, it shapes a national narrative. If it overcorrects, it can appear partisan. Crisis protocols are meant to defend electoral integrity; they can just as easily distort it.

Conflict magnifies the stakes further. During armed confrontation, platforms attempt to stop incitement, clamp down on hate speech, and limit graphic content. But they also remove eyewitness testimony, censor reporting, and obscure human rights abuses. Automated filters—trained on imperfect data—misclassify war documentation as violence or propaganda. Governments pressure platforms to promote patriotic messaging or suppress dissent. Civil society groups beg them to preserve evidence of atrocities. Moderators face impossible decisions with irreversible effects.

The common pattern is opacity. When platforms intervene, the public rarely learns why. Statements are vague: "inauthentic behaviour", "misinformation", "violating our community standards". Appeals are slow or non-existent. Researchers trying to audit decisions face secrecy. Those who are silenced have little recourse. When emergency rules affect millions of posts, accountability collapses.

It is tempting to blame platforms alone, but governments exploit the uncertainty. Emergency powers expand discretion, sometimes indefinitely. Courts may be bypassed. Takedown requests multiply, often without transparency. Platforms comply to avoid legal jeopardy, especially when operating in multiple jurisdictions. Citizens face a double blind: they cannot see whether a removal was a platform choice, a government order, or a pre-emptive gesture to fend off political heat.

The philosophical dilemma is sharp. Speed saves lives during crises; hesitation can cause real harm. But rules written in haste often outlast the emergency. After a health scare, platforms find it easier to keep suppressing medical controversy than to reopen debate. After an election, they continue dampening political virality. Crisis protocols harden into permanent architecture.

Some scholars argue for "crisis governance charters"—predefined playbooks agreed upon by platforms, regulators, and civil society. These would specify triggers, oversight, error tracking, and sunset clauses. In theory, this would trade improvisation for legitimacy. In practice, crises are unpredictable, and governments are reluctant to bind themselves. Platforms likewise prefer discretion. They believe they must be free to act fast and learn later. Citizens are asked to trust that the right judgment was made.

There is also the problem of narratives: what counts as harmful information? In democracies, competing parties accuse each other of misinformation. In authoritarian states, dissent is labelled destabilising. Platforms operating globally cannot rely on one definition of truth; they must choose which government's version to follow. A post removed as misinformation in one country may remain visible elsewhere. That inconsistency is not a bug—it is political geography in digital form.

The accountability gap becomes most visible at the edges: whistle-blowers who claim posts were suppressed for political convenience; journalists who find their reporting repeatedly flagged; activists who watch their documentation disappear. Platforms promise appeals, but in emergencies those processes slow or vanish. People lose their speech rights precisely when speech is most consequential.

At the same time, crisis protocols can genuinely prevent harm. Rapid takedowns can limit coordinated harassment. Visibility limits can reduce bloodshed during volatile moments. Labelled corrections can slow the spread of false health advice. The problem is not the existence of emergency tools, but the absence of safeguards around them.

A more resilient model would include layered accountability: independent audits of removals, public metrics of error rates, timelines for restoring suppressed material, and clear records of state requests. Platforms could publish *after-action reports* detailing what worked, what failed, and what changed permanently. Governments could subject emergency orders to judicial review. None of these changes require revealing sensitive data; they simply require admitting that digital crisis management is a form of governance, not customer service.

The deeper question is cultural. Societies are still learning how to navigate collective truth when information moves faster than verification. Platforms were built for sharing, not adjudication. Governments were built for deliberation, not instantaneous response. Crises demand speed, but democracy demands scrutiny. The two can coexist, but only if the systems handling information treat citizens as stakeholders, not problems to be managed.

As the world faces more emergencies—climatic, political, medical—the default will remain centralised, rapid, and opaque unless people demand otherwise. The infrastructure now exists to shut down speech within minutes, coordinate messaging globally, and steer public perception with unprecedented precision. Whether that infrastructure is used to protect or to control will depend on rules that do not yet meaningfully exist.

What begins with a rumour about poisoned water can end as a precedent for digital authoritarianism. The hardest part is that citizens may never know which line was crossed, or when.

Transparency that Matters

A user discovers her post has vanished. No explanation, no warning, no appeal link—just absence. She checks her inbox, scans her notifications, and refreshes the page. Nothing. It is a small loss for the platform, but a profound one for her. She has been judged, but she does not know by whom or by what rule. She does not know whether it will happen again. And because she cannot see the system, she cannot challenge it.

This is the quiet heart of transparency: not spectacle, not PR, but the ability for ordinary people to understand the forces that act upon them. Digital speech is mediated by infrastructure most citizens cannot inspect, and most platforms would rather not explain. They gesture towards openness—

"community standards published online", "quarterly transparency reports", "partnerships with fact-checkers"—but much of this is symbolic. Real transparency is operational, not decorative. It explains *how decisions are made*, *how often they go wrong*, and *what recourse exists* when the system fails.

Platforms remove millions of posts each day, often with automated filters that are fallible, biased, and occasionally absurd. A breastfeeding image becomes pornography; a war crime video becomes "graphic content"; a political joke is flagged as extremism. When this happens, users are not simply annoyed—they are excluded from a civic space that increasingly functions as public square, workplace, and archive. Yet most "transparency" documents do not reveal how often these mistakes occur. Platforms publish global takedown numbers that are vast but meaningless. A million removals says nothing about whether the rules worked, merely that the machinery was active.

What people need are error rates: how many decisions were overturned on appeal, how many flagged posts were later restored, and how many removals were made solely by machines. These metrics would illuminate the reliability of the system. Instead, they are buried. Appeals data, when shared at all, arrives in aggregate summaries that smooth out the stories of wrongful silencing and bureaucratic limbo. A functioning justice system does not only declare verdicts; it records mistakes.

The second missing ingredient is escalation paths. When someone believes they have been wrongly punished, there should be somewhere to go—and someone accountable at the other end. Currently, most appeals do not involve humans. They are routed through automated queues and judged by criteria that the platform refuses to disclose. Even when people reach a human moderator, that moderator is often temporary staff following inflexible checklists. The process resembles customer service for a lost parcel, not adjudication of speech rights.

Imagine if newspapers handled libel this way—opaque, unappealable, and silent. The outrage would be immense. Yet platforms govern speech on far greater scale, with fewer safeguards. Transparent escalation paths would change that. Users should know: how their appeal is reviewed, how many human checks occur, and whether independent oversight exists. Even the most privacy-conscious intelligence agencies publish some version of this structure. Platforms that shape public discourse can do the same.

The third pillar—dataset lineage—is the most technical and the least understood. Nearly every moderation decision now depends on machine learning. These systems do not apply human law; they apply statistical judgements based on examples they were trained on. If the dataset is biased, the enforcement will be biased. If the dataset excludes certain languages, dialects, or cultural contexts, the model will fail on those groups. This is not theoretical. Research repeatedly shows that hate speech detectors struggle with reclaimed slurs, satire, minority languages, and AAVE. Yet platforms rarely disclose what data their models were trained on, who labelled it, or how representative it is.

Dataset lineage would make these systems contestable. It would allow independent researchers to audit bias. It would let civil society verify that classifiers reflect society, not the prejudices of outsourced labellers. Crucially, it would allow users to question outcomes—not just accept the verdict of an inscrutable machine.

Why do platforms avoid this? They fear giving adversaries clues about how to evade detection. They fear revealing the sheer volume of errors. They fear admitting that their technological sophistication is, in many areas, brittle. But secrecy does not eliminate criticism; it intensifies distrust. When a sexual assault survivor has her testimony removed as "adult content", or when a journalist's reporting disappears as "misinformation", opacity turns injury into suspicion.

Some platforms have started publishing transparency dashboards. But many are immaculately designed emptiness—charts without context, numbers without interpretation. A report that "two million posts were removed for extremism" tells nothing of quality. Were they accurate? Could users appeal? Did governments request those removals? How many were reinstated? Without such details, transparency becomes theatre.

Useful transparency must be boringly specific. It names error categories. It publishes monthly appeal success rates. It clarifies whether takedowns were automated or manual. It discloses which governments issued legal orders and how many were rejected. It logs the average time to restore wrongly removed content. These are metrics citizens can understand, journalists can scrutinise, and lawmakers can debate.

Consider what standardised reporting might look like. Every major platform could deliver quarterly statements with consistent fields:

False positives: percentage of content wrongly removed and subsequently restored.

Appeal turnaround: median time from appeal submission to decision, separated by content category.

Model coverage: languages and regions where automated tools are deployed, and where they are absent.

Human oversight: proportion of moderation actions reviewed by people, not machines.

Government orders: number received, number declined, and legal basis invoked.

Dataset lineage: sources of training data, including whether local communities participated.

None of these disclosures reveal platform secrets. They reveal competence.

Researchers and journalists could compare systems across jurisdictions. Users could see whether they are treated fairly. Advocacy organisations could detect discrimination. And platforms would have incentives to reduce mistakes rather than conceal them.

Some critics argue that transparency empowers bad actors: trolls learning how to avoid bans, propagandists studying detection thresholds. Yet secrecy already fails to stop them. The people most harmed by opacity are ordinary citizens, not professionals of manipulation. If platforms treat speech as a governed space, citizens deserve the equivalent of parliamentary records: clear, structured, and auditable.

There is also a philosophical dimension. Transparency is not just protection—it is dignity. When a person knows why they were judged, they remain a participant in the system, not its victim. Even a justified punishment feels fairer when the rule is visible. Justice must not only be done; it must be seen to be done.

The alternative is invisible governance—rules that apply without explanation, punishments delivered without reason, and evidence hidden from view. That model was once the hallmark of authoritarianism. Today it appears in sleek corporate products, wrapped in brand language about safety and trust. Politeness does not make it benign.

Transparency that matters is not a corporate favour; it is a democratic norm. If platforms wish to host public conversation, they must be accountable to the public. Citizens should know how many mistakes occur, how disputes are handled, and who bears responsibility. Anything less is rule by software fiat.

None of this demands perfection. Mistakes will happen, especially at global scale. The point is not to shame platforms for errors, but to illuminate them. Only visible failures can be corrected. Only measurable bias can be reduced. Only recorded removals can be audited. A moderation system is a justice system in miniature; it deserves the same scrutiny.

The next decade will be defined by whether citizens can see the infrastructures that govern their speech. If transparency remains ornamental—vague blogs, glossy dashboards, selective anecdotes—distrust will deepen. If transparency becomes operational—standardised, comparable, and comprehensible—public confidence may follow.

And yet, the incentives remain misaligned. Platforms fear lawsuits. Governments prefer discretion. Users often do not realise how many decisions happen in the shadows. Without pressure, change will be slow. But the pressure is growing. Researchers demand data. Regulators demand accountability. Users demand explanations.

Perhaps the real question is simple: if platforms are confident their systems are fair, why not show the evidence?

Silence is an answer, too.

Chapter 6

Money, Payments, and Platform Borders

A dissident newspaper can survive without social media. It can survive without search indexing. It can even survive when its website is blocked, slipping through mirrors and proxies until someone finds it. But it cannot survive when every payment processor refuses to touch it. Servers cost money. Reporters must be paid. Legal fees arrive on schedule, even when freedom does not. Silence the money, and the speech falls quiet. In the modern information war, financial choke points often achieve what censorship cannot: quiet, deniable, devastating compliance.

Money has always been a border. The difference now is that those borders are programmable, automated, and sometimes invisible. Platforms shape not only what people can say, but whether they can earn, donate, subscribe, or transact. When a creator loses access to payouts, their audience does not disappear; their livelihood does. When a civic group cannot accept donations, its message becomes a wish rather than a campaign. The old model imagined censorship as a government blocking words. The new model often begins with a platform blocking payments.

This chapter follows the movement of money through digital systems and shows how those movements define the limits of speech, participation, and power. Payments infrastructure decides who may build an institution, who may raise funds at scale, who may turn influence into income, and who may be quietly throttled without a single post removed. The public sees content; the platforms see cash flow.

The first mechanism is the payment switch. Block a post and the speaker can rephrase it. Block an account and the speaker can create a new one. But block the money—cut off merchant services, subscription rails, donation platforms—and you end the enterprise. Some governments know this well. Rather than banning a controversial organisation by law, they pressure payment firms to drop it. The firm complies "voluntarily", and the state has what it wants without judicial scrutiny. A handful of API calls can accomplish what a repressive statute once required. The result looks commercial, not political, which is precisely why it works.

Next come the app stores, the customs checkpoints of the global internet. Every app seeking entry must pass inspection: security scanning, legal compliance, content policy, and sometimes local politics. A developer might write one piece of code, but it becomes many different apps, each tailored to a region's demands. In one country, a VPN app is perfectly legal; in another, it is contraband. Store policies become living borders, changing overnight with regulatory pressure or diplomatic tension. App stores are rarely described as policing speech, yet their choices dictate which tools people may use to speak at all.

Advertising markets add a softer kind of control. Ads do not silence speakers directly—they starve them or nourish them. A platform can quietly decide that certain categories of political speech cannot be monetised. A brand safety system can block entire topics as "sensitive", whether or not they are newsworthy. Entire communities have discovered that their content is allowed, but unprofitable. Visibility remains, but viability disappears. The public never sees a takedown notice; the income simply dries up.

Behind these decisions sit compliance stacks: KYC checks, anti-money laundering filters, sanctions lists, fraud scores. To financial institutions, these are risk controls. To dissidents, journalists, and activists, they can be bars of a cage. A bank need not say "we find your speech objectionable"; it can simply cite risk policy. Platforms and fintech gateways enforce these rules algorithmically, flagging certain geographies, networks, or surnames as high-risk. Because the logic is opaque, those affected do not know whether they are judged for what they say, where they live, or what they are presumed to be.

Yet borders also invite escape routes. Gift cards, prepaid vouchers, peer-to-peer transfers, stablecoins, crypto rails—these form parallel economies for people who are excluded from official systems. Remittances move across continents through messaging apps; donations flow through tokens when traditional processors refuse. These workarounds carry new vulnerabilities: scams, volatility, surveillance, and the constant threat of shutdown. But they demonstrate a deeper truth: when platforms close one gate, people build another.

Money, payments, and platform borders matter because they change who can participate in public life. They decide who may sustain a movement, who may build a business, who may turn an audience into an institution.

A silenced bank account is as effective as a silenced voice. And while content moderation is debated in parliaments and newsrooms, financial moderation often operates in shadows, framed as fraud prevention rather than political choice.

The chapter that follows shows how payment switches can disable speech, how app stores act as customs authorities, how advertising systems entangle profit with politics, how fintech gateways enforce digital sanctions with silent precision, and how parallel economies emerge when the official rails narrow. It asks a simple but unsettling question: what does free expression mean when the infrastructure that sustains it can be turned off without a word?

The borders of the digital world are no longer drawn only around what you can say. Increasingly, they are drawn around what you can earn, buy, or support. To understand modern censorship, we must follow the money.

The Payment Switch

A dissident newspaper in the twentieth century could survive extraordinary pressure. If the state seized the printing press, the editors found a new one; if censors blacked out their columns, they distributed pamphlets; if the police shut down distribution, couriers carried copies by hand. Speech was fragile, but money was tangible; supporters placed coins on tables, lawyers accepted envelopes, and paper still existed. Today, a publication can reach millions without printing a single sheet—but if its payment processor closes the account, its voice evaporates. There is no ink to buy, no server to host, no staff to pay. The website remains online, yet the institution underneath is starved.

That is the paradox of digital free expression: the most powerful tool of censorship is not the removal of words but the removal of revenue. A platform might tolerate provocative speech, but refuse to pay the person who speaks it. A government may claim to value open debate, yet quietly pressure a bank to drop a troublesome organisation. The public sees only the silence that follows, not the switch that was flipped. To restrict information, it is often more effective to block the money than the message.

Payment infrastructure was not designed as a political instrument. It was built for fraud detection, risk scoring, and transaction security. Yet these systems sit at the hinge of speech and sustainability. Unlike content moderation—messy, public, and endlessly debatable—financial exclusion happens quietly. A button is pressed, a policy invoked, and the flow of funds stops. No headlines, no courtrooms, no dramatic confrontation. Just a black hole where support used to be.

Consider how donation platforms have become lifelines for independent media, grassroots organisations, creators, and movements. Crowdfunding is not merely commerce; it is collective will converted into financial capacity. When a donation processor withdraws service, it is not just a lost revenue stream—it is the removal of a civic oxygen supply. A news outlet that cannot receive reader support cannot pay journalists. An activist group that cannot collect funds cannot mount legal defences. A humanitarian project that loses its payment gateway cannot respond to emergencies, even if public support remains overwhelming.

Platforms know this power. Governments know it too. In some countries, the fastest way to neutralise a civil society organisation is not to draft a ban, but to call a bank. The financial firm rarely fights back; risk departments are conservative by nature, and reputational exposure is avoided at all costs. A request that would provoke a constitutional crisis if delivered to a newspaper editor becomes mundane when delivered to a payment processor. The same hands that fight fraud and terrorism financing are now enlisted to limit dissent. The line between risk management and political convenience blurs.

Not all payment shutdowns originate with states. Platforms themselves apply moral, commercial, or reputational filters. A creator may gain a vast following on a video site, yet discover their payouts suspended because advertisers dislike the topic. A musician might sell millions of streams but see their earnings withheld due to identity verification issues that never resolve. The punishment appears technical, not ideological, which makes it harder to challenge and easier to justify. The audience hears the music; the artist never sees the royalties.

For small organisations, this fragility is existential. A sudden freeze on payments can collapse operations in days. The organisation may still have a loyal audience, powerful arguments, and international support—yet without access to funds they become spectators to their own disappearance. In some jurisdictions, even a rumour of regulatory scrutiny can push fintech firms to pre-emptively disengage. It is safer to over-comply, safer to sever connection, safer to drop the edge case than defend the principle.

Financial platforms often describe these decisions as neutral, citing terms of service rather than public policy. But neutrality is a myth when access to payments determines who can operate. A digital bank that refuses accounts for whistle-blowers is not neutral; a crowdfunding platform that blocks environmental activism after political pressure is not neutral; a creator economy platform that demonetises minority communities while leaving dominant voices untouched is not neutral. Payment switches shape the civic sphere just as surely as content filters do.

Because these decisions take place far from public scrutiny, accountability is minimal. Users receive vague emails: "Your account has been suspended for violation of policy." They are invited to appeal into a void, where responses are automated and timelines indefinite. Evidence is rarely disclosed; reasoning is redacted as proprietary. Even regulators struggle to obtain transparency, because payment processors position themselves as technical intermediaries, not arbiters of speech.

There is a deeper philosophical tension beneath this surface. Digital platforms have fused expression with infrastructure. To publish is to host. To build a movement is to process transactions. To exist as an independent creator is to accept platform-mediated payments. These structures create extraordinary freedom—anyone can start a publication or a business in minutes. But they also create dependency: if a single company decides you are a risk, you vanish.

Supporters often point to alternative funding methods. Why not move donations to cryptocurrency? Why not use prepaid gift cards, stablecoins, or informal remittances? These workarounds show ingenuity, but they are not universal. They require technical literacy; they impose fees; they expose users to scams; they attract regulatory suspicion. More importantly, they require the public to change habits, which most will not. The payment switch works precisely because mainstream financial rails are frictionless, trusted, and familiar. When access is cut, the fallback options are narrow and uneven.

Even well-resourced organisations fear financial exclusion. Large media outlets, global NGOs, and political campaigns negotiate with banks as carefully as they negotiate with legislators. Payment access is strategic infrastructure: a single disruption during a critical moment—an election, a humanitarian crisis, an investigative exposé—can derail entire operations. Quiet pressure applied at the right moment can achieve political goals without ever requiring a public ban.

Some defend payment controls as necessary. Platforms must comply with sanctions, anti-money laundering rules, and fraud checks. Governments argue that dangerous groups exploit financial systems to cause real harm.

These dangers are not imaginary; there are legitimate reasons to regulate transactions. But the problem is not the existence of rules—it is the opacity of their application. When a civic group is treated like a criminal enterprise, but given no evidence and no appeal, the legal justification becomes irrelevant. Power without transparency is indistinguishable from abuse.

There is also a subtle shift in how financial systems evaluate risk. Algorithms look for patterns, not contexts. A journalist reporting on extremist groups may trigger the same filters as the extremists themselves. A charity operating in a sanctioned region may be flagged alongside money launderers. False positives are inevitable, yet the responsibility to contest them lies entirely with the accused. Without visibility into scoring logic, they are trapped: presumed risky until proven safe.

The payment switch therefore creates its own geography of silence. Regions with tighter financial surveillance see more shutdowns. Diaspora groups sending remittances face suspicion. Minority communities reliant on crowdfunding find themselves disproportionately flagged. Marginalised voices—the very people who benefit most from digital expression—become the easiest to financially undermine.

The pressure does not have to be overt. A platform can discourage certain activities simply by increasing friction: additional verification checks, delayed payouts, elevated fees, mandatory security reviews. None of these measures break the rules; they merely break momentum. For a small organisation, a six-week delay in receiving funds is as damaging as a ban. The public never learns that a financial lever was pulled.

The result is a form of censorship that hides in plain sight. Users are not told that a voice is suppressed; they simply stop seeing new work. Movements seem to lose energy. Creators fade from feeds. Journalists announce "funding difficulties". The silence looks organic, even voluntary. In reality, a handful of private firms performed acts that once required entire ministries.

The payment switch raises uncomfortable questions. Should financial platforms be allowed to unilaterally determine who can earn a living? Should governments be able to weaponise compliance departments, using risk language to mask political suppression? Should the right to transact be considered part of the broader right to speak? If speech is free but funding is not, is the freedom meaningful?

There are paths forward. Transparency is the first: publish reasons for shutdowns, disclose error rates, allow independent audits. Appeals must involve humans, not auto-generated emails. Differentiation matters: a journalist investigating extremism is not an extremist; a charity supporting civilians in a conflict zone is not a combatant. Regulators could demand due process, so that financial exclusion cannot be imposed through insinuation. Civil society groups can build support funds and legal defences for those who are wrongly targeted. None of these solutions are simple; all are necessary.

The larger lesson is that digital speech and digital finance are no longer separable. To speak at scale is to join an economy. To silence a speaker, you can disrupt that economy. The payment switch is the most powerful border in the platform world because it works quietly, efficiently, and without public debate.

Some borders are drawn in code, others in law, and others in money. The most dangerous are those that appear automatic—those that look like neutral security measures while shaping who may participate in society. When a donation link fails, when a creator's income evaporates, when a civic group cannot receive funds, we should ask not just what happened, but who demanded it.

If the future of free expression depends not only on what we are allowed to say, but whether we are allowed to sustain ourselves while saying it, how should societies respond? The world has spent decades debating the boundaries of speech. Perhaps it is time to debate the boundaries of payment—and who controls the switch.

App Stores as Customs

A developer can publish an idea to the world in the time it takes to compile code. Yet the same app, unchanged, may appear instantly in one country's store, linger for weeks in another, and never surface at all in a third. Nothing about the software varies: the code is identical, the icon the same. What differs is the border it encounters. The app store is not merely a catalogue; it is a frontier post. Every submission is inspected, stamped, and either waved through or quietly turned away. For billions of users, this is the only route into the digital marketplace. And, like any border, it enforces rules—some visible, others opaque.

Developers understand this more keenly than most citizens understand their own customs systems. They fill in forms. They declare what their app contains. They answer probing questions about encryption, labour laws, payment flows, user-generated content, political material, gambling mechanics, and data collection. Their work is scanned by automated systems, and if flagged, interrogated by humans. The rejection notices read like bureaucratic verdicts: insufficient safeguards, inappropriate content, or—most frustrating of all—non-compliance with local regulations. These rules do not originate solely from corporate policy. Many are demands of national governments, quietly baked into review checklists. The result is a hybrid border: commercial at the surface, sovereign beneath it.

For consumers, this border is invisible. They search for a podcast app and download whatever appears. Yet what appears is curated by national context. In one jurisdiction, health apps must partner with accredited medical providers; in another, apps offering encryption must include key-escrow mechanisms; in a third, content relating to politics is unavailable around election periods. Nothing is announced. Users simply never see what isn't allowed. The silence looks natural.

Framing app stores as customs is more than metaphor. Like customs officers, reviewers inspect goods before entry, enforce lists of prohibited items, and apply local tariffs—in this case, commissions and payment rules. They require disclosures about ingredients: which SDKs are used, which tracking libraries are embedded, which external services are called. They seize contraband: malware, spyware, unlicensed gambling mechanics. Sometimes, they even demand modifications: remove this feature, shift that button, change this payment flow. Only then can the developer receive their entry stamp.

The analogy deepens when considering regional variants. Major mobile ecosystems maintain distinct stores for different geographies. The China edition is not the France edition, which is not the Brazil edition. Apps that operate globally discover that their code lives parallel lives: allowed in one region, restricted in another, legally compelled to alter behaviour in a third. These are living borders—constantly updated, politically responsive, and commercially entangled. When sanctions tighten, apps vanish. When child-protection rules change, age gates appear overnight. When new data-localisation laws emerge, foreign cloud storage becomes non-compliant, and developers are forced to build in-country infrastructure or withdraw completely.

Consider a small meditation app. It uses a third-party library to manage subscriptions, which happens to include analytics features prohibited under a new privacy law. The developer may not even know. The app is scanned, flagged, delayed. In the meantime, a competitor passes through customs smoothly, gaining market share. The border has reshaped competition without a single courtroom involved. The audience learns nothing of this hidden sorting. To them, the winning product simply appears superior.

Platform review teams insist they are neutral. Their enforcement, they argue, protects users from fraud, malware, and harmful content. Often, that is true. Yet neutrality erodes when governments lean on these private gatekeepers. A regulator contacts a platform; a review team updates internal guidance; what was once acceptable now violates "regional policy". No law changes. No public debate occurs. The store transforms into a de facto censor, under the banner of safety.

Even when the objective is positive—child protection, healthcare accuracy, consumer rights—the instruments are blunt. Automated scanning systems misjudge satire as extremism, educational health games as medical advice, and encrypted messaging tools as suspicious. Developers appeal, but appeals are slow and opaque. Decisions arrive with the bureaucratic finality of border control: no explanation beyond a generic clause, no escalation path, no accountability. When the livelihood of a small studio depends on a store listing, the cost of contesting is enormous. Many simply comply.

The power imbalance is stark. Two or three firms control nearly all mobile distribution worldwide. If both reject an app, it effectively ceases to exist. The web is theoretically an alternative, yet mobile operating systems steer users relentlessly toward app stores—nudging, warning, and disabling features to ensure compliance. Access to users is thus mediated by a small number of private companies tasked with interpreting not only corporate guidelines but national politics.

In some countries, the store itself is weaponised. Political satire apps disappear. News outlets find themselves unable to update their listings. Privacy tools face endless delays. Financially sensitive apps—donation platforms, remittance tools, cryptocurrency wallets—meet heightened scrutiny. Developers report being asked for additional documentation that never resolves, or told to consult regulatory bodies that offer no clear pathway. The customs metaphor tightens: undesirable goods are not seized publicly; they are simply held indefinitely at the border.

The store's review process shapes global discourse in quieter ways too. When an app includes a premium subscription, store policies dictate how payment is collected. In some regions, platforms mandate in-app purchases with steep commissions. Developers who refuse are removed. This is economic customs enforcement: a tariff on access. Countries have begun contesting this, arguing for domestic competition and payments independence. The irony is rich—a sovereign state demanding sovereignty inside a private border.

Behind the scenes, automated tools scan codebases for banned APIs, outdated permissions, or references to restricted regions. Machine learning models monitor screenshots for inappropriate imagery. Logs are inspected for data-sharing patterns. It is industrial-grade customs at a planetary scale, conducted in milliseconds. But scale brings error. Innocent apps receive warnings for imaginary violations. Harmful apps slip through because bad actors learn how to mimic compliance. It is cat-and-mouse, just like any border.

Developers try to adapt. They maintain localisation teams, compliance officers, and regional partners. They strip sensitive features from certain countries—maps without borders, chat apps without group messaging, browsers without incognito modes. They create separate builds for separate jurisdictions. Over time, the "same app" becomes many different apps, splintered by policy. The border fragments the digital landscape, one quiet restriction at a time.

Some argue that this fragmentation is justified. Each nation has the right to enforce its own laws. Platforms should not override democratically enacted rules. Others counter that many restrictions stem not from democratic process but from opaque demands. Still others note that app stores operate as monopolistic gatekeepers with minimal public accountability. The tension is unresolved: national sovereignty, corporate sovereignty, and user autonomy collide inside a review queue.

For users, these dynamics have civic consequences. Activism apps may exist in one country but not another. Independent media may be accessible on one handset and missing entirely on another. Educational resources may be blocked where governments fear their content. Citizens do not vote on these outcomes. The decisions are made elsewhere, in a mixture of corporate policy, political pressure, and compliance anxiety.

The customs metaphor also reveals a truth about digital mobility. A traveller crossing a physical border might hide a forbidden book in a suitcase. But an app cannot be smuggled past a store. Even when citizens resort to sideloading—installing apps outside the official store—operating systems erect obstacles: security warnings, restrictions on background services, disabled notifications. The message is clear: stay within the authorised marketplace.

Yet some borders generate their own resistance. Parallel stores emerge—unofficial, unregulated, and often unsafe. Governments launch national app stores to ensure local control. Developers flock to open-web technologies to escape gatekeeping altogether. The store border holds, but it cracks at the edges.

The most profound question is about legitimacy. Who should decide which apps a citizen can install? Is it a corporation headquartered elsewhere? A regulator issuing quiet demands? Or users themselves? At the moment, the answer is a muddle. The public is told that store policies are for safety and quality. Sometimes they are. Sometimes they serve strategic interests that have little to do with user welfare.

Customs systems are judged by transparency and accountability. App stores rarely provide either. Their rules change without notice. Their appeal systems rely on canned responses. Their enforcement may be inconsistent or politically responsive. A digital border that controls expression, commerce, health, and education ought to meet higher standards than "internal policy".

As global tensions rise around digital sovereignty, app stores will become more contested, not less. Nations will demand their rules be enforced. Platforms will resist, then accommodate, then over-correct. Developers will complain, adapt, and compromise. Users will continue to live inside invisible perimeters that decide what tools they may access. The border will grow more complex, more dynamic, more consequential.

At some point, societies will have to choose: should these borders be public law or corporate protocol? Should users have rights when apps are denied entry? Should developers receive due process? Should review systems disclose error rates and political requests? These are not niche questions for technologists. They are civic questions for everyone living in a world where the digital marketplace is the public square.

If app stores are the customs posts of the modern world, who gets to write the customs code? And what happens to a society when most of its borders are invisible, unaccountable, and updated overnight with no public record?

Ad Markets as Soft Power

A political movement can have millions of supporters, volunteers in every city, and a message honed for the national moment. Yet if the major advertising platforms deny its campaigns, restrict its targeting, or brand it *unsafe*, the public may never see it. The movement still speaks, but its voice is muffled, heard only by those already listening. Meanwhile, a commercial brand with a generous budget and approved creative can reach the same audience in minutes. Nothing about speech has changed. Only the plumbing of promotion has.

Advertising markets once felt like infrastructure—dull, technical, automated. But in the age of digital platforms, they are closer to geopolitical instruments. The buying rules, eligibility standards, political restrictions, and brand-safety filters shape public discourse as surely as editorial decisions in a newsroom. A post that reaches ten people matters little; a post boosted to ten million can sway a nation. Control over amplification is control over attention, and attention is the currency of modern speech.

The paradox of the digital public square is that most voices are free to speak, yet few are free to be heard at scale. Platforms insist that amplification is a commercial service, not a civic right. Their policies are framed as business rules: advertisers must comply with brand safety, consumer protection, and political transparency. Yet when these rules intersect with national politics—when campaigns are silenced, advocacy groups demoted, or civic education throttled—the economic veneer wears thin. Ad markets become instruments of soft power: subtle, deniable, and immensely effective.

Brand safety appears innocuous. Platforms do not want advertisements placed next to extremist propaganda or violent content. But brand safety is a broad category, and its operationalisation is delegated to machine-learning classifiers trained on shifting definitions of harm. The result is a form of algorithmic caution that sweeps in more than the intended targets. A human rights group documenting police violence may find its adverts banned because the footage is graphic. A mental health charity discussing suicide prevention is flagged for sensitive content. By protecting brands from reputational risk, platforms quietly restrict the visibility of non-profits and civic actors. Advertisers pay; dissenters explain themselves to automated systems that rarely listen.

Political advertising is even more fraught. Some platforms require identity verification, government-issued documents, and region-specific disclaimers. Others ban political ads outright, forcing campaigns to rely on organic reach that algorithms may never surface. The assumption is that political spending online is inherently dangerous, prone to manipulation. There is truth in that. Yet the consequence is that challenger parties, activists, and minority movements are disadvantaged, while established players with mainstream media access retain their megaphones. Efforts to clean up the system can entrench power as easily as dismantle it.

National regulation further complicates the picture. Governments demand that platforms restrict foreign-funded political ads, prohibit "divisive" content, or allow state agencies priority access to ad-buying tools. Some states insist that only registered parties can advertise on civic issues. Others expand the scope so broadly that environmental groups, religious charities, or immigration advocates fall under "political influence". The definitions creep. Soft power becomes policy.

For platforms, political compliance is not just a legal matter but a business necessity. Ad revenues depend on licences, tax agreements, and regulatory goodwill. When a government signals displeasure, platforms often adjust their policies before any law is passed. The shift is subtle: tightened keyword bans, increased documentation requirements, stricter creative review. These changes are rarely announced loudly. They appear in updated policy pages, unseen by the public but felt by those denied access.

Behind all this is the architecture of automated auctions. Advertisers bid for user attention, and algorithms decide whose message wins. These auctions are supposed to be neutral—highest quality ad at the lowest cost. But "quality" is a platform-defined metric. It might favour content predicted to generate positive engagement, meaning cheerful, consensus material travels farther than challenging, complex speech. A civic education campaign that warns people about disinformation may receive lower scores because it dwells on negativity. The algorithm is not malicious; it is simply designed to maximise pleasant clicks. But pleasant clicks do not always serve democracy.

There is an additional tension between corporate incentives and national aims. Platforms thrive when advertisers spend freely. If a government demands that certain political campaigns be throttled, platforms may comply to protect market access. Conversely, if a ruling party's political ads are lucrative, a platform might interpret the rules flexibly. State-backed messaging becomes just another profitable client. The border between commerce and propaganda blurs.

Some platforms offer ad libraries and transparency dashboards. In theory, these tools reveal who pays for political messaging and how audiences are targeted. In practice, they are incomplete. Ads vanish once they stop running. Targeting criteria are summarised vaguely. Content categorisation is patchy. Researchers struggle to audit the system, and citizens rarely know what messages are being whispered to their neighbours. The democratic expectation—that political persuasion should happen in daylight—is lost in a haze of micro-targeting and proprietary secrecy.

Even when platforms insist on neutrality, they cannot avoid editorial power. Choosing which ads are allowed, which keywords are banned, which targeting parameters are visible, and which groups are flagged as sensitive—all of this is policy. All of it shapes which ideas circulate. In some countries, advocacy campaigns for LGBTQ+ rights are deemed adult content and forced behind age walls. In others, feminist organisations find their promotions restricted for "social issues" that require special labelling. A bureaucratic classification can sideline a social movement without ever mentioning its name.

Advertisers have also become geopolitical actors. State media outlets buy ads to polish national reputations abroad. Intelligence agencies run influence campaigns designed to appear as grassroots activism. Political consultants create shell companies to mask funding sources. Platforms respond by tightening verification, but every tightening introduces collateral damage. Small civic groups that cannot navigate the paperwork are locked out. Authoritarian states adapt quickly; democratic actors, slower and poorer, lose ground.

At the edges of the market, creative resistance emerges. Advocacy groups switch to merchandise sales, podcast sponsorships, or crowdfunding platforms less prone to politicised filtering. Some rely on encrypted messaging apps to bypass advertising altogether. Yet these workarounds have limits. The mainstream public—busy, distracted, algorithmically curated—rarely sees messages that are not paid to reach them.

The question, then, is about power without visibility. When a newspaper rejects an advert, it is a public editorial decision. When a platform blocks a campaign, only the advertiser knows. There is no headline, no public argument, no democratic accountability. The censorship is silent, procedural, and deniable. It hides behind dashboards and keyword lists. Citizens rarely suspect that the ads they do not see have been filtered out. They assume the absence is ordinary.

Some argue that platforms should ban political advertising entirely. If all civic speech must be organic, the logic goes, no one can buy influence. But organic reach is not neutral. Algorithms privilege those who already have attention, often larger, wealthier actors. A ban may protect incumbents. Others propose regulated equal access—public ad credits for registered campaigns, mandatory transparency for all targeting, independent oversight of takedowns. The challenge is execution. Platforms resist intrusive regulation. Governments differ on what constitutes fairness. And in the meantime, ad markets continue shaping discourse quietly.

There is also a philosophical tension at the core: should commercial platforms serve as democratic infrastructure? They were not designed for civic responsibility. Their incentives are simple—maximise engagement, protect the brand, avoid regulatory crises. Yet they have become our public squares. Their advertising markets are now tools of influence comparable to broadcast television and print media. But unlike traditional media, they operate without editorial boards, without public charters, without constitutional duties. They are private markets with public consequences.

The limits of soft power become visible only when they fail. A political ad slips through that incites violence, spreads harmful conspiracy theories, or targets minorities. Outrage erupts. Investigations ensue. Platforms tighten rules once again. But for every scandal that surfaces, countless quieter decisions shape what societies see. Most of those choices are never scrutinised.

If the border of speech once lay at censorship—deciding what could not be said—it now lies at amplification, deciding what will not be heard. Digital ad markets are the customs posts of attention: they inspect messages, stamp some through, and hold others back. They are not merely commercial services. They are levers of influence.

When the architecture of persuasion is governed by opaque rules, when powerful actors can buy favourable access while civic voices are stifled, and when national agendas seep quietly into corporate policy, the public sphere becomes an unmarked borderland. Citizens live in it without seeing the fences.

The uncomfortable question remains: who should control the megaphone of modern politics—the state, the platforms, or the people themselves? And if the answer is shared responsibility, how do we build systems where that responsibility is visible, contestable, and democratic rather than quietly auctioned to the highest bidder?

Fintech Gateways

A crowdfunding campaign can be spirited, creative, and backed by thousands. Yet a single error message—*payment declined*—can stop it dead. No police raid, no censorship notice. Just an invisible financial membrane, quietly refusing to carry funds across. Moments later, the campaign's momentum evaporates. Supporters assume it failed to catch fire. In truth, it was frozen at the gateway.

Modern finance leans heavily on software. Every wire transfer, debit-card swipe, or digital wallet transaction travels through a stack of automated checks. These systems are designed to prevent fraud, laundered money, and sanctioned actors from crossing borders. They are necessary. They also serve as de facto border guards, deciding who may move money and who may not. Unlike traditional censors, they rarely justify themselves. Code does not hand out legal justifications. It simply enforces.

KYC—know your customer—is the first gate. Banks and payment platforms verify identity before money flows. They ask for passports, proof of address, and sometimes biometrics. The stated purpose is straightforward: stop criminals from hiding behind shell identities. But the logic scales far beyond that. Migrants with unclear paperwork, dissidents protecting their anonymity, or citizens in unstable states find the gate closed. Access to the formal economy becomes a privilege, not a universal right. The platform's interface delivers a friendly message: *Your documents could not be verified.* The consequences can feel anything but friendly.

AML—anti-money laundering—adds the next filter. Here the goal is to detect suspicious patterns: transfers at odd hours, rapid movement of funds, or transactions between flagged regions. Banks model risk through algorithms trained on historical data. The models are imperfect, so caution overwhelms leniency. They lock first, ask later. Charities working in conflict zones face constant interruptions. Researchers paying sources in sensitive countries struggle to reach them. When risk signals overlap with geopolitics, the filter grows even tighter. A banking system designed to police global crime becomes a perimeter for national power.

Then there are sanctions lists: names, addresses, organisations, entire countries. A platform that allows transactions involving them risks penalties, licence loss, even criminal liability. Compliance is automated. A match means a freeze, no questions asked. Innocent names that resemble sanctioned individuals are caught as collateral. Appeals exist, but the process moves at bureaucratic speed. For people whose livelihoods depend on smooth financial access, weeks of waiting might as well be exile.

These systems are rarely noticed until they fail. For most users, payments feel instantaneous. But speed conceals architecture. Under the surface, a network of banks, processors, and compliance vendors collaborate to vet every movement of money. They exchange logs, freeze accounts, and share risk scores. The infrastructure is designed to scale. If a government updates its sanctions, millions of transactions adjust overnight.

This is programmable borders at their most efficient: lines of code that push geopolitical decisions into databases and filters. A single policy change ripples across hundreds of millions of users. The enforcement is silent, total, and non-negotiable. When a payment platform excludes a country, its citizens may find they cannot buy basic services online, access cloud storage, or pay subscription fees. Their digital lives shrink instantly. Global connectivity was a promise; compliance turns it conditional.

From a security perspective, the logic is compelling. Financial crime funds terrorism, corruption, and weapons trafficking. States have a legitimate interest in preventing that harm. Platforms that refuse cooperation risk becoming offshore havens. Yet there is an unavoidable trade-off when systems that fight organised crime also sweep up ordinary people. Risk models ignore context. Code cannot distinguish between a journalist paying a source and a criminal laundering cash. It measures patterns, not intentions.

Even when citizens trust the goals of compliance, they may not trust its implementation. The algorithms are opaque; appeals pathways are labyrinthine. A person whose account is frozen receives a templated email. Customer support is triaged by bots. Information asymmetry is total. The system knows everything about the user; the user knows nothing about the system. The imbalance resembles immigration control without a courthouse: a border checkpoint that can detain your funds indefinitely, with no public defender in sight.

There is also a democratic question: who writes the rules? Banks implement national directives, but platforms operate globally. A sanctions decision made in one capital can shut down accounts in another. Sometimes the decision originates from a company seeking to avoid regulatory pressure rather than any explicit law. Financial actors pursue self-protection, not international consistency. The result is policy creep: beyond fighting crime, systems enforce political aims, foreign policy, or reputational considerations. Compliance becomes a shield for private interests.

Fintech startups often discover these tensions the hard way. They launch with ambitions to make payments borderless—fast, cheap, inclusive. But as they grow, regulators demand KYC, AML, and sanctions checks. The dream of frictionless finance collides with legal reality. Their systems re-centralise. Gateways that once promised openness now rely on the same compliance vendors as legacy banks. Innovation bends to geopolitics.

There is no simple path around these constraints. Privacy-preserving technologies exist—zero-knowledge proofs, selective disclosure credentials—but banks and regulators move cautiously. They want assurances, audit trails, accountability. Distributed ledgers offer transparency, yet crypto markets have had their share of fraud, creating paradoxes: tools that promise liberation become magnets for scams, prompting even tighter controls. The arms race continues.

For citizens under authoritarian rule, fintech gateways can be both lifeline and trap. Digital wallets allow people to receive support from abroad even when local banks are compromised. But those wallets must partner with licensed processors, who must obey government demands. A quiet phone call from a ministry can trigger a mass account freeze. No public announcement, no trial, just vanished balances. To withdraw money safely, people rely on informal networks—cryptocurrency exchanges, gift card resale, or physical cash transfers. These work, but they erode the very financial protections that compliance was meant to provide: audit trails, consumer rights, recourse.

Philosophically, the tension lies in reconciling two goods: security and autonomy. Societies need guardrails against criminal finance, but they also need accessible economic participation. When gateways default to suspicion, the unbanked suffer most—refugees, students, itinerant workers, and anyone with inconsistent documentation. The digital economy treats them as risk rather than opportunity. Their exclusion is not an accident; it is an operational outcome.

In affluent countries, the consequences are easier to dismiss. A flagged transfer is annoying, not existential. But for those living at the edge—where online income pays for schooling or daily food—a frozen account is crisis. When humanitarian aid is routed digitally, compliance delays can halt medicine deliveries. The border is not theoretical. It touches lives.

If fintech gateways are to remain legitimate, they need transparency that citizens can understand. Not regulation numbers or legal citations, but meaningful explanations: why a transfer was blocked, how to appeal, how long it will take, and what criteria determine risk. Systems should distinguish between malign actors and ordinary people caught in false positives. Technology could help—privacy-preserving identity checks, human review for high-impact cases, and redress channels that respond in hours, not weeks. But implementing this costs money. When profit margins strain, user rights shrink.

The future may bring programmable compliance: smart contracts that lock or free funds based on verified conditions, or digital identities that reveal only what is necessary for a transaction. Yet these innovations come with their own political questions. Who controls the underlying identity credential? Can citizens contest errors? Will alternative financial systems remain open to those who distrust government databases?

What started as financial plumbing has become geopolitical infrastructure. Every payment tells a story about who is trusted, who is ignored, and who is forbidden. The gatekeepers are not uniform; they are banks, fintechs, API providers, and compliance algorithms. They cooperate across borders, often more effectively than governments themselves. They hold power because their decisions are invisible.

In a world where speech and commerce converge—where subscription platforms fund journalism, where donations sustain activism—control over money is control over voice. The border is not just a line between currencies; it is a lever that shapes public life. And as more of society moves onto digital rails, the question grows sharper: if financial inclusion is a precondition for digital citizenship, who decides who belongs?

Parallel Economies

A journalist in a sanctioned state writes articles that the world is eager to read. Foreign publications want to pay her. Banks will not. Every transfer triggers a compliance alarm. So a friend abroad sends her a string of numbers by encrypted message: a gift card code for an international retailer. She buys food and medicine, and then sells part of the balance informally to cover rent. The payment system said she should be unreachable. Yet value reached her anyway. Not through the front door, but through the side alley.

For all the rhetoric of borderless digital economies, official rails have become thicker with checkpoints. Compliance stacks, sanctions lists, and platform rules funnel money through narrow channels. When those channels close, people do not stop transacting; they find parallel routes. The more formal finance hardens, the more creative the workarounds become.

Gift cards sound mundane: birthday presents, corporate perks, small indulgences. But they also serve as a covert remittance system. A card loaded by someone in London can be redeemed in Lagos or Johannesburg, and its value can be resold locally for cash. No international bank transfer, no SWIFT message, no flagged transaction. The route is slow and sometimes inefficient, but it works. In places where financial controls choke dissent, gift cards fund clandestine reporting, humanitarian projects, and even political campaigns. Their banality is their advantage. No one imagines revolution arriving in denominations of £25.

Stablecoins offer a flashier alternative. They promise the stability of a traditional currency, the speed of crypto rails, and the global reach of the internet. A donor in Berlin can send funds to an NGO in Beirut in minutes, bypassing banks that would otherwise block the transfer. For families divided by conflict, stablecoins have become modern remittances. Some use them as emergency savings, holding value in a currency beyond the reach of local inflation.

But the promise of stability depends on trust. Who guarantees that a digital token claiming to represent a pound or a dollar can actually be redeemed for one? Some issuers publish audits, maintain reserves, and seek regulatory approval. Others do not. Users in distressed economies are often those least positioned to scrutinise financial nuance. A stablecoin that collapses is not a speculative loss—it is a month's groceries, a semester's tuition, or a clinic's medicine.

Alongside gift cards and stablecoins sits a broader universe of alternative rails: peer-to-peer crypto swaps, informal hawala networks, prepaid vouchers, digital goods traded for cash, gaming currencies redeemed on grey markets. They are improvised, decentralised, and resilient. Each transaction is a quiet act of defiance against a system that insists only certain people may move money. Parallel economies turn the border upside down: instead of proving identity to a bank, users prove trust to each other.

These ecosystems are not uniform. Some are sophisticated, using encryption, escrow services, and reputation scores. Others are crude, depending on handshakes and personal referrals. All of them run on human relationships rather than institutional authority. That makes them adaptable but fragile. If a trusted broker disappears with everyone's funds, there is no regulator to call. If a wallet provider shuts down, balances vanish. The very invisibility that protects users from state surveillance also isolates them from consumer rights.

Governments see these channels as threats. They bypass tax collection, undercut capital controls, and can enable criminal finance. Some states ban gift card resale, restrict crypto exchanges, or mandate registration for peer-to-peer traders. Yet enforcement is partial. You cannot easily outlaw a code printed on a receipt or forbid a person from selling a digital balance for cash. The tighter the restriction, the more inventive the workaround. Borders encourage smuggling of goods; financial borders encourage smuggling of value.

Philosophically, parallel economies expose an uncomfortable truth: access to money is not just a financial question, but a political one. If official channels exclude people—because of nationality, paperwork, or reputation—then inclusion becomes a matter of autonomy. In many countries, freelancers, creators, and small merchants use stablecoins not because they distrust banks, but because banks distrust them. The requirement to supply formal identification, bank statements, and reference letters turns a simple act—receiving payment for work—into a bureaucratic obstacle course.

This is not only a story of hardship. It is also a story of innovation. Developers build wallets that run on low bandwidth; open-source projects create bridges between blockchains and fiat; diaspora communities maintain informal clearinghouses to support relatives. When traditional rails fail, societies invent new ones. The ingenuity is impressive. But it carries a cost: fragmented systems, inconsistent protections, and exposure to scams. Parallel economies are lifeboats, not cruise ships.

Corporate platforms face their own dilemmas. Some ban crypto altogether to avoid regulatory scrutiny. Others embrace it and become de facto gateways between regulated and unregulated finance. A social network might allow creators to withdraw earnings in stablecoins when banks refuse to pay them. A gaming platform might turn digital items into hard currency, functionally acting as a global exchange. These arrangements blur the line between entertainment product and financial institution. They expand inclusion but also import systemic risk.

When gift cards and tokens become currencies of necessity, what happens to accountability? If a researcher funds medical outreach through prepaid vouchers, how do donors verify the funds were spent ethically? If activists in exile pay organisers inside a country using crypto swaps, how do they prevent infiltration or fraud? Transparency is difficult without records. Ironically, systems meant to evade surveillance also impede trust-building.

The tension between resilience and risk runs through every parallel economy. They empower the excluded, but expose them to predators. They protect privacy, but sometimes shield criminals. They resist censorship, but weaken regulatory safeguards. The question is not whether they should exist—they already do—but how societies should understand them.

Designers of alternative rails often talk about sovereignty: giving individuals control over their own assets. For some, sovereignty means financial freedom. For others, it means operating beyond the reach of hostile rule. Yet sovereignty without structure can be perilous. If a stablecoin issuer fails, there is no central bank to stabilise the collapse. If a gift card resale market implodes, users have no legal claim.

Still, parallel economies offer something the formal system often forgets: dignity. When institutions shut people out, these channels say: you still matter. You still have agency. A society that relies entirely on formal rails is brittle; one that allows for redundancy is more resilient. After natural disasters, conflicts, or financial crises, informal networks often restore commerce long before banks reopen. A gift card code sent over a messaging app can be the difference between hunger and survival.

The border metaphor matters here. Official finance treats identity as a gate: prove who you are, or stay outside. Parallel economies treat identity as context: who vouches for you, who trusts you, who you have helped. One is legalistic; the other is communal. Neither is perfect. But in a world where compliance is increasingly automated and unforgiving, communities will build whatever bridges they can.

The open question is how these parallel systems evolve. Will they grow into regulated alternatives with consumer protection and transparency? Will governments co-opt them through central bank digital currencies? Or will they remain in the shadows—useful, risky, and always at the edge of legitimacy? As long as borders exist, formal or informal, people will find ways to cross them. The tools may change—from numbered banknotes to blockchain wallets—but the impulse remains constant: when survival and dignity are on the line, no barrier is absolute.

Chapter 7

Data Localisation and the New Mercantilism

A president announces a sweeping new digital sovereignty law. The speech is filled with patriotic cadence: foreign clouds are national vulnerabilities, data is a strategic resource, and keeping citizen records "within our borders" is a matter of dignity. The applause is loud, the headlines approving. Yet the next morning, in a basement far from the capital, nothing has changed. The national tax authority still stores its records on a server farm owned by a foreign vendor. The health ministry still depends on software patched overnight from another continent. The data may sit inside the country, but the power to run, update, and secure it remains elsewhere.

This contradiction lies at the heart of the new mercantilism. Governments talk about local control, but control is not where the cables terminate. It rests in code, contracts, and expertise. The concrete box of a data centre can be national; the systems inside often belong to someone else.

Data localisation began as a defensive reflex. If information is the new oil, then why let it flow to foreign refineries? Yet localisation is more than caution. It is industrial policy and bargaining leverage. A rule that forces tech giants to build infrastructure on national soil promises jobs, investment, and a seat at the negotiating table. It can also become a velvet glove for something sharper: the belief that information is safer when the state can reach it.

There are practical arguments too. Local hosting can lower latency and improve reliability. Patients want their medical records handled under domestic law. Banks demand predictable compliance. Companies fear extraterritorial subpoenas. These concerns are real, not rhetorical. Countries with fragile geopolitics see foreign data centres as single points of failure. If a submarine cable is cut or a foreign jurisdiction intervenes, essential services could blink offline. Localisation can look like prudence.

But prudence has a price. The first cost is complexity. A government can require domestic storage, but global cloud platforms are not Lego bricks to be rearranged at will. Most services are designed with distributed architecture. Forcing them into a geographic box means building bespoke partitions—harder to maintain, slower to update, and more vulnerable to subtle bugs. Many institutions discover that localisation produces symbolic sovereignty rather than substantive autonomy. The data is here; the dependency remains there.

Hence the rise of sovereign clouds and on-premise partitions: an attempt to create controlled environments that mimic global infrastructure without surrendering to it. Some countries demand that only locally vetted engineers may access the servers. Others insist on encryption keys held exclusively by a national authority. These measures sound decisive until a major outage hits and foreign engineers, flown in quietly under emergency exemptions, restore the system. Sovereignty is not an address; it is capability.

Behind the rhetoric of digital borders stands a compliance supply chain—auditors, integrators, and vendors who translate laws into operational controls. They write the checklists, configure the dashboards, and sign the certificates that declare a system "local". The real border appears in contracts: whose tools monitor the network, whose policies trigger alerts, whose staff have privileged access. A ministry may own its hardware, but if every critical update arrives from a foreign helpdesk, which flag truly flies over its data?

This supply chain often becomes a hidden form of lock-in. Once a public agency commits to a specialised architecture to satisfy localisation rules, switching vendor becomes painful. The country that hoped to resist digital dependence finds itself more entangled. Talent gaps make this worse. Running secure, large-scale data infrastructure requires experienced engineers, cybersecurity teams, and 24/7 operations. Many governments rely on the same multinational firms they hoped to constrain. The border shifts, but remains porous.

Localisation can also be performative. When a regulation mandates "local copies" of data, companies comply by storing encrypted blobs on domestic servers while processing everything elsewhere. Policymakers claim victory; engineers shrug. Citizens believe their privacy is protected; in practice, little has changed. The country bears the cost of storage and power without gaining meaningful control.

Yet dismissing localisation entirely misses the point. Some data should be local. Critical infrastructure cannot depend entirely on foreign clouds. Sensitive records deserve legal protection that travels no further than necessary. The question is not whether to localise, but when—and at what depth. Blind mandates treat all data as strategic, inflating cost and distorting innovation. Thoughtful governance distinguishes between categories: personal data, industrial secrets, public sector systems, and commodity analytics. If everything is sensitive, nothing is.

There is another path emerging: data embassies. A country can store backup systems in a trusted foreign state, protected by diplomatic agreements and mutual recognition. The idea sounds like science fiction, but captures a pragmatic truth. Some nations cannot sustain world-class infrastructure alone; they need allies. A secure data embassy allows continuity if domestic facilities are disrupted—by natural disaster, cyberattack, or political instability. It is sovereignty through cooperation, not isolation.

Such arrangements require preconditions: shared legal norms, reciprocal oversight, and clear accountability. Without them, a data embassy is merely outsourcing in ceremonial dress. But when done well, these pacts challenge the crude binary of "everything must stay here" versus "let it float in the cloud". They assert that sovereignty can be distributed rather than confined.

The deeper story behind localisation is competition for leverage. Countries want bargaining power against digital giants whose platforms shape economies. Forcing physical presence turns abstract corporate influence into something tangible: data centres that can be taxed, audited, or sanctioned. Some governments use this power for transparency; others use it to pressure companies into censorship and surveillance. Localisation can be a shield for rights or a sword against dissent.

Businesses, meanwhile, face a patchwork of rules. Hosting one dataset across five jurisdictions may require five compliance architectures. Each new border multiplies risk. Some firms simply withdraw from small markets where compliance costs exceed revenue. Citizens find themselves excluded from global services—not because of politics, but because their nation demanded a level of control it cannot realistically enforce.

The irony is sharp: laws meant to protect sovereignty can reduce autonomy. If local industries cannot scale, they depend harder on foreign investors. If public agencies cannot secure talent, they invite foreign contractors deeper into the system. If infrastructure becomes too costly, governments turn to turnkey "national cloud" solutions sold by the very companies they hoped to contain.

Still, there are good reasons not to dismiss localisation as protectionist theatre. It forces a reckoning with the political economy of data. When a foreign firm handles a country's health or tax records, it holds power. Not military power, but operational power: the ability to disrupt, to delay, to deny. States that rely blindly on offshore infrastructure are not sovereign in any meaningful sense. The strategic instinct behind localisation—retain some control over core systems—is rational.

The challenge is to separate necessary localisation from performative nationalism. Necessary localisation builds capacity: training engineers, funding security teams, and designing layered architecture with clear failover plans. Performative localisation builds headlines: encryption keys in a local safe, servers in a patriotic colour scheme, grand declarations of independence while the printer jams because the vendor forgot to renew a licence.

In the century ahead, data policy will resemble trade policy. Nations will negotiate reciprocal access, impose tariffs on cloud usage, and demand transparency about supply chains. Some will form regional alliances, pooling infrastructure the way they pool defence. Others will try to go it alone, discovering that isolation breeds fragility.

As frontier technologies grow—AI, genomics, smart grids—the stakes rise. A state that cannot store, process, and secure its data risks being a client rather than a sovereign. Yet a state that walls off everything risks stagnation. The future will not be defined by a single model. Some countries will choose fully domestic infrastructures; others will hybridise; a few will embrace global clouds with strict oversight.

Readers should expect something more textured than slogans. Localisation is neither salvation nor folly. It is a tool—sometimes necessary, sometimes wasteful, sometimes dangerous. Like tariffs or export controls, it expresses power relationships through technical rules that appear neutral.

This chapter follows those entanglements. It traces why states keep data at home, what sovereignty looks like in the cloud era, how laws become dashboards, and where the traps lie. It also confronts the strange notion of data embassies—the promise of sovereignty without isolation. Behind each policy lies a simple question with no simple answer: when a nation says "our data", what does *our* mean—location, control, capability, or consent?

Turn the page, and the rhetoric resolves into architecture, contracts, and code. The slogans fall away. What remains is the real borderwork of the digital age: invisible, intricate, and profoundly political.

Keep It Here

A minister cuts a ribbon at a new national data centre. Cameras flash, politicians beam, flags hang beside humming racks. The message is unmistakable: this is sovereignty rendered in steel and silicon. Yet the celebratory image hides a more complicated truth. Data localisation is often sold as a patriotic act, but its real engine is economics as much as nationalism. "Keep it here" sounds like a call to digital self-defence; in practice, it is industrial strategy with the language of security.

For many governments, localisation laws are the fastest way to compel global firms to invest. A requirement that citizen data must sit on domestic soil drives the building of server farms, the hiring of local technicians, and contracts with national cloud providers. It is a tariff without tariffs: a rule that turns foreign demand into domestic infrastructure. Storage mandates masquerade as privacy shields, but they also serve as quiet industrial policy—one that makes technology multinationals pay rent in the form of jobs and hardware.

Security is the public rationale, and at times a convincing one. Central banks fear that a foreign subpoena could freeze national payment systems. Defence agencies imagine a crisis where a cloud region goes dark. Hospitals do not want life-or-death systems dependent on decisions made in a distant jurisdiction. Latency becomes geopolitics: the shorter the distance the data travels, the less exposed to foreign disruption. Local storage promises faster access, fewer geopolitical choke points, and a sturdy line of accountability. If a breach occurs, the state knows where to knock.

This logic deepens in countries with precarious geography. Island states worry about submarine cables. Landlocked nations fear transit dependencies. Rival powers watch each other's digital arteries. In these places, localisation is not symbolic theatre. It is continuity planning. A cloud region five thousand miles away offers scale and convenience; a private cluster forty minutes from the capital offers reassurance when the wind shifts.

Yet storing data at home only solves problems at the surface. Latency improves, but the software still needs to be maintained. Updates still cross borders. Encryption keys may be located domestically—or perhaps not.

The physical presence of a server does not guarantee that a government can control, audit, or repair it without foreign cooperation. Data centres are not forts. Their sovereignty depends on who can reboot them at three in the morning.

This is the hidden bargain behind "keep it here". Localisation creates bargaining leverage. A company with no assets in a country can shrug off a regulatory order. A company with a billion pounds of equipment and a national payroll cannot. Data localisation transforms an abstract platform into a tenant. States gain leverage: to request logs, to demand algorithmic disclosures, or to impose fines with teeth. Some use that leverage for accountability; others for coercion. In many capitals, the private conversation is blunt: if you want access to our market, build inside our borders.

But leverage cuts both ways. Once infrastructure is in place, governments become dependent on the companies that operate it. Migrating a national identity database or healthcare system is not trivial. If relations sour, retaliation may risk disruption. Governments find themselves entangled with the very giants they sought to discipline. Localisation promises autonomy; sometimes it breeds reliance.

For businesses, localisation is often a tax in disguise. Maintaining parallel data stacks for every jurisdiction is costly and brittle. A global service forced to build miniature replicas in dozens of countries spends less on innovation and more on compliance. Smaller markets may be abandoned entirely, their citizens collateral damage of geopolitically ambitious policy.

And still, localisation spreads. Legislators favour it because it is visible. A minister can tour a data centre and claim victory. Citizens believe their information is safer when it sits at home. Whether the servers run on imported hardware, foreign operating systems, and proprietary clouds is an awkward detail left for the footnotes.

There are subtler motivations at work. Localisation preserves investigative reach. When data sits offshore, a domestic subpoena is a suggestion, not a command. Mutual legal assistance treaties are slow and uncertain. For law enforcement, keeping data inside the jurisdiction means faster access to evidence, fewer diplomatic delays. Civil liberties groups counter that such proximity enables abuse, turning legal process into convenience. The same infrastructure that shields data from foreign powers makes it easier for domestic ones to reach.

The privacy argument is similarly double-edged. Supporters say personal data stored at home is less exposed to foreign espionage. Critics note that localisation often comes with weaker protections, especially in countries with fragile rule of law. Data that cannot leave the country is also data that cannot flee an abusive state. In some regimes, localisation is less a firewall against external threats than a net for catching internal ones.

Security engineers point out another problem: concentration is risk. A data centre cluster designated as "sovereign" becomes a single high-value target. A small number of jurisdictions can harden such facilities; others cannot. Cooling failures, ransomware, and insider threats do not vanish at the border. When governments insist on local copies of everything, they quietly assume responsibility for infrastructure they may not be prepared to defend.

Still, to dismiss localisation as political theatre is shortsighted. The instinct behind it is centuries old. Nations that cannot protect their own infrastructure invite influence. In the industrial age, the security of railways, ports, and telegraphs mattered. In the digital age, data pipelines matter too. A country whose tax records or hospital networks reside entirely overseas has traded sovereignty for convenience. That trade is not always wise.

The question is not whether data should sometimes stay home, but how to design policies that resist both panic and performative politics. Some states have begun to categorise data, rather than sweeping everything into a single mandate. Critical national records receive strict domestic hosting; mundane analytics live in global clouds. Encryption and key management provide control without sacrificing scale. Tokenisation allows data to be processed abroad without exposing its raw form. These hybrids reflect a grown-up understanding: sovereignty is not a binary. It is layered.

There are moments when the logic of localisation becomes humane rather than nationalistic. When earthquakes or floods threaten infrastructure, local hosting means recovery crews are minutes away. When undersea cables are cut, hospitals do not go dark. When foreign courts demand user information for political prosecutions, companies can refuse without risking entire service bans. Local presence becomes a shield for rights, not merely a lever of state power.

But there is also a darker trajectory. Some governments pair localisation with vague "critical information infrastructure" laws that allow sweeping surveillance. Others force companies to store decryption keys on demand. A data centre becomes a silent witness: every request logged, every movement tracked. The same rule that protects citizens from extraterritorial intrusion can expose them to domestic overreach.

The motif repeats: localisation is a tool, not a destiny. It can nurture domestic industry, harden security, and create negotiating power. It can also enable censorship, raise costs, and entrench dependence. The nuance lies in governance: transparency about access requests, independent oversight, and clear limits on retention. Without these, "keep it here" becomes an excuse for authorities to reach into systems that would otherwise resist.

Technologists sometimes speak of "data gravity"—the idea that data, once collected, exerts a pull on the tools and services around it. Perhaps the same is true politically. When data lives within a country, it draws investment, scrutiny, and ambition. Universities build cyber programmes. Courts learn to adjudicate digital evidence. Local talent rises. The gravitational pull of keeping data here shapes whole ecosystems.

Yet gravity can trap as well as attract. A country that mandates local infrastructure but lacks research capacity becomes a perpetual customer of foreign providers. Hardware is assembled domestically but designed elsewhere. Engineers follow playbooks written in another language. Sovereignty is performed, not lived.

There is no universal formula for localisation done right. Each society must weigh latency against cost, sovereignty against flexibility, privacy against reach. But one insight should unsettle both sceptics and enthusiasts: the location of data matters less than the location of control. A server in national territory secured by foreign keys delivers drama, not autonomy. A distributed architecture governed by domestic law and cryptographic restraints can be sovereign without being parochial.

The global map of data borders will not settle soon. Countries will tighten, relax, and reinvent. Some will claim victory too early; others will discover that keeping data at home is only the opening move in a much longer game. But the question that pushed legislators to demand localisation will not disappear: in a world where information is both a resource and a weapon, what must remain within reach?

"Keep it here" is no longer a slogan. It is a test of power, trust, and competence. The next sections follow those tests to their difficult edges, where patriotism meets engineering, and where the border is drawn not by flags, but by who can log in.

Cloud Sovereignty

A government CIO stands in a glass-walled data centre, the air cold and dry, the floor humming with redundant power lines. Behind her, a row of beige cabinets hosts what officials proudly call a *sovereign cloud*. The logo on the casing belongs to a foreign hyperscale provider, repainted in national colours. The hardware was shipped from abroad. The engineers who will patch and upgrade the software fly in every quarter. The minister points to the blinking lights and declares victory: the nation has taken back control of its data.

It is a scene repeated around the world. Countries want clouds that are both modern and sovereign. The demand is simple: world-class infrastructure without geopolitical strings attached. What they receive is often a partitioned slice of a global service, fenced off by legal contracts and virtual air gaps. It feels decisive, yet the reality is murkier. Sovereign clouds are, at their best, carefully negotiated compromises. At their worst, they are theatre—sovereignty as branding.

The difficulty is that cloud autonomy has layers. There is the question of who owns the servers. Then, who controls the encryption keys. Then, who writes the operating system. Then, who can compel updates or backdoors through legal orders overseas. A patriotic badge on the front panel does not answer these questions. Real sovereignty is a chain of custody, not a press release.

In many cases, governments want more than reassurance—they want bargaining power. Regional cloud instances, operated with local partners and staffed by vetted personnel, claim to deliver it. Control of keys stays within the jurisdiction. Customer support is handled by citizens subject to national confidentiality laws. Access logs, audit trails, and shutdown rights are governed by domestic courts. On paper, these are substantive gains.

But sovereignty can evaporate in a single clause. If the provider retains remote management rights, a foreign authority could still compel changes. If patches are distributed from a global control plane, code flows across borders even when data does not. If the hardware supply chain is opaque, a server may phone home to firmware signed elsewhere. Governments often discover that their "sovereign" cloud remains a client of an unseen empire—updates, tools, and vendors that lie outside national reach.

The practical motives behind sovereign clouds are not romantic. Hospitals want to be confident that patient records will not vanish if diplomatic relations sour. Banks need guarantees that sanctions do not abruptly freeze their own citizens' funds. Security services ask whether foreign law enforcement could secretly subpoena data. To these actors, sovereignty is not a slogan. It is operational continuity, legal clarity, and a buffer against extraterritorial control.

Yet building an entirely indigenous cloud—hardware, software, protocols, chips—is beyond the capacity of most states. Even giants rely on international supply chains. So governments choose middle paths: joint ventures with global providers, on-premises partitions operated by local teams, or public-private "trusted clouds" that promise compliance with strict national rules. These arrangements bend the global cloud into a shape a sovereign can accept, without pretending that isolation equals competence.

There are philosophical tensions too. The cloud's value comes from scale: global redundancy, shared innovation, rapid deployment. Sovereignty is about exclusivity: controlled access, national jurisdiction, local accountability. Many policymakers want both simultaneously. They soon learn that a cloud trimmed to satisfy political demands risks losing what makes the cloud efficient. Isolated regions lag behind in features. Security patches arrive late. Tools developed for global use do not port cleanly. Autonomy becomes stagnation.

National security officials rarely accept that argument. To them, sovereignty is a risk calculation, not a luxury. They point to outages in foreign regions that cascade across continents. They invoke espionage scandals, leaked cables, and sudden sanctions. Their stance is blunt: dependency is vulnerability. The cloud they seek is less a product than a bunker.

Others push back. Civil liberties advocates warn that localising both data and cloud operations gives governments too much reach. A sovereign cloud can be a shield against foreign intrusion—but also a cage for domestic dissent. The same architecture that limits external subpoenas can deliver effortless internal surveillance. Once access conditions are set by secret directives, public oversight becomes a polite fiction.

Corporate leaders add their own cautions. Sovereign clouds require deep trust in the local partner. If that partner lacks engineering talent or financial resilience, the country inherits a brittle dependency disguised as self-reliance. Disaster recovery, cyber defence, and compliance tooling are not simple tasks. A compromised sovereign cloud can fail faster and more decisively than a global one, because there is no larger system to absorb the shock.

Even so, the idea keeps spreading. Ministries want procurement checkboxes ticked. Parliaments want headlines. Citizens want reassurance that their data is not floating in a legal no-man's land. The political reward of *doing something* is immediate; the technical burden arrives slowly. Some of the most ambitious sovereign cloud programmes are more symbolic than structural—local logos on global machines.

There are, however, models with substance. Some states require domestic control of root encryption keys, audited by independent regulators. Others mandate that cloud management systems must operate from inside national borders, with explicit legal firewalls preventing foreign interference. A few have invested in training local engineers, rather than outsourcing everything to the original vendor. In these cases, sovereignty becomes skill rather than slogan.

Substantive autonomy also means the ability to switch vendors. If a sovereign cloud is merely a locked-down version of a hyperscaler's platform, migration is hard. If it is built on open standards, with portable workloads and transparent APIs, the country retains exit options. The right to leave is the truest form of control. Otherwise, what looks sovereign is merely captive, a gilded cage with a patriotic crest.

There is a parallel story in on-prem cloud partitions. Banks, tax authorities, and defence agencies have long hosted critical systems on private infrastructure. The novelty is the attempt to wrap those systems in cloud-like tooling—virtual machines, automated deployment, elastic scaling—while maintaining physical control. These "private clouds" are meant to deliver modern convenience without exposing data to external jurisdictions. They often succeed, but the trade-offs are sharp: less elasticity, slower innovation, and security responsibilities that cannot be outsourced.

Every sovereign cloud therefore grapples with a paradox: the more a country controls, the more it must competently manage. Owning the keys means guarding them. Local patches mean local incident response. Physical servers mean physical risk. True autonomy demands investment not just in hardware, but in people, governance, and law.

The symbol of sovereignty is a data centre. The substance is a constitutional settlement about who can command it. Courts, parliaments, regulators, and civil society all matter more than the colour of the server racks. A cloud is only sovereign if the rules governing its access are clear, enforceable, and accountable.

Some countries are discovering that partial sovereignty may be enough. Encryption, decentralised key management, and mutual legal assistance reforms can provide protection without building isolated platforms. Others are learning that the political theatre of sovereign branding breeds complacency—leaders believe they have secured autonomy when they have merely purchased a controlled illusion.

The future will not be tidy. Cloud sovereignty is becoming a battleground for competing visions of global order: open networks, managed alliances, or fractured blocks. Each path carries its own risks. Isolation breeds stagnation. Blind dependency breeds vulnerability. Manufactured symbolism breeds self-deception.

The question that lingers beneath every procurement meeting and press conference is deceptively simple: who can turn the servers off? If the answer is someone outside the nation's laws—or someone inside them, without oversight—the cloud is not sovereign. It is merely convenient, until the day it is not.

That uncomfortable truth has only begun to reshape digital power. The coming sections follow its consequences, from contracts to cryptography, and how states learn—sometimes too late—the difference between a cloud they can claim and a cloud they can command.

The Compliance Supply Chain

The border did not appear as a fence or a filter. It arrived as a spreadsheet. It came from a reputable audit firm, full of green ticks and red flags, columns of controls translated into procurement language. A platform that yesterday served customers across borders now discovered, through page thirteen of a certification report, that a field in its database needed encryption using a locally approved module. Until that change was shipped, the service was non-compliant. So the engineers halted rollout, legal counsel drafted new terms, and a button quietly flicked to "off" for users in the affected jurisdiction. No courtroom, no parliamentary drama—just a dashboard.

This is the hidden architecture of digital borders. Laws rarely enforce themselves; they are mediated by the people who interpret them and the software that operationalises their meaning. Policymakers announce statutes. Auditors define controls. Integrators choose vendors. Vendors translate rules into features, APIs, and configuration settings. Somewhere along this chain, sovereignty becomes code. Whether a service may operate, process payments, or store data is decided not in the legislative chamber, but in the continuous integration pipeline.

Most citizens imagine compliance as a question of obeying the law. In the cloud era, it is a question of fitting into the compliance supply chain. A bank that wants to use a foreign analytics provider must verify that identity proofs meet domestic standards. It needs proof of encryption, attestations of physical security, guarantees of data deletion timeframes, and dashboards showing real-time risk. These are not abstract ideals; they are contractual obligations written in technical language. Government regulators, once content with static reports, now demand telemetry. Trust has turned machine-readable.

The rise of the compliance supply chain is not accidental. When infrastructure becomes global and borderless, the state responds with paperwork that bites. A jurisdiction cannot physically inspect a cloud server farm three continents away. But it can require certifications issued by accredited auditors, who themselves rely on standardised checklists. Those checklists, in turn, shape system architecture. Compliance becomes a design constraint, not a periodic chore. An application that cannot prove its controls cannot ship.

A striking irony lies in the opacity of this process. The public sees a law passed to protect privacy or secure critical data. They do not see the months of consultancy work that transform vague legislative principles into concrete technical demands. Government guidance often arrives in the form of best-practice documents, ISO references, and sectoral standards. Integrators then translate those guidelines into vendor recommendations. The result is a cascade: from law to standard, from standard to contract, from contract to software deployment. At each stage, choices are made—some conservative, some expedient, some driven by commercial interest.

This supply chain confers enormous power on auditors and consultancies. They do not merely measure compliance; they define its shape. A firm that controls a widely recognised certification can determine which cloud services enter a market and which are effectively banned. A single line in a compliance checklist—say, a requirement that all administrators be citizens—can force foreign vendors out entirely. The border is drawn not in a treaty, but in a spreadsheet cell.

There are benefits to this system. In principle, it professionalises risk. Instead of arbitrary decisions by overworked civil servants, compliance becomes a verifiable process, subject to rules and documentation. Dashboards standardise oversight. Logs offer audit trails. A government can demand that a data controller demonstrate encryption, key management, and access policies with screenshots and timestamps, rather than polite assurances. This is sovereignty expressed through automation.

Yet automation cuts both ways. The very dashboards that provide visibility also constrain interpretation. A compliance officer in a multinational firm may not fully grasp the local legal culture; instead, she ticks the boxes her software provides. If the risk is not captured in the checklist, it hardly exists. When auditors evaluate firms, they evaluate documentation, not lived practice. A company with impeccable paperwork can still be dangerously insecure. A company with sound engineering but poor paperwork is deemed non-compliant. Over time, compliance becomes theatre: immaculate dashboards, brittle reality.

An additional tension emerges when the compliance supply chain becomes a business. Vendors build tools to satisfy rules. They lobby for those rules to remain or expand. If encryption must meet a particular certification, vendors selling that certified module gain market share. If data deletion must be provable through specific logs, platforms offering such logging become indispensable. Law shapes markets, and markets in turn shape law. The border becomes a commercial moat.

This phenomenon is particularly visible in localisation mandates. A regulator might require that sensitive data remain on domestic soil. That sounds simple, even intuitive. But someone must verify that data never crosses the border—no backups, no telemetry, no remote debug sessions. Auditors demand a control. Integrators specify a product. Vendors produce a dashboard that promises visibility. The company buys the product, configures the dashboards, and reports compliance. Whether the rule is substantively effective becomes secondary; what matters is that the dashboard shows green.

There are darker edges to this machinery. Compliance supply chains can quietly exclude smaller innovators. A start-up that wants to sell analytics to banks may face hundreds of pages of security and governance requirements. Meeting them demands lawyers, consultants, and months of engineering. Established giants absorb these costs easily; challengers cannot. A law written to protect citizens ends up sheltering incumbents. The border hardens into oligopoly.

Yet governments often view this trade-off as acceptable. In their eyes, the risk of non-compliance is too high: data breaches, covert foreign influence, criminal misuse. They do not trust markets to self-police. So the state relies on the compliance supply chain as a substitute for direct enforcement. A foreign cloud provider can operate only if it contracts with a local auditor; that auditor must prove adherence to national standards. The arrangement creates leverage without building physical infrastructure. It is a regulatory choke point.

For companies, the consequence is a growing lattice of contractual obligations. Each jurisdiction demands its own proofs. Some require onshore storage. Others mandate escrow of encryption keys. Others insist on government access under sealed orders. Contracts proliferate. Dashboards multiply. The global platform fragments into a quilt of local instances, each decorated with compliance artefacts. Engineers begin to speak of jurisdiction-specific deployments, where code paths differ subtly to satisfy local rules. The border is not at the firewall; it is in the source tree.

The philosophical question is whether this is governance or delegation. When auditors and integrators decide how to interpret the law, they effectively legislate. They create de facto standards that may be stricter or looser than the statute intended. Who elected them? They are not accountable to voters. They answer to clients and professional associations. Their incentives are conservative: avoid risk, avoid scandal, avoid change. Innovation chills, not through censorship, but through caution.

At the same time, some of the most meaningful protections for citizens have emerged from this system. Mandatory breach disclosure, encryption at rest, two-factor authentication—these were once optional. Compliance regimes made them standard. The supply chain of governance, if well designed, can raise the baseline without requiring governments to micromanage technical systems. Contract clauses can do what legislation cannot: adapt quickly.

The problem is invisibility. Public debate fixates on dramatic interventions—bans, fines, takedowns. The real machinery of control is quieter. It is the risk engine that flags a workflow as non-compliant and locks accounts until remediation. It is the automated audit that sends a report to regulators when a server enters the wrong region. It is the procurement portal that refuses to accept a product lacking a certain certification. Citizens do not see these systems. Yet they shape what services are available, which apps fail to launch, and which foreign firms withdraw.

Sometimes the border works too well. When a misconfigured rule triggers a false violation flag, an entire service can be taken offline. Engineers scramble to prove compliance to software that has misunderstood a log entry. A charity that hosts mental-health helplines can vanish for hours. The people harmed never learn that the culprit was an automated compliance gate. They assume incompetence; the platform blames the auditor; the auditor blames the standard. Responsibility diffuses until it evaporates.

And still, the trend accelerates. As data volumes grow and supply chains digitise, governments lean on compliance to tame complexity. No ministry has the staff to inspect thousands of firms manually. Dashboards are scalable. APIs are scalable. Third-party auditors are scalable. The border becomes a managed service.

But where automation creates efficiency, it also invites new forms of power. A dominant vendor offering automated compliance tooling can become the quiet governor of a digital economy. If the tool declines to certify a competitor's product, the competitor dies. If the tool updates its requirements in response to legal shifts, companies scramble to adapt. A software release can have the effect of law.

The unresolved tension is whether democracies can oversee these hidden borders. Transparency reports for content moderation are now common. Transparency for compliance controls is not. The public does not know how many services were blocked, or on what grounds. Legislators rarely understand the mechanics well enough to question them. Regulators depend on the very experts they are meant to supervise.

A future of accountable compliance will require more than dashboards. It will require mechanisms for challenge, appeal, and public scrutiny. Companies must be able to contest erroneous flags. Citizens must know when access is denied due to compliance rules, not technical glitches. Independent bodies must audit the auditors.

Until then, the compliance supply chain will continue redrawing borders from behind glass doors: contracts as control surfaces, dashboards as checkpoints, and spreadsheets as silent instruments of sovereignty. The next sections follow where that logic leads, and what happens when the line between law and software finally dissolves.

Trade-offs and Traps

The politician cut the ribbon on a new "sovereign data centre", cameras flashing as he announced the triumph of national autonomy. On the tour that followed, journalists were shown an immaculate server hall: racks humming, lights blinking, the floor polished to a mirrored shine. What they did not see was the control plane—a dashboard hosted abroad, maintained by foreign engineers, relying on proprietary firmware. The data sat physically on domestic soil, yet every critical operation depended on external expertise. Independence was a stage set.

This ambiguity lies at the heart of modern localisation. Governments demand that data be kept within borders, hoping to gain security, bargaining leverage, or industrial advantage. Firms dutifully comply, building local instances and hiring local staff. But the reality is messier. Localisation costs money. It creates vendor dependence. And without deep technical talent, the entire exercise risks becoming performative: a story of sovereignty rather than its substance.

The first trade-off is economic. Data localisation requires infrastructure—data centres, redundant networking, energy, cooling, and the engineers who keep it all alive. Cloud providers amortise these costs globally, spreading them across millions of customers. A national variant shrinks that base dramatically, driving costs up. Some governments subsidise the build-out; others require foreign firms to invest. Either way, the price lands somewhere: on taxpayers, businesses, or end-users. Localisation that looks simple on legislative paper becomes, in practice, a negotiation between budgets and ambition.

The second trade-off is security. Politicians often speak as if physical proximity ensures control, but security is about people, processes, and software—not just geography. A database stored domestically is still vulnerable if its administrators are remote, its patches come from abroad, and its monitoring tools are proprietary. A breach in a sovereign cloud run by foreign contractors is a breach all the same. Worse, some rushed localisation projects skip basic hardening because meeting deadlines matters more than robustness. Citizens inherit the risk.

Then comes technical dependence. A nation that localises data often must choose a cloud provider that offers regional tooling: encryption key management, compliance dashboards, edge caching, and disaster recovery. Building local equivalents is expensive and slow. Most governments accept the trade: they own the hardware and the address, while the cloud giant owns the soul of the system. The arrangement resembles franchising rather than sovereignty. If the provider withdraws support or raises prices, the nation finds itself cornered—locked into proprietary interfaces and formats.

Talent is the quietest trap. The world's best cloud architects and security engineers cluster in firms that build global systems. Local markets may not have enough skilled professionals to design, operate, and audit sovereign-infrastructure deployments. When governments mandate localisation faster than talent can be trained, operators fill the gap with consultants. Foreign experts fly in, configure the system, and leave. Local administrators inherit complexity they cannot fully maintain. Sovereignty becomes a managed service.

None of these trade-offs are theoretical. When a major platform is forced to run a local instance for regulated sectors, its engineers split the codebase. Features that rely on global analytics, machine learning, or AI moderation fail silently because the local environment lacks the necessary telemetry or models. Users on the local instance receive poorer performance, fewer safety tools, and slower product updates. Governments may insist on local processing for privacy, but often, ironically, receive degraded privacy protections: threat models shrink; anomaly detection weakens; patch cycles lag. A border imposed for safety can produce new vulnerabilities.

A further tension lies in bargaining leverage. A government may believe localisation gives it the upper hand in negotiations with large platforms. If data sits within reach, it can be seized or legally accessed. But the same dependency cuts both ways. A platform running a bespoke deployment can threaten quiet withdrawal, leaving hospitals, banks, or public services scrambling. Contracts become weapons. Sovereignty becomes conditional.

To separate necessary localisation from performative policy, hard questions must be asked. First: what is the specific risk that localisation mitigates? If the concern is unauthorised foreign access, is geographic storage the right control, or would strong encryption and key isolation provide more meaningful protection? Second: who operates the local infrastructure? If the answer is the same foreign provider, meaningful control may be illusory. Third: what are the lifecycle costs of autonomy? Budgets must account not just for installation, but for continuous security updates, skilled staffing, and long-term maintenance.

Fourth: what is the exit strategy? If the nation wants to avoid vendor lock-in, it must insist on data portability, open standards, and transparent APIs. Many countries fail to negotiate these rights. Once data and workflows are embedded in proprietary systems, leaving is prohibitively expensive. Localisation morphs into dependency, visible only when leverage is tested.

There are successful models. Some countries have built strong domestic cloud ecosystems by pairing localisation mandates with investment in talent pipelines, research centres, and open-source initiatives. Others create hybrid sovereign clouds: critical workloads remain domestic, while low-risk tasks run on public hyperscalers. The key is clarity of purpose. Localisation is not an ideology; it is a tool. Used well, it strengthens resilience. Used poorly, it becomes theatre.

The hardest trap is psychological. Policymakers and the public derive comfort from the idea that data is "here". It is tangible, patriotic, measurable. "Here" suggests control. Yet digital systems are not factories; they are layered abstractions. Data sovereignty can disappear in a few lines of code: who holds the keys, who operates the orchestration plane, who patches the hypervisor? Geographic location is only one part of the security story. Sometimes, the least visible layers matter most.

A government that wants genuine sovereignty must interrogate the stack. Does it own the encryption keys? Are access logs stored locally and reviewed by accountable teams? Can it audit the firmware supply chain? Can it compel the vendor to repair vulnerabilities promptly? Does it have the human expertise to judge the answers? These are the uncomfortable questions that transform symbolism into substance.

Localisation can also distort industrial policy. When laws require data to be hosted domestically, platforms may limit or delay entry into smaller markets. Local start-ups, unable to bear compliance costs, may abandon innovation in data-heavy sectors. Citizens receive fewer services, not more choice. National champions may emerge, but sheltered from competition, they can stagnate. A law aimed at economic growth may produce its opposite.

Some defenders of aggressive localisation argue that sovereignty requires sacrifice. Better a slower, costlier system than dependency on foreign clouds. Others counter that true independence lies in interoperability: the ability to migrate between providers, layer domestic controls atop global infrastructure, and audit systems rigorously. Both positions contain truth. The debate is not about whether localisation is good or bad, but about when it is necessary, and at what price.

There is also geopolitics. Localisation can serve as leverage in diplomatic negotiations. A state may threaten to tighten data controls to extract concessions from foreign firms or governments. The data centre becomes a bargaining chip. But brinkmanship carries risk: if the bluff is called, citizens may lose access to critical services overnight. The cost of performative sovereignty is paid by users, not policymakers.

The path forward demands intellectual honesty. Localisation is not a magic shield. Nor is it inherently naïve. It is a strategic choice with costs and trade-offs that must be weighed transparently. Citizens deserve to know when a law protects them and when it merely looks protective. They deserve leaders who ask: Are we building capacity, or buying appearances? Are we gaining control, or rearranging dependencies? Are we protecting rights, or narrowing them by accident?

The traps are subtle because they play on national pride and public fear. "Keep it here" sounds reassuring. But sovereignty is not a slogan; it is a practice. It requires engineers, auditors, contracts, keys, and exit strategies. Without those, localisation becomes a border drawn in sand: impressive until the tide comes in.

Data Embassies

When a government stores its most sensitive records in a foreign data centre, it sounds like the opposite of sovereignty. Yet that is precisely what some nations have chosen: they treat another country's servers as if they were their own soil, complete with legal protections, jurisdictional shields, and contractual firewalls. The idea is simple and audacious. If embassies protect diplomats abroad, why can't they protect data?

This notion of a *data embassy* emerged from a profound fear: the risk that a nation's digital identity could vanish overnight. A cyber-attack, natural disaster, or hostile occupation could wipe out civil registries, tax records, land titles, medical systems, and court archives. For a modern state, this is more than technical inconvenience; it is an existential threat. Without the data that documents who owns property, who is a citizen, who carries criminal liability, or even who is alive, a government loses continuity. In the twentieth century, nations stored critical archives in vaults and archives. In the twenty-first, the vault is another country's cloud.

The metaphor works because embassies themselves are a delicate legal fiction. A patch of foreign territory is treated as sovereign space through mutual recognition. Data embassies borrow this logic but invert it. The servers remain physically abroad; sovereignty travels with the data. This inversion reveals a larger geopolitical shift: power is becoming portable. If the nation can move its identity to a safe jurisdiction, it can survive a crisis, even one that takes its territory offline.

But metaphors can be seductive, and data embassies are not magic. They require precise preconditions, careful engineering, and trust deeper than any marketing slogan. Without those, the embassy becomes a warehouse—safe only until someone decides it no longer is.

To function as a true extension of national sovereignty, a data embassy needs four foundations: legal recognition, cryptographic control, operational independence, and political continuity.

Legal recognition means the host state formally accepts that the data and systems housed inside are off-limits. The host country agrees not to seize the data, search it, or compel access. This is not merely courtesy; it must survive adversarial tests. If a foreign court orders the host to seize encrypted records belonging to another state, the embassy arrangement should hold. Without that protection, the embassy is a data centre with a diplomatic nickname.

Cryptographic control is the second foundation. The embassy must be sealed with encryption keys held only by the home country. If engineers in the host country can access plaintext data, sovereignty becomes a handshake rather than a guarantee. True control means the host provides power, cooling, and connectivity—but no visibility. The home state must be able to rebuild itself from those encrypted archives without asking permission.

Operational independence is harder. Embassies need maintenance: hardware replacements, software updates, security patches, and staff. If a foreign vendor controls these, the embassy's autonomy hinges on that vendor's loyalty. Some states mitigate this by co-locating embassy servers within private or government-run facilities abroad, using their own administrators or automated deployment pipelines. Others rely on agreements with major cloud providers, trusting that the business model will sustain the arrangement longer than politics might. Both approaches carry risk.

Political continuity is the most fragile requirement. What happens if the host state's government changes? An agreement between friendly administrations may not survive a diplomatic freeze. Embassies rest on long-term trust, not just technical controls. In this sense, the data embassy is a bet: the home country wagers that the host will remain a friend when it matters most.

These preconditions reveal a paradox. Data embassies promise resilience by distributing risk across borders, yet they deepen dependence on another jurisdiction. A state bets that one disaster—natural or political—will not happen everywhere at once. The logic is similar to storing gold abroad, but digital sovereignty is easier to revoke than property rights. A foreign government could cut power, revoke legal protections, or quietly copy data. The embassy is only as strong as the host's willingness to enforce the fiction.

Yet dismissing data embassies would be a mistake. They solve a problem that cannot be ignored: modern states are brittle. When national digital identity systems go offline, life stops. Passports cannot be issued. Hospitals cannot confirm allergies or prior diagnoses. Borders cannot verify travellers. In a crisis, paper backups are too slow and too shallow. Data embassies provide a lifeline.

The idea extends beyond emergency planning. Two countries might agree to host each other's critical systems, creating a mutual insurance pact. Smaller states might pool resources to create shared embassies in neutral jurisdictions. Regional blocs might negotiate multi-country redundancy, giving each member the ability to recover from catastrophe. In a world where infrastructure can be physically targeted, this redundancy is not paranoia; it is prudence.

But pitfalls abound. First is transparency. Citizens rarely understand where their data lives or which country ultimately protects it. Governments may tout sovereignty while quietly outsourcing backups to a foreign hyperscaler. If secrecy cloaks dependence, democratic accountability evaporates. Citizens deserve candour: if their government is betting the continuity of the state on another nation's goodwill, they have a right to know.

Second is control of encryption. A data embassy secured with weak key management is not an embassy—it is a liability. Who holds the keys? Are they distributed across multiple trusted custodians? Can the home state recover the system without foreign assistance? If any answer is "no", sovereignty is compromised.

Third is the silent creep of vendor lock-in. The embassy may rely on proprietary software, proprietary monitoring tools, proprietary backup systems. In theory, the home country could migrate elsewhere. In practice, doing so might take years. The country becomes dependent not only on the host state, but on the corporate entity that maintains the technical stack. Sovereignty becomes a subscription service.

Even the diplomatic metaphor has limits. Embassies involve human staff, national flags, and well-understood norms. Data embassies are invisible: racks of machines indistinguishable from ordinary infrastructure. At a moment of crisis, a foreign government might hesitate to defend an institution that only exists on paper and in code. And if the host comes under pressure from a powerful ally, the embassy could be quietly compromised without leaving fingerprints.

Despite these risks, data embassies hint at a compelling vision: sovereignty as something portable, distributed, and resilient. Instead of tying national identity to one fragile geography, a government creates a network of safe harbours. Continuity becomes a function of architecture rather than luck.

But real resilience demands more than symbolism. It requires agreements that survive geopolitical strain, encryption that outlasts vendors, and operational independence that does not disappear when budgets tighten. Some nations are beginning to ask the right questions. Others still chase headlines.

The deeper issue is philosophical: can sovereignty truly be outsourced? Is a country still sovereign if surviving catastrophe depends on another state's power grid and diplomatic goodwill? Or is sovereignty evolving into something more interdependent—an agreement among nations that continuity matters to all?

There is no tidy answer yet. Data embassies force states to rethink borders themselves. They show that a nation's core can live outside its territory and that resilience may require trust beyond patriotism. New forms of sovereignty are being invented in server rooms and reinforced through contracts, keys, and cryptographic proof.

Whether these embassies ultimately protect national identity or merely relocate its vulnerabilities will only be known in the moment they are tested. The question is not whether they can work, but whether nations are honest about what it takes to make them real.

Chapter 8

Virtual Nations and Diaspora Networks

Someone lights a candle before a webcam. A crowd of strangers from different continents bow their heads in unison. A moderator reads a list of names to be honoured. There are rituals, dress codes, sanctions for disruptive behaviour, and a treasury that supports members in need. It looks nothing like a state, yet it functions suspiciously like one. No land, no flag, no army—just rules, culture, loyalty, and shared memory moving across fibre-optic cables.

Communities without territory have always existed, but the digital age has turned this from anomaly to norm. Today, millions of people pledge allegiance not to geography but to networks: fandoms, collectives, diaspora groups, and online polities that are far more cohesive than many official nations. Their members don't simply chat; they legislate, adjudicate, police, celebrate, and sometimes secede. They have diplomats—admins who negotiate alliances with other communities—and exiles—users banned for violating sacred norms. The map of influence is no longer drawn only by borders on land, but by clusters of servers, social groups, and encrypted channels.

The central puzzle is simple and provocative: what happens when the most meaningful citizenship is digital, not national?

For some people, the country that matters most is the one where their friends are, where their earnings come from, where their identity lives, and where disputes are settled. That "country" is often a platform—a place that takes a cut of income, arbitrates conflicts, and issues penalties with more efficiency than any municipal court. A user who loses access to a messaging service, payments account, or gaming platform may suffer more real-world harm than losing voting rights in a distant capital.

This quiet shift carries profound consequences. If states once monopolised belonging, they now share the stage with virtual nations—some playful, some serious, some powerful enough to move money, culture, and politics across continents. These new formations raise unsettling questions: How do you recognise a nation that has no land? Who grants it dignity, rights, or representation? And when digital communities collide with traditional governments, whose rules prevail?

The story begins with communities that behave like micro-states. Many large online groups—open-source projects, fandom societies, blockchain networks, competitive gaming leagues—write constitutions, adopt judicial procedures, elect leaders, and collect dues. Some redistribute funds to members in hardship; others supply education, housing, or healthcare subsidies funded by donations. These are not fantasies. They are operating systems for collective life. The rules are encoded in documents and software, and enforcement is swift. Platforms provide the police—moderation tools, blocklists, the ban. Members speak of "citizenship", not as metaphor, but as lived identity.

Territory is no longer soil. Territory is server space.

Yet the most powerful digital polities are not always self-contained. Diaspora communities act as their own kind of nation: resilient, multilingual, scattered across time zones but tied by blood, history, and obligation. Long before the internet, diasporas moved goods, money, and knowledge across borders. Now they route encrypted messages, crowd-fund legal defence, translate news that governments try to suppress, and provide remote schooling for children cut off from home. They are lifelines when states fail. At their best, diasporas are bridges; at their worst, they fracture from within, exporting rivalries and factional propaganda as efficiently as they export capital.

These networks are not evenly distributed. Some arise from disaster—war, persecution, economic collapse. Others form out of aspiration: migrants seeking opportunity but maintaining allegiance to the place they left. In either case, the internet erases the silence that distance once imposed. A village can argue through WhatsApp. A revolution can be planned across continents. A government can lose legitimacy while its exiles grow stronger abroad.

Meanwhile, platforms quietly became nations of their own. A payments service collects taxes in the form of fees. A cloud provider stores vital records for millions. A social network verifies identity, issues credentials, and adjudicates complaints more swiftly than bureaucracies. The average person spends more time under platform governance than state governance:

rules about speech, behaviour, commerce, privacy, and punishment are enforced through dashboards and algorithms, not parliaments. If you violate the law of a country, you may face a court. If you violate the law of a platform, you may vanish without appeal.

This raises a disorienting but necessary thought: citizenship may no longer be tied to passports but to platforms. A person can change countries without moving an inch—simply by switching networks.

Some communities reject platform dependence altogether. They dream of digital secession: federated social networks, self-hosted communities, decentralised currencies, and governance through code. The rhetoric is romantic—freedom from corporate control, independence from governments, resilience through distribution. But secession demands hard realities: stable funding, reliable infrastructure, conflict resolution, and norms that survive bad actors. Many digital breakaway projects collapse not through attack but through exhaustion. Running a country, even a virtual one, is harder than declaring one.

Still, the impulse matters. It reveals dissatisfaction with centralised rule—platform or state—and faith that collective intelligence can build alternative systems. When federated communities succeed, they do so not through slogans but through meticulous engineering and stubborn stewardship. They blend the velocity of the internet with the patience of constitutional design.

Hovering over all of this is the question of recognition. In the physical world, nationhood carries criteria: population, territory, government, capacity to enter relations. In the digital world, these tests crumble. Some online polities are larger than small countries. Some have better governance. Some wield greater economic power. Yet none have automatic legitimacy. States rarely know how to treat them. Companies rarely want to. And citizens, torn between multiple loyalties, navigate identities that are layered rather than singular.

If a virtual polity negotiates with a government, who signs the agreement? If a diaspora runs schools and courts in exile, is it a community or a nation waiting for land? If a platform controls identity, payments, and arbitration for a billion users, is it still a business—or something closer to sovereignty?

There are no quick answers. But ignoring these questions is impossible. Across the world, people increasingly live as members of multiple nations: one with a flag, others with passwords. They belong to a geography, but also to a network. When disasters strike—natural or political—they may turn to each with different expectations. A physical state provides hospitals and passports. A virtual one provides income, trust, and continuity.

This chapter traces the shape of these emerging polities. It will profile communities that legislate without land, diasporas that wield quiet power, and platforms whose influence resembles government more than commerce. It will examine the fantasies of digital secession and the practical governance challenges that follow. And it will confront the hardest question of all: who grants rights and recognition to nations that exist only in the cloud?

The world is already full of them. Most operate in the background, too small or too peaceful to attract attention. Others gain momentum and become political forces. None of them look like the nations that ruled the nineteenth or twentieth centuries. They do not conquer territory; they absorb attention, loyalty, and infrastructure. They do not mint flags; they mint tokens. They do not issue passports; they issue credentials. Their diplomacy takes place in APIs and community forums. Their wars—when they erupt—are fought through moderation, propaganda, and code.

Some will fade. Some will fracture. Some will remain harmless. But a few will matter, deeply and permanently. In a century defined by climate displacement, economic migration, and platform dependence, millions may find belonging not where they were born, but where they connect.

The question is no longer whether virtual nations exist. They do. The question is what kind of world emerges when citizenship itself becomes portable, divisible, and programmable—and when more people feel at home in a network than in a state.

Communities as Polities

A stranger joins an online forum to ask for help paying for a family member's surgery. Within hours, anonymous users send donations, cross-check the hospital, verify the documents, and vote to match funds from a community treasury. They do it not as charity, but as duty. A constitution—literally called that—outlines who qualifies for assistance, how votes are counted, and what penalties apply if someone abuses the system. Every participant lives in a different country, yet their shared norms are clearer and more enforceable than the laws of some states. The community has no flag, no capital, no land. But it has citizens, courts, budgets, rituals, and legitimacy.

This is not an outlier. Across the digital world, large communities operate as micro-states in everything but territory. They legislate codes of conduct, enforce rules, run elections, collect dues, settle disputes, and honour traditions that bind members into a coherent political body. Some Reddit subcommunities maintain welfare funds. Open-source projects set immigration rules—onboarding protocols for new contributors—and judicial processes to resolve conflict. Even fandom groups establish tribunals, archives, and ceremonies. The building blocks of sovereignty have migrated into chat rooms, wikis, and Discord servers.

The simplest definition of a polity is a group of people with rules, identity, and governance. By that standard, many online communities count. The harder question is legitimacy. What gives these rule-bound communities the right to govern? The answer is not territory. It is consent, participation, and continuity: three attributes that many offline governments have struggled to maintain.

Rules come first. Almost every major community publishes written codes that resemble constitutions: charters that specify acceptable behaviour, sanctions, appeals, and rights. These are not symbolic. They are enforced through moderators, automation, and peer judgement. In some spaces, users elect moderators or vote on changes to the rulebook. In others, founders act as benevolent monarchs, delegating power but retaining ultimate authority. The diversity mirrors the world: democracies, oligarchies, technocracies, emirates of code.

Yet rules alone do not make a polity. Rites matter. Online communities cultivate ceremonies—annual events, communal milestones, insider vocabulary—that transform crowds into cultures. A gaming server might host memorials for deceased players. A long-running forum may publish annual "state of the community" addresses. Rituals signal belonging and continuity across generations of users. Without them, the space feels transactional; with them, it feels like home.

Redistribution cements the bond. When a community shares resources—not only money, but labour, expertise, and emotional support—it crosses the threshold from interest group to polity. Members care about one another's welfare, not just shared topics. Cryptocurrency networks, mutual aid groups, open-source foundations, and creator collectives all maintain treasuries to fund work, support contributors, or help individuals in crisis. That is taxation, budgeting, and welfare policy in miniature.

Of course, communities are fragile. Many collapse under the weight of their own politics. Factions form. Administrators burn out. Powerful personalities hijack decision-making. Some devolve into tyranny: founders become despots, dissenters are expelled, and rules shift to protect insiders rather than the community. The failures resemble failed states because the underlying dynamics are the same: concentrated power, weak accountability, and fragile legitimacy.

Legitimacy is where the digital domain is most novel. In physical states, legitimacy is inherited from history, elections, or force. In digital polities, legitimacy comes from participation. Members choose to stay. If governance is unjust or incompetent, they can defect—sometimes en masse—to rival communities or fork the entire system. A community that loses its members is dead, no matter how well-crafted its constitution. Exit is the ultimate veto.

That dynamic makes digital polities more fluid and, paradoxically, often more responsive. Leaders know that loyalty is voluntary. If rules are unfair, users can migrate to another platform or start their own. Forking is a constitutional right, enforced by code and social norms. In the open-source world, a project that ignores its contributors risks splintering; history is full of forks that became more vibrant than the parent. In creator economies, moderators who abuse power watch their audience vanish overnight. The threat of exit disciplines authority in a way physical borders rarely allow.

Still, consent is not a perfect shield. Power concentrates quickly in digital communities: administrators with technical control can lock out dissenters, erase criticism, or rewrite history. Without checks and balances, a virtual polity becomes a fiefdom. And because most communities rely on external platforms, sovereignty is always conditional. If the host service decides to shut them down, years of governance and culture can vanish in seconds. Digital micro-states live at the pleasure of platform empires.

This precariousness raises a deeper philosophical question: can a polity be legitimate if it can be deleted?

Members often behave as if the answer is yes. They invest time, labour, money, and emotion because the community gives them something the physical state does not: agency. In many countries, citizens feel powerless to influence national politics. In online communities, they can propose legislation, debate openly, and see change happen quickly. The bureaucracy is smaller. The stakes feel personal. The signals of belonging—reputation, trust, recognition—arrive faster. The community becomes the primary locus of democratic life, even if the passport says otherwise.

The result is a quiet shift in political imagination. Millions of people now experience self-governance through screens. They join communities where citizenship means participation, not paperwork. They learn that borders are constructed, not fixed; that authority must earn legitimacy; that governance is a skill, not a mystery. Some users discover they are better citizens online than offline. Others find that online life prepares them to demand more from real-world institutions.

Yet digital polities also amplify old tensions. Rules can be weaponised to purge dissent. Redistribution can create hierarchies of who is "worthy". Charismatic leaders can become cult figures. Communities can spiral into insularity, ideology, or conspiracy. The freedom to exit does not abolish the damage done inside. Legitimacy is fragile, and the absence of territory does not eliminate the darker side of human social behaviour.

What distinguishes successful digital polities is not perfection, but resilience. They evolve. They refine constitutions, rotate leadership, invest in dispute resolution, and preserve institutional memory. Some appoint ombudspeople; others publish transparent audits of moderation outcomes. These are the markers of a maturing state, not a hobby group.

The most intriguing cases are those that bleed into the physical world. A diaspora forum organises scholarships for students in another country. A mutual aid network buys medical equipment. An online guild runs a democratic council and funds community centres. These actions force a reconsideration of what sovereignty means. Does a state require soil, or is sovereignty the ability to coordinate resources, resolve disputes, and protect members?

Territory still matters—but less than it used to. In the digital sphere, communities claim jurisdiction over behaviour, identity, and memory, not land. They govern attention and resources. They create laws in text and code. They decide who belongs. Legitimacy comes from performance, not flags.

This trajectory invites a final, unresolved question: if a community without territory can legislate, redistribute, and protect its people, what stops it becoming a nation in everything but name—and what happens when millions choose allegiance to these invisible states over the ones they were born into?

Diaspora as Bridge

A government shuts down social media during a crisis, hoping silence will smother dissent. Inside the country, feeds freeze and messages fail. Yet hours later, videos resurface abroad: translated, mirrored, and reposted from accounts on the other side of the world. The blackout works locally but not globally. Expatriate students in Toronto, taxi drivers in Dubai, nurses in Berlin, and coders in Singapore stitch together a narrative that the state cannot fully contain. Their phones become relays; their communities, informal newsrooms. What was meant to vanish instead multiplies. The bridge is the diaspora.

Diasporas have always been conduits—of culture, of capital, of memory. The digital world simply gives them reach and speed that once required ships and postal networks. Today, a WhatsApp group in London can fund an ambulance in Lagos. A Discord server in Melbourne can teach protesters in Hong Kong how to bypass surveillance. Facebook pages run in Stockholm can translate court transcripts for families in Kabul. The crucial insight is not that information and money travel across borders, but *how* they travel: through trust networks rooted in identity and obligation, rather than formal institutions. When states falter or platforms restrict, diasporas route around the breakage.

This routing takes many forms. The obvious one is news. Diaspora groups coordinate VPN access, mirror blocked websites, subtitle videos, and archive evidence before it disappears. Trusted intermediaries verify sources, contextualise rumours, and connect distant reporters to audiences hungry for fact over propaganda. A single diaspora journalist with a Telegram channel can become a lifeline for millions.

Money follows. Remittances already dwarf many countries' foreign aid receipts; digital payment tools simply tighten the loop. Diasporas use mobile transfers, stablecoins, and informal ledgers to wire funds into places where banks are slow, corrupt, or politically constrained. Cryptographic tools allow them to send money into zones where the state or platform wants it stopped. Families survive because cousins abroad refuse to let the lights go out.

Tools come next. When regimes censor platforms or throttle connections, diaspora engineers distribute VPN configurations, mesh-network kits, and privacy guides in multiple languages. They assemble secure laptops for journalists, smuggle hardware through airports, and maintain cloud backups in case servers are seized. They solve the problems of distance by making it irrelevant.

In this way, diasporas behave like parallel governance systems: they provide infrastructure, finance, intelligence, and resilience. They are not merely spectators to homeland politics; they are participants and, often, protagonists.

But every bridge carries risk. Diaspora communities tend to be more politically engaged—and sometimes more radical—than those who never left. Distance can harden identity. The homeland becomes a memory filtered through trauma, nostalgia, or selective retelling. Factions emerge, each claiming to represent the "true" nation. In extreme cases, diasporas fuel conflict by channelling money, propaganda, or weapons to hardliners who face no local consequences for escalation. The same connectivity that enables humanitarian support can also amplify division.

Trust, too, is a double-edged sword. Diasporas rely on social capital to move resources quickly, but trust can be exploited. Scammers pose as activists; intelligence services infiltrate groups; governments monitor foreign students and pressure families at home. Fear stalks the WhatsApp thread. Where bridges exist, so do gatekeepers, and gatekeepers are vulnerable to manipulation.

States understand the power of diasporas, which is why they try to court, control, or criminalise them. Some launch digital consulates to maintain influence and extract remittances. Others threaten relatives to silence critics abroad. A few embrace them as economic partners, offering tax incentives for investment and voting rights for expatriates. The relationship is transactional: diasporas provide capital and legitimacy; states offer belonging and protection. When trust erodes, the bridge becomes a battleground.

Yet even the fiercest attempts at suppression rarely succeed completely. When a government bans VPNs, diaspora coders build steganographic tunnels. When propaganda floods the feeds, diaspora fact-checkers crowdsource debunks. When borders close, people still find ways to talk. The bridge survives because technology lowers the cost of connection and identity raises the will to use it.

There is a deeper philosophical thread here. Diaspora networks challenge the idea that political community stops at the border. Citizenship becomes less about residency and more about participation. A teacher in Paris who spends her evenings distributing emergency funds to families in Beirut may feel more politically active than a voter in her district. Belonging becomes polycentric: a citizen of one state, a citizen of another nation, a citizen of a dozen digital communities. The modern world allows multiple allegiances, layered rather than exclusive.

This emotional geography complicates traditional diplomacy. When crises unfold, foreign ministries speak to each other, but diasporas speak first and faster. Their version of events often sets the narrative long before officials draft statements. They raise money before governments send aid. They warn of atrocities while newsrooms are still seeking confirmation. They are early-warning systems and humanitarian responders, operating without permission.

And yet, diaspora bridges are fragile. Coordination is hard. Secure communication requires digital literacy that not everyone has. Factionalism can fracture trust and paralyse action. A few influential figures can dominate discourse, silencing moderates. When disinformation spreads within the diaspora, it spreads with the authority of kinship. Not every bridge leads to safety.

What determines whether a diaspora supports resilience or deepens division is governance—not of territory, but of discourse. The healthiest diaspora networks build transparent rules for funding, verification, and conflict resolution. They publish sources. They enforce civility. They resist the temptation to romanticise struggle or villainise neighbours. Over time, they behave not just as bridges, but as institutions.

If physical borders once separated people from their homeland, digital tools stitch them back together. The result is a world in which sovereignty is porous, narratives are contested, and power is dispersed across continents. Diasporas do not merely witness change; they enact it. They are unofficial diplomats and unofficial media, unofficial banks and unofficial infrastructure.

But an unresolved tension remains: what happens when a diaspora's influence eclipses that of those living inside the country? Who speaks for a nation—the people who stayed, or the people who left? And if the answer is both, who arbitrates when their visions collide?

Platform Citizenship

A traveller loses his passport overseas. The embassy is closed for the weekend, the hotline goes unanswered, and the emergency desk quotes a wait of several days. Yet within an hour, the traveller has reactivated his bank cards through a mobile app, signed a rental agreement using an identity service trusted by local businesses, and checked into a hotel where the receptionist accepts digital credentials in lieu of physical documents. His legal identity is stranded, but his *platform* identity keeps life moving. In a quiet, mundane way, loyalty shifts from the state that issues papers to the company that keeps the lights on.

The more our lives migrate online, the more our rights, access and recognition migrate with them. Identity, once a matter of birth certificates and border stamps, becomes a constellation of logins and verifications. Platforms ask for trust and, in return, offer continuity. For millions, losing a national ID is a crisis. Losing access to email, payments, or cloud storage can be catastrophic. A person may have a citizenship in law, but *platform citizenship*—the right to transact, communicate and prove one's existence—often matters more in everyday life.

This inversion is most visible where institutions are weak. In countries where government systems fail, residents turn to global platforms for services the state cannot reliably provide. Cloud accounts serve as personal archives. Mobile money replaces failing banking systems. Ride-hailing apps track identity and reputation more consistently than police records. With each substitution, the relationship of obligation changes: people depend less on government and more on corporations with customer support centres on the far side of the planet.

Consider payments. Stateless refugees fleeing conflict zones may lose passports, but many can continue receiving remittances through digital wallets tied to phone numbers or platform accounts. Migrant workers may be unbanked in their host country, but their earnings flow through superapps that allow them to pay rent, buy groceries and send money home. The contract is implicit: platforms safeguard your funds in exchange for absolute procedural compliance. They do not ask about nationality; they ask for correct credentials. And unlike states, they can lock you out in a heartbeat.

Identity follows a similar pattern. Some people trust a platform login more than a government ID because the former is accepted globally while the latter is not. A national identity card might let you open a bank account in your home town; your email login can open one halfway across the world. Your passport may be valid for ten years; your platform account might be valid for life—unless a security system flags suspicious behaviour or an opaque policy changes without warning.

Then comes dispute resolution. Governments promise rights processed through courts and bureaucracy; platforms promise tickets processed through algorithms and moderators. A bank account frozen by the state is a political act. A payment account frozen by a platform may be an automated fraud detection trigger. Both leave you powerless, but only one offers an appeal form with a response time of "possibly never". In practice, many users treat terms of service with the reverence once reserved for legislation. Violations lead to digital exile: no access, no money, no voice. A ban from a major platform can matter more than a fine in a court.

None of this is accidental. Platforms have quietly accumulated the three pillars of citizenship: identity, economic participation and protection (or its functional equivalent). They verify who you are. They allow you to earn, spend and save. They mediate disputes, even if imperfectly. They may not call you citizens, but the architecture behaves like a civic system—rights conditional on compliance, duties defined by policies, and enforcement built into code.

Some will object that states still wield force, collect taxes and define borders. That is true, yet platforms often enforce their will with greater immediacy. A government must pass laws, deploy police or request judicial orders. A platform can disable an account globally with a few keystrokes. The border crossing of the twenty-first century may be less about land checkpoints and more about whether a payment processor approves your transaction or a cloud provider accepts your login. Borders shift from maps to dashboards.

There are benefits. Platforms can be more accessible and efficient than states, especially for those historically excluded. They innovate faster, serve globally, and skip the national chauvinisms that undermine public institutions. People with marginalised identities may find more rights—and more dignity—in online communities than in their official homelands. A person rejected by their country can build a livelihood online that no state can fully choke. For many, platform citizenship feels fairer because its rules apply to everyone—or at least to everyone the system can see.

But dependence has a cost. Platforms are not democracies; they are firms with shareholders, incentives and risk managers. They can change rules without consent, ban users without explanation, and experiment with behavioural policies that affect millions. Their appeals systems are often slow, fragmented, or non-existent. Where a state must justify coercion, a platform may justify nothing at all. One wrongful ban can freeze a creator's income, erase a business or erase a decade's work. In this light, platform citizenship resembles feudalism more than democracy: rights granted conditionally, revocable on a whim.

There is also the geopolitical tension. A country may issue a passport, but a platform issues access. When sanctions hit, platforms often act faster than governments. A state seeking to punish dissidents might fail to penetrate encrypted channels, while platforms can—under government pressure or corporate caution—silence accounts across continents in seconds. Citizens find themselves trapped between two authorities: one territorial, one transnational. Neither fully accountable.

For the user, loyalty flows toward whoever can actually solve problems. When a platform resolves a dispute, protects an account or restores payments, gratitude accumulates. When a state fails to provide services and platforms fill the gap, legitimacy migrates quietly. The person who trusts their cloud storage more than their national archive has already shifted allegiance, even if they carry the same passport as before.

Yet platform citizenship remains incomplete. Users cannot vote on policies. They cannot compel transparency. They cannot demand proportionality in enforcement or due process in moderation. Their rights are privileges, contingent on profitability and compliance. And when platforms collapse, are sold, or pivot to new strategies, users discover how little power they really possess. A digital landlord can evict an entire population overnight.

So the question becomes: should platforms be treated as civic institutions? Some argue yes. If platforms govern identity, economy and speech, then they should be bound to the obligations of states—due process, non-discrimination, transparency, the right to appeal. Others recoil at the idea of ceding civic authority to corporations and prefer to restore state capacity instead. But the reality is that millions already live inside platform jurisdictions, whether anyone acknowledges it or not.

The deeper tension is not whether platforms *should* hold power, but what happens now that they do. If states reclaim authority, how will they compete with services that are faster, global and relentlessly user-centric? If platforms accept civic responsibilities, how will they balance rights with profits? And if neither side adapts, what happens to the billions whose identities, incomes and social lives depend on systems they cannot influence?

The most unsettling possibility is also the most realistic: that platform citizenship becomes the default, normalised by convenience, cemented by dependence, and invisible until a crisis hits. Only then will people notice that the institutions they rely on are governed not by constitutions, but by terms of service; not by citizens, but by shareholders.

And the open question, still unresolved, is this: when sovereignty is exercised through code rather than law, who protects the citizen when the platform becomes the state?

Digital Secession

A disgruntled community spends weeks protesting an opaque moderation decision. Appeals vanish into silence, customer support responds with canned replies, and volunteers who held the community together lose their access without explanation. Then, abruptly, the group migrates. Posts reappear on a federated platform they now control. Familiar names return, governance votes are held, and the rules are rewritten in public. It feels like liberation—until the server collapses under traffic, bills arrive, and the arguments begin over who is responsible for security, backups and abuse reports. Freedom is exhilarating; sovereignty is exhausting.

Digital secession—the act of exiting a dominant platform for a space one owns or governs—has always carried a romantic vocabulary. "We'll build our own platform." "We'll run our own servers." "We'll take back control." But every act of independence exposes the difference between leaving and sustaining. A community can quit a platform in minutes. Running an alternative that works, at scale, for ordinary users is another matter entirely.

The idea is not new. Email was a federated system long before social media existed: anyone could run a server, anyone could send a message, and no single company held the keys to the network. The early web was the same. Small forums, self-hosted blogs and open protocols created a loose public sphere where central power was limited. What changed was convenience. Centralised platforms solved spam, scaling, security and design in ways that self-hosting rarely managed. Users traded autonomy for reliability, and most never looked back.

Now, the pendulum swings again. Outrage at unilateral moderation, algorithmic opacity and data harvesting drives communities to seek exits. Some join federated systems like Mastodon or Matrix. Others revive old technologies: mailing lists, independent forums, IRC. A few build their own software entirely. The dream is simple: to leave the jurisdiction of a corporate sovereign and enter a digital republic of one's own.

But secession is not a switch; it is an ongoing institution. Running a server means patching security vulnerabilities at 3 a.m. It means moderating harassment, handling legal complaints, and storing user data responsibly. It means uptime, backups, encryption, latency and a budget. When a federated instance grows large, it inherits liabilities once shouldered by the corporations it rejected. Donations rarely keep up with costs. Volunteers burn out. Governance disputes erupt. For many, exit becomes a cycle: migrate, rebuild, fracture, migrate again.

The obstacles are not merely technical. They are social. Centralised platforms offer network effects: everyone is already there. Leaving means persuading peers, family or customers to move too. Most will not. A federated platform that cannot reach the people who matter offers autonomy without audience. This is why so many projects begin with bold manifestos and end with quiet decay. Without sustained participation, sovereignty becomes an empty flag.

Yet federated platforms reveal something powerful. They show that alternatives are possible. They prove that communities can enforce their own norms, design their own interfaces and decide who they wish to federate—or defederate—with. Instead of one universal space, there are thousands of neighbourhoods, each with its own rules. In this ecosystem, *leaving* becomes a credible threat. If a platform treats users poorly, rivals exist that embody different principles. Exit creates pressure, even if it does not always create paradise.

Self-hosting, the purest form of digital secession, pushes the idea further. When individuals or collectives run their own infrastructure, each person becomes their own jurisdiction. Files sit on servers they physically control. Messages travel through systems they administer. No corporation can lock them out; no algorithm can bury their speech. But here, romance meets reality again. Most people do not want to be system administrators. They want things that work, with minimal effort and predictable support. Self-hosting succeeds for the technically skilled, the ideologically committed, or the very small community. At population scale, convenience wins.

The tension is familiar from political theory. A city-state offers autonomy but demands responsibility. An empire offers stability but concentrates power. In the digital context, federated platforms resemble confederations of small states; centralised platforms resemble imperial administrations.

Users must choose not only where power lies, but who bears the burden of making things function.

The practical question, too often ignored, is governance. If a community secedes, how will it make decisions? Who arbitrates disputes? Who holds administrator privileges? When a rogue moderator abuses power, what recourse exists? The architecture of independence often rests on a few trusted individuals—and trust is brittle. In many breakaway communities, the new sovereigns become as opaque as the old, only without the safety net of customer support.

Financial models add another layer of fragility. Without advertising or venture capital, federated platforms depend on donations, memberships or volunteer labour. Some thrive through collective funding. Others languish. A sovereign server that cannot pay its bills is not sovereign for long. The same applies to legal risk: if authorities demand logs or issue takedown notices, operators need counsel, procedures and policies. A server run on goodwill may crumble under pressure a corporation would absorb routinely.

Still, to dismiss digital secession as fantasy misses its virtue. It injects competition into a world drifting toward monopoly. It showcases new experiments: community-owned platforms, co-operative hosting, public-interest infrastructure. It creates pockets of innovation overlooked by commercial giants. And it protects vulnerable groups when mainstream platforms fail them. Independence may be fragile, but it can be life-saving.

There is also a strategic insight. The power of digital secession does not lie solely in exit; it lies in *credible exit*. When users know they can leave, they negotiate better terms with platforms. Corporations cannot rely entirely on captive audiences; they must earn trust. Sovereignty becomes a spectrum, not a binary: from full self-hosting to multi-homing (using several platforms), to maintaining portable data and interoperable formats. The more frictionless the exit, the more accountable the centre.

Perhaps the most important lesson is that independence is collective. A lone user cannot secede meaningfully; a community can. Tools that make migration easy—portable social graphs, exportable data, interoperable protocols—are the real infrastructure of autonomy. Without them, exit is symbolic. With them, exit can reshape the equilibrium of power.

And the unresolved question remains: will digital secession ever scale beyond subcultures and activists? Could millions live in federated networks sustainably, or will convenience always pull them back to the central platforms they distrust? Independence offers dignity and self-determination. Dependence offers simplicity and reach. Between them lies a fault line that every future community must navigate.

The promise of secession is that people may one day choose their digital governments as consciously as they choose their physical ones. The risk is that most will not choose at all, drifting back to the comfort of central authority until the next crisis reminds them what it costs to be governed by systems they cannot influence.

Recognition and Rights

A virtual polity holds an election. Ballots are counted, rules are codified, and leaders are sworn in for a fixed term. Citizens debate proposed amendments, approve budgets, and distribute funds from a shared treasury. Yet outside their borders—elastic, digital, nowhere—no state acknowledges their sovereignty, no court recognises their constitution, and no international body invites them to speak. They exist by consent of their members and by tolerance of the platforms they occupy. Their legitimacy is real to those who built it, but invisible to powers that traditionally grant it. The paradox is stark: they behave like nations, but remain legally weightless.

This is the central tension of recognition in the digital age. For centuries, territory anchored legitimacy. Land could be mapped, borders patrolled, sovereignty enforced. But when political life migrates into networks rather than land, what counts as recognition? If thousands of people follow rules, elect representatives, and invest real resources into collective projects, are they simply a fan club with good branding—or something closer to a micro-state? The answer depends not only on what they build, but who accepts that it exists.

Some virtual polities pursue formal recognition from the offline world. They draft charters modelled on constitutions, create ministries, issue identity documents, and even collect membership dues. But law is stubborn. International recognition is not awarded for enthusiasm or symbolism; it is granted through treaties, diplomacy, and a thick history of realpolitik. A digital community may produce governance with the elegance of a Scandinavian parliament, yet still be treated as a hobbyist association because no sovereign state chooses to acknowledge its status.

Beyond the legal vacuum lies a deeper question: what does recognition look like when territory is irrelevant? In practice, legitimacy is a layered phenomenon. A polity may be unrecognised by nations yet recognised by platforms, payment networks, or civil society groups. A fundraising platform might allow them to collect dues; a cloud provider might sign enterprise contracts; a local court might accept evidence they produce. Each interaction grants a sliver of status. Recognition accumulates not through a single proclamation, but through networks of trust.

In some cases, platforms themselves become gatekeepers of status. A virtual community that survives an internal crisis, or negotiates platform rules with professional sophistication, earns credibility. When administrators demonstrate responsible governance—transparent budgets, fair moderation, appeals processes, child-safety protocols—outsiders see them as institutions rather than subcultures. In this sense, legitimacy emerges from competence. A well-run online polity can appear more orderly than a failing municipal council.

Yet competence alone does not guarantee survival. Recognition is always conditional. Platforms can suspend accounts, payment processors can cut off funding, and cloud providers can terminate servers. A community may have written the most meticulous constitution ever drafted in a chatroom, but if a single corporation controls the infrastructure they depend on, sovereignty is brittle. The community exists at the pleasure of forces they do not elect. This is the existential vulnerability of many virtual polities: if the host withdraws permission, the state collapses overnight.

This fragility encourages some communities to seek alternative forms of representation—forms that do not require permission from states or platforms. Public legitimacy can come from journalism, academic research, NGOs and advocacy networks. When respected institutions treat a digital polity as a serious actor, its claims gain weight. A diaspora group coordinating humanitarian aid, or a digital collective documenting human rights abuses, may acquire moral authority that no platform can erase. Here, recognition flows from relevance: if a community delivers tangible value to the real world, others treat it as legitimate regardless of its legal status.

Representation can evolve further. Virtual polities may delegate ambassadors, draft public briefs, or appear before parliamentary committees. They might file amicus briefs, present expert testimony, or join multi-stakeholder bodies shaping internet standards. None of this grants formal sovereignty, but it constructs influence. The key insight is pragmatic: international life is full of actors who are not states—corporations, NGOs, standards bodies, religious organisations—and they exercise power without territory. Virtual polities may join this category, not as recognised nations but as recognised stakeholders.

Still, the question of rights remains. If digital citizens pay taxes into a shared treasury, vote in elections, and abide by laws, what protects them from malicious administrators, arbitrary expulsion, or disappearance of funds? In physical states, constitutions, courts and human rights treaties provide remedies. In virtual states, the primary safeguards are contractual—terms of service, codes of conduct, and social norms. A platform's appeal system may function as a court; a peer-review process may substitute for oversight. But such systems lack the moral force of law. No one is obliged to respect them.

This creates a peculiar contradiction. Virtual citizens can grow deeply attached to their polity. They may work, socialise, protest and form identity within it. Yet they remain legally unprotected. A change of platform ownership, a policy shift, or a data breach can erase their history. Communities that appear stable can disintegrate with shocking speed. The rituals of statehood—elections, flags, ceremonies—mask the fragility beneath.

A few digital polities attempt to harden their rights by embedding them in technology. Distributed ledgers, transparent treasuries, and open-source governance tools aim to reduce the power of administrators. If expenditure is publicly logged, corruption is harder. If code enforces rules, authority is less arbitrary. But code introduces new risks. A bug can freeze funds; a poorly written smart contract can lock citizens out of their own property. "Trust the code" may sound like rule of law, yet it offers no comfort when the code fails. In the worst cases, immutability makes mistakes irreversible.

Others pursue recognition through culture rather than infrastructure. They create symbols outsiders care about: art, memes, charitable projects, public campaigns. They personify their polity with ambassadors, spokespeople and narratives. In a connected world, attention confers status. If journalists cover a digital community as a meaningful political actor, people outside the community start to treat it as one. Recognition becomes social before it becomes legal.

But even cultural recognition has limits. It can exaggerate factions, reward provocation, and overlook diligent but unglamorous governance. A colourful micronation with flamboyant leaders may attract attention; a quiet collective managing a refugee translation network may be more deserving of recognition but receive less. Public legitimacy is not automatically moral legitimacy.

The most effective path to recognition, though still uncertain, lies in forming alliances. Virtual polities that partner with NGOs, municipal governments or universities gain access to legitimacy by association. A diaspora digital network that collaborates with a city council on emergency alerts gains a foothold in civic life. A decentralised research community that contributes data to public institutions gains credibility. Recognition becomes practical: if you help solve problems others care about, they treat you as a peer.

Yet even these pathways raise hard questions. Who decides which virtual polities deserve recognition? The largest? The oldest? The most ethical? The least controversial? Every criterion reflects values and power. States may ignore digital minorities; platforms may reward profitable communities; NGOs may prioritise issues aligned with donors. Recognition is political, not neutral.

And the central dilemma remains unresolved: can a digital polity secure rights without anchoring itself in traditional law? Some explore hybrid models. They incorporate as co-operatives, charities or associations, gaining limited legal personality. They sign contracts, employ staff, and manage funds transparently. This provides recourse when disputes arise and reduces dependence on platform goodwill. Yet it also brings bureaucracy, registration fees, and obligations that volunteers never imagined when they founded a forum.

There is no single blueprint. Some communities aspire to constitutional maturity; others prefer informal governance. Some seek formal power; others prefer moral authority. What unites them is the search for recognition that reflects what they already are: real communities with real stakes, even if their territory is made of servers and their citizens log in from around the globe.

As digital polities expand, the boundaries of representation will stretch with them. Courts may eventually confront disputes between citizens of virtual states; legislatures may consult digital assemblies; platforms may negotiate with federations rather than individuals. Or these ambitions may falter, leaving recognition as a patchwork of informal accommodations.

For now, the question hangs open: who has the authority to say a digital polity is merely a hobby, and who has the insight to see the beginnings of a nation? The answer will not be written in charters alone. It will emerge from practice—how these communities govern, how they protect their citizens, and how much the rest of the world chooses to take them seriously.

Chapter 9

Security, Stability, and the Open Internet

A submarine cable snaps on the floor of the Atlantic. In a handful of coastal cities, the internet slows to a crawl; in others, it disappears entirely. Flights land late, hospitals shift to paper, traders shout across desks instead of tapping keyboards. The failure is mundane—saltwater, steel, and bad luck—yet the consequences ripple through economies that barely know the cable exists. Few people ever see the infrastructure that keeps the digital world alive. Fewer still appreciate how fragile it can be.

That fragility is why states increasingly treat platforms not as websites, but as critical infrastructure. A messaging service with a billion users is indistinguishable, in effect, from a telecommunications provider. An outage during an election is no longer an inconvenience; it's a national security incident. Citizens expect platforms to behave like utilities even when they are designed like startups: always available, resilient under attack, transparent in crisis. Safety is assumed. Failure is scandal. The internet's original ethos—distributed, experimental, best-effort—now collides with a world that demands reliability closer to aviation than academia.

This shift produces a revealing tension. The open internet was never meant to be run like a single machine. It is a federation of networks, protocols, reputations, and norms. Yet when something goes wrong—a massive hack, a sovereign-scale cyberattack, a cloud region collapsing—governments look for a switch to flip and a building to blame. The instinct is centralisation: a command centre, a national cloud, a regulator with teeth. But centralisation brings its own fragility. When you create a single point of control, you also create a single point of failure.

A more robust approach treats security as *risk-by-design*. Systems that fail gracefully, segment blast radius, and degrade rather than detonate. Federation limits contagion. Rate limits slow abuse. Kill switches prevent compromised machines from turning into weapons. None of these measures are glamorous. They rarely inspire venture capital hype or viral headlines. Yet they are the quiet engineering of stability: the difference between a temporary glitch and a cascading collapse.

The chapter ahead examines how platforms, protocols, and governments grapple with this engineering mindset. It opens with the logic of critical infrastructure—why states increasingly expect redundancy, incident response plans, and disaster exercises. The internet has grown too essential to rely on goodwill. Hospitals, utilities and emergency services run across privately owned clouds and messaging apps. Power without accountability is unacceptable; accountability without preparedness is cosmetic.

From there, the lens widens to design. Some architectures absorb shock. Others magnify it. Centralised platforms promise simplicity but demand trust in the centre. Federated systems distribute responsibility but struggle with consistency. No structure is perfect; the question is what risks you choose. A tightly integrated network may offer polished performance, yet it becomes irresistible to attackers and regulators alike. A loose federation may appear chaotic, yet fragments of it can survive when others fail. Stability is not the same as uniformity.

This naturally leads to a hard question: *what does openness look like under stress?* Open protocols have survived mass surveillance, criminal abuse, and state pressure, yet their resilience is uneven. Critics argue that fragmentation is inevitable—that governments will wall off their citizens, platforms will build private gardens, and open standards will wither. But that prophecy ignores the stubborn power of interoperability. When systems speak a common language, borders never fully close. People route around blocks. Networks reconfigure. Information leaks. The open internet bends under pressure, but it rarely breaks.

Still, survival is not enough. A healthy internet is not defined by the absence of catastrophe, but by the presence of pluralism. Interoperable diversity allows communities, companies and nations to build systems that reflect their values without forcing uniformity. You can have strict privacy in one place, open experimentation in another, and commercial scale in a third—so long as the connective tissue remains intact. The test of a mature digital civilisation is whether difference can coexist without fracture.

That ideal requires measurement. Freedom online is often treated as abstract, ideological, or unknowable. In reality, it leaves fingerprints: latency spikes that hint at throttling, blocklists that expand quietly, verification queues that stretch into weeks, appeal response times that shrink or grow depending on who is complaining. Citizens can watch these signals the way environmentalists watch coral reefs and glacier melt. A free internet has a pulse, and the data is public if people choose to monitor it.

The deeper thread uniting this chapter is responsibility. The internet is now infrastructure, but it is still an idea. It was built on openness, and openness will survive only if defended with the same seriousness that societies apply to water systems and power grids. Rules matter, but architecture matters more. When systems are robust by design, freedom does not rely on luck.

Read on, then, with a simple premise in mind: stability and openness are not rivals. They are partners. The future of the internet will belong not to those who centralise control, but to those who distribute resilience.

Critical Infrastructure Mindset

A messaging app fails for half an hour. Memes stall, emojis vanish, and a few million teenagers complain. That is the cliché. The reality looks very different. Ambulance dispatchers cannot reach crews. Families abroad lose contact during a disaster. Small traders miss settlement windows and take unexpected losses. In some cities, teachers now distribute assignments, attendance, and safeguarding messages through the same platforms children use for gossip. When the service drops, so does a layer of the social fabric. An outage can feel like an attack.

This is why states have begun to treat dominant platforms—not just social networks, but payment rails, cloud infrastructure, identity services and messaging systems—as critical infrastructure. In practice, the threshold is simple: if the failure of a private service can cause public harm, governments will demand reliability. Electricity grids, water pipes, and air traffic networks operate under this logic. Now software does too. A tiny team with global reach can accidentally hold the stability of cities in its hands.

The transformation of platforms into infrastructure happened quietly. It was not ordained by law or designed through committees. It emerged from convenience. Citizens adopted the fastest, cheapest, most intuitive tools. Institutions followed. Public agencies sent alerts through private APIs; hospitals entrusted patient records to clouds; courts used commercial messaging for remote hearings. The state outsourced resilience to companies whose DNA is iteration, not obligation. For years, that bargain held. Then shocks arrived: ransomware, botnets, disinformation campaigns, cloud region failures, geopolitical cyberattacks. Suddenly, governments understood that trust without control is wishful thinking.

From that moment, platforms inherited a new social contract. It demands three things: redundancy, transparency, and preparedness. Redundancy means that failure in one part of the system cannot cascade through the rest. A single data centre fire must not erase medical histories. A regional outage should not cripple national emergency response. Yet redundancy is expensive and invisible. Shareholders resent costs they cannot see; users rarely notice the infrastructure that keeps services alive. Only during disaster does the public understand why engineers built entire parallel systems they hoped never to use.

Transparency is harder still. When critical infrastructure falters, citizens expect timely, honest information. For years, platforms treated outages as PR crises: brief posts, vague apologies, forced smiles. That era is fading. Regulators now require incident reports, timelines, and forensic explanations. In some countries, platforms must notify government agencies within hours. Silence triggers suspicion. The public assumes that anything concealed is worse than it seems. With power comes scrutiny.

Preparedness is the most demanding pillar. True readiness means practising failure—literally breaking things on purpose to test recovery. Banks and airlines run war games. Energy grids simulate coordinated attacks. Cloud providers quietly copy this playbook: chaos engineering, failover rehearsals, backup capacity on different continents. Yet many social platforms still behave as if resilience will magically emerge from scale. It does not. When resilience is an afterthought, disruption becomes a teacher, and the price of each lesson is paid by society.

This raises an uncomfortable question: if platforms perform state-like functions, should they be treated like utilities? Some argue yes: impose the same duties of care, reporting standards, and disaster recovery requirements that water and power companies face. Others warn that bureaucracy will freeze innovation and fortify incumbents. A regulated infrastructure mindset may lock in the giants and smother challengers. The trade-off is real. A fleet of small, creative startups rarely provides nationwide reliability. A handful of regulated behemoths rarely fosters experimentation.

The cultural gap between Silicon Valley and critical infrastructure is equally stark. Startups celebrate "move fast and break things"; airlines never do. Engineers raised on A/B testing and quick deployment cycles now find themselves writing playbooks for black swan events, negotiating with intelligence agencies, and planning for cyberattacks orchestrated by nation-states. This is not the world they were trained for. Yet it is the world they have inherited.

There are successful adaptations. Messaging platforms have built "degraded modes" that allow essential functions even when full services collapse. Payment systems now include offline fallback for natural disasters. Hospitals run mirrored databases across clouds and on-premise systems to prevent data loss. Some governments require platform operators to prove that no single point of failure can compromise national continuity. The mindset is simple but demanding: if a service is essential, it must handle the worst day, not just the best one.

Still, the boundary of "essential" is contested. Is a gaming network critical infrastructure if it keeps teenagers occupied during lockdowns? Does an AI translation service become infrastructure when courts rely on it to communicate with asylum applicants? What about cloud GPU clusters that train defence models or run election monitoring software? The state's definition expands as society's dependence deepens. That expansion is not a conspiracy; it is a consequence of convenience winning.

The expectations placed on platforms now stretch beyond uptime. They extend into incident response: how quickly a service detects intrusion, isolates damage, coordinates with law enforcement, and communicates with the public. The world watched as ransomware paralysed hospitals, oil pipelines, and shipping companies. Each time, response speed became a public safety issue. Platforms no longer manage just data; they manage harm.

This shift has political implications. As platforms become infrastructure, failure becomes geopolitically exploitable. A hostile state does not need to bomb power grids if it can disrupt cloud APIs or identity providers. Companies that once sold photo-sharing apps now negotiate with intelligence agencies. Private engineers become first responders to international conflict. The boundary between corporate security and national defence has blurred.

Citizens feel this change instinctively. When the internet falters, modern life hesitates. People queue outside banks, teachers print worksheets, shelves empty faster because logistics systems lag. No one voted for a world where private systems carry this responsibility. Yet abandoning them is no longer possible. Their integration into daily life is too deep. The question is not whether they *should* be infrastructure, but how we ensure they behave like it.

The critical infrastructure mindset demands humility from engineers and vigilance from governments. It forces a societal reckoning: convenience built the digital world, but resilience will decide whether it survives stress. Platforms that embrace that duty may become trusted civic institutions. Those that resist will find that public patience is short and political appetite for regulation is long.

The next frontier is uncomfortable but inevitable: expecting private networks to withstand the pressures traditionally reserved for national utilities. Whether platforms welcome that role or fight it, the responsibility has already arrived.

Risk-by-Design

When a bridge fails, it does not collapse all at once. Engineer it well, and damage remains local: a span buckles, a joint cracks, the structure groans but stands. Poorly designed systems do the opposite. A single fault cascades through the whole. The digital world, for all its speed and sophistication, still struggles with that ancient truth. Too many platforms behave like brittle monoliths. A malfunction in one component knocks down everything it touches, and sometimes everything beyond. Risk-by-design asks a different question: what if we built systems to fail safely, not perfectly?

The instinct in technology has long been scale first, resilience later. Centralise user data, centralise authentication, centralise reputation, and pray that the centre holds. It works—until it doesn't. When a major identity provider stumbles, thousands of dependent services suddenly cannot log users in. When a cloud region dies, entire industries flicker. The blast radius of a mistake is not measured in downtime, but in people: delayed ambulances, lost coursework, halted payrolls. Risk-by-design reverses the logic. Instead of assuming systems stay healthy, it assumes they get sick, and builds immunity into the architecture.

Federation is the most visible expression of that philosophy. Rather than one colossal service, you have many independent nodes following a shared protocol. If one instance collapses—through attack, mismanagement, or political coercion—others continue. The network bends but does not break. Email is the classic model. No single server controls global communication; hundreds of thousands collaborate. Even if a major provider vanishes, the system lives on. Attempts to suppress messages in one jurisdiction cannot easily silence the rest. Federation mirrors federalism: diversity within unity.

Yet federation is not a utopian cure. It imposes friction. Users migrate between instances; moderation differs; reliability varies. Some hate that inconsistency. But resilience is rarely elegant. A garden of hardy plants looks messier than a lawn of identical turf, yet it survives drought. Centralisation offers convenience and consistency at the cost of fragility. Decentralisation trades polish for durability. Risk-by-design asks citizens, companies, and states to decide which trade they are willing to make.

Rate limits are another method of controlling blast radius. They sound modest: cap how quickly a user, bot, or system can demand resources. In reality, they are an essential line of defence. Without rate limits, a mundane error in code can generate millions of requests per second, crippling a platform. A malicious actor can scrape private data at scale, impersonate thousands of accounts, or hammer an API until it folds. Rate limits do not ban misuse; they slow it. They turn catastrophes into incidents and give engineers time to react. They are the firebreaks of software.

Properly used, rate limits become a language of trust. A bank gives its payment partners a generous allowance; a hobbyist app receives less. Emergency services gain priority bandwidth; suspicious newcomers start small. The limits adapt—expanding as trust deepens, shrinking when anomalies appear. In a world where botnets and automation make attack almost effortless, friction becomes protection. Without it, one compromised device can impersonate an army.

Then there are kill switches—the most controversial tool in the resilience toolkit. A kill switch shuts down part of a system intentionally to prevent wider damage. Used ethically, it is a tourniquet: painful, temporary, life-saving. If a payment network detects cascading fraud, better to halt a segment than allow billions to leak. If a messaging platform discovers a vulnerability that exposes private data, temporary shutdown can protect users while a fix deploys. The public rarely loves kill switches. They look authoritarian. But the alternative—silent exploitation while engineers hope for a miracle—is far worse.

Kill switches raise a deeper question: who decides when to pull them? In private companies, the choice often belongs to executives or on-call engineers. Yet when platforms underpin public life, the stakes escalate. Hospitals, courts, even militaries rely on commercial clouds. A hasty shutdown in the name of "safety" could paralyse vital services. Conversely, refusal to shut down during an attack could expose millions. Risk-by-design forces institutions to confront their governance gaps. It demands rules, oversight, and rehearsals—not improvisation during crisis.

Resilience is not only a technical matter. It is cultural. Some companies celebrate the myth of uninterrupted growth. Reliability is a marketing claim, not a duty. Others embrace the awkward reality that failure is inevitable. They build "circuit breakers" that prevent runaway processes, shadow copies of critical data, and manual overrides if automated systems panic. Engineers run disaster drills: simulated data corruption, sudden region loss, or mass login failures. When the real crisis arrives, their muscle memory saves them.

Contrast this with systems that pretend failure is impossible. When a single engineer accidentally deletes a production database and there is no backup, the world learns how thin the margin really was. When a content delivery network deploys flawed code that breaks the websites of newspapers, banks, and airlines simultaneously, we see how centralisation amplifies risk. These incidents are warnings: complexity without containment becomes a liability.

Risk-by-design borrows from epidemiology. If contagion is inevitable, reduce transmission. If infection spreads, isolate it. If immunity exists, strengthen it. Federation isolates outbreaks of failure. Rate limits slow their spread. Kill switches sever infected limbs to protect the body. The metaphor is not poetic; it is practical. A digital ecosystem is healthier when failure is local, recoverable, and visible.

There is, however, a philosophical tension. Society loves seamlessness. Users prefer services that "just work" and trust the giant that provides them. Resilience strategies often make the seams visible—divergent servers, throttled requests, temporary shutdowns. The public sees inconvenience, not protection; friction, not foresight. Leaders face the same perception gap: investing in redundancy is thankless, until disaster strikes. Then everyone asks why more was not done.

Risk-by-design exposes an uncomfortable truth: fragility is fast. The shortest path to growth is to centralise everything and hope for the best. Safety is slow. It demands compromise. It demands scepticism. It demands humility in engineering cultures often addicted to bravado. But history gives no reward to the brittle. Bridges fall. Networks fail. Resilient systems endure not because they are perfect, but because they are prepared.

The future of the open internet depends on this mindset spreading—not only among platforms, but among governments and citizens. When states design digital services, they too must anticipate failure. When journalists use cloud tools to publish, they should ask how easily those tools can be silenced. When hospitals move records online, they should demand proof of backup. Risk-by-design becomes a civic expectation, not an engineering footnote.

What happens when a global platform adopts true risk-by-design? Outages shrink from days to minutes. Attacks injure but do not cripple. Political pressure to censor or control becomes harder to enforce because there is no single choke point. Transnational communication remains possible even in crisis. In other words, resilience becomes a defence of freedom.

And yet the incentives remain misaligned. Investors reward velocity, not prudence. Users complain about delays, not fragility. Regulators arrive after catastrophe, not before. So the question lingers: who will demand risk-by-design before the next failure arrives—and how much damage will it take for everyone else to follow?

Openness Under Stress

The triumph of the internet was never that anyone could speak. It was that everyone could listen. From the first publicly shared web pages to encrypted messaging and peer-to-peer networks, openness was more than a technical choice; it was a political one. Yet openness is most interesting when it is under threat. When a government blocks a site, when a platform bans an application, when hostile traffic floods a server, the question becomes painfully simple: does the system break, or does it bend?

Pick almost any moment of geopolitical tension, and the open internet becomes a battlefield long before physical borders shift. During protests, dissidents scramble to share live streams before censors intervene. When state media collapses under a data breach, independent bloggers become the public record. Under stress, openness faces two simultaneous attacks: deliberate interference from those who fear it, and accidental overload from the people who depend on it.

The myth is that an open system is inherently fragile. In truth, openness is closer to a forest than a fortress. Individual trees burn, yet the ecosystem survives. Centralised platforms promise security through control: one company, one policy, one gatekeeper. Open protocols offer security through plurality: many nodes, many routes, many custodians. The result is not tidy. It does, however, endure.

Consider the humble Domain Name System. It has been attacked, exploited, and manipulated for decades. Yet it persists because no single organisation holds its keys. Authoritative servers are distributed across continents; caches live on laptops and routers; root operators share responsibility. When a government orders a national block, traffic often reroutes. When a misconfigured update knocks out a provider, other resolvers take the load. Users might complain of slow pages or stubborn errors, but the global system remains intact. A closed alternative would be easier to police—and easier to break.

Openness survives because it is harder to kill than to govern. Countries that want total control discover the limits quickly. Deep packet inspection can throttle protocols, but encrypted tunnels slip past. IP blocklists create whack-a-mole economies of proxies and mirrors. Even the most sophisticated censorship relies on infrastructure companies cooperating, devices obeying, and engineers staying silent. History shows that none of those hold indefinitely.

Yet romanticising resilience is dangerous. Open protocols are not invincible. They can be poisoned, jammed, and captured. A distributed network does not guarantee justice; it merely distributes power. Attackers use the same openness to coordinate botnets, scrape data, or spread propaganda. Censors adapt. Platforms cave. The struggle is ongoing.

This is where architecture matters. Openness without redundancy is merely hope. Openness with thoughtful engineering becomes resistance. Peer-to-peer protocols turn every user into a broadcaster, making censorship costlier. Content-addressable storage means a file can survive without a central host. Caching ensures that popular resources live near users even if their origin disappears. These are not abstract design patterns—they are lifelines.

Political pressure reveals another strength of open systems: no single negotiation can silence them. A government might threaten a company, but cannot threaten an entire protocol. Telegram, Signal, Tor, Mastodon, BitTorrent—their operators differ, their politics diverge, yet their underlying principle remains: let people connect without asking permission. Even when a platform retreats or self-censors, the protocol persists for the next builder.

The inevitability of fragmentation is another myth worth dismantling. There is a fashionable fatalism among technologists: the open internet is collapsing into rival blocs, and nothing can be done. But fragmentation is not destiny; it is a policy choice. When regions impose digital borders, they are telling their citizens: trust us more than the world. When companies wall off their ecosystems, they are telling users: your freedom threatens our margins. Fragmentation benefits gatekeepers, not societies.

History offers a different lesson. Interoperability has a habit of sneaking back in. Proprietary messaging apps discover users want to reach friends elsewhere. Courts and regulators begin to ask why exported goods must be interoperable, but digital services need not be. Activists pressure for portability. Developers build bridges. The temptation to centralise is strong, but the incentives to reconnect often return stronger.

Open protocols are also surprisingly adaptable. When governments block one port, engineers tunnel through another. When entire address ranges are banned, systems switch to domain fronting or encrypted packet padding. Some of these tactics become cat-and-mouse games; others become standard practice. Censorship forces innovation, and innovation spreads beyond the places that needed it first.

The deeper truth is that the internet was designed for hostility. Its founding engineers feared nuclear attack, not advertising or surveillance, yet the architecture they built—packet switching, distributed routing, decentralised trust—still protects against modern threats. Openness was not a concession to idealism; it was a survival strategy.

Still, openness demands stewardship. Open-source projects wither without maintainers. Protocols stagnate without governance. A distributed network is not egalitarian if only a handful understand its workings. The open internet survives attacks well; it survives apathy poorly. Citizens who rely on it must care enough to fund it, fix it, and defend it.

There is a quieter pressure too: corporate consolidation. Even if the protocols remain open, their use increasingly flows through commercial platforms. Cloud providers host the nodes. App stores gate the clients. Search engines index the content. A censor might not need to block a protocol if it can persuade intermediaries to stop serving it. The architecture is open, but the ecology is not. Resilience demands diversity not only in code, but in ownership.

Where does this leave the future? Somewhere between fear and determination. Yes, powerful states want digital borders. Yes, companies would prefer customers to stay in walled gardens. But every time a government tries to switch off the internet, citizens discover tools to route around it. Every time a closed platform grows too controlling, someone builds an alternative—and sometimes millions follow.

Openness under stress reveals character: of systems, of engineers, of societies. The internet's original promise was that knowledge could cross borders even when people could not. That promise still holds, but only because countless individuals work to keep it true. The next time a crisis arrives—from censorship to conflict to corporate retreat—the question will not be whether fragmentation is inevitable. It will be who is willing to defend the fragile, stubborn infrastructure of freedom, and how far they are prepared to go.

Pluralism, Not Uniformity

Uniformity has always tempted engineers and policymakers alike. One protocol, one platform, one global rulebook: tidy, predictable, optimised. The rhetoric is seductive—if only everyone used the same system, the internet would be safer, faster, fairer. Yet history teaches a sharper lesson. Monocultures fail. When the world depends on a single crop, a single bank, or a single communications channel, stability becomes an illusion. One vulnerability becomes a global event. Diversity, inconvenient and untidy, turns out to be the safer bet.

This is the paradox at the heart of digital governance. Societies want the benefits of interoperability—people everywhere connecting, collaborating, and trading—without surrendering to a monoculture that collapses under its own weight. The problem is not too much diversity; it is the wrong kind. Balkanisation, where nations build isolated digital fortresses, strangles innovation and suppresses dissent. Corporate walled gardens do something similar, enclosing users in proprietary ecosystems. But interoperable diversity—pluralism backed by open standards—creates resilience without fragmentation. It is possible to have many flowers without building a thousand separate gardens.

On the ground, pluralism looks ordinary. A student in Nairobi trades design files with a firm in Manchester. A diaspora community in Berlin streams news from an independent broadcaster in Kyiv. A researcher in São Paulo queries open datasets hosted in Singapore. None of this requires uniform software or identical platforms. It requires compatibility: shared protocols, portable data, mutual recognition. The communication layer stays open while the applications vary. This, not forced sameness, delivered the internet's golden age.

The danger of uniformity is clearest when a dominant platform fails. When Facebook suffered a global outage in 2021, businesses lost sales, public health agencies lost channels, and millions of people had no access to messaging. The event lasted hours, not days, yet it exposed how deeply societies had fused everyday communication to a single corporate network. A healthy digital ecosystem should treat platforms like shops on a high street—convenient, replaceable—not like the only road into town.

Pluralism protects against political coercion as well. A regime can pressure one platform into silence, but cannot easily suppress thousands of independent nodes using open protocols. A company can impose biased moderation rules, but cannot rewrite standards that everyone else implements. Power disperses. No single boardroom, ministry, or investor controls the public square.

This does not mean chaos. Interoperability demands rules—technical, social, and sometimes moral. Healthy diversity is cooperative, not atomised. Competing services can innovate on design, business models, and culture while still speaking a common digital language. Email is the classic example: Gmail, Fastmail, Proton, and niche self-hosted servers all coexist. Users send messages across providers without caring where the other person's mailbox lives. Each provider can specialise without isolating its community.

Contrast this with messaging apps that lock conversations behind proprietary walls. When a platform becomes a closed island, switching costs grow abusive. Users stay not because they love the service, but because leaving severs social ties. In the analogue world, this would be like a telephone company preventing customers from calling friends on another network. It is absurd in principle, yet normalised online.

Pluralism also moderates error. A single central database is easy to corrupt, whether through malice or incompetence. Distributed systems, by contrast, force consensus. A bogus certificate or manipulated blocklist does less damage when checks and redundancies exist across multiple providers. Even a dominant actor must persuade rather than dictate.

How, then, can we judge healthy variance? There are concrete criteria.

First, portability. If users can move their data, contacts, and identity between services without starting life from scratch, the market rewards quality instead of captivity. Services must compete on merit.

Second, transparency. Pluralism works when decision-making happens in daylight. Open standards, clear APIs, published moderation rules—all allow scrutiny. Secrecy breeds suspicion and hidden dependencies.

Third, substitutability. When many providers can implement the same protocol, outages and censorship lose their bite. If one node goes dark, another picks up the signal.

Fourth, participation. Standards should not be dictated solely by large firms or powerful states. Small providers, civil society groups, and independent developers must have a seat at the table. A diverse network cannot be governed by a monoculture of voices.

Finally, accountability. Pluralism is not a licence for abuse. The ability to fork code or switch providers means communities can reject services that behave irresponsibly. In a plural system, exit is meaningful.

Critics argue that pluralism introduces friction. They are correct. Interoperable diversity is messier than uniformity. It requires negotiation, engineering discipline, and political will. Some will see this as inefficiency. Yet friction is often the price of freedom. A world with only one bank is efficient until the day it fails. A world with only one newspaper is orderly until the day it lies.

Pluralism respects cultural differences as well. A privacy-focused cooperative in Helsinki does not need the same features or governance as an entertainment giant in Seoul. A community-run server in Nairobi can tailor its policies to local needs without losing contact with the wider world. Uniformity would crush this nuance.

There is a deeper philosophical point. Democracy is not designed for speed; it is designed for legitimacy. The internet's original designers understood that consensus, even when slow, beats command-and-control. Federated systems echo this political instinct. When disagreements arise, participants can fork, extend, or innovate without begging permission. Divergence becomes a source of progress.

Still, pluralism is no panacea. A world of incompatible standards masquerading as "choice" serves no-one. Too much fragmentation leaves citizens trapped in digital micro-states with no bridges between them. Too much centralisation leaves them dependent on global gatekeepers. The virtuous middle—interoperable, competitive, transparent—is difficult to govern and easy to erode.

The coming decade will test whether societies choose monoculture or pluralism. As governments regulate platforms and companies build new networks, the temptation to consolidate power will be strong. Yet citizens have leverage too. They can demand portability, punish lock-in, support open standards, and choose providers that honour consent rather than exploit inertia.

Pluralism asks more of us: more patience, more participation, more critical thought. It is slower than uniformity, cheaper than fragmentation, and fairer than monopolies. Its virtue lies not in elegance, but in endurance. One system to rule the world has always been a fantasy. Many systems that speak to one another—that is a civilisation.

Measuring Freedom

Authoritarianism rarely begins with a midnight knock at the door. It begins with a slower signal: a popular website that suddenly loads more slowly than it used to, a livestream that stutters for no clear reason, a messaging app that cannot deliver videos on the day of a protest. There is no announcement, no public decree. Instead, the internet's pulse changes. Freedom fades in milliseconds.

This is the uncomfortable truth about digital rights: they are not visible in constitutions or slogans, but in latency graphs and error logs. A society may celebrate free expression on paper while throttling it in practice. The most revealing indicators of liberty are technical. They are also measurable by ordinary people.

For decades, citizens relied on journalists, lawyers, and activists to warn when the state crossed a line. Today, engineers and data scientists increasingly join them. A censorship event can be captured in a spreadsheet: the timing of DNS failures, the sudden increase in packet loss, the systematic blocking of virtual private networks. Together, these traces form a civic seismograph—quiet, quantitative evidence that pressure is rising beneath the surface.

Consider blocklists. Most users never see them, yet they govern who gets heard. Blocklists decide which URLs, hashtags, or entire applications can reach the public. A government may claim it targets only foreign propaganda or fraud, but a closer look often reveals a creeping expansion.

News sites disappear. Opposition forums fail to resolve. Even apolitical tools—file-sharing services, encrypted messengers—are throttled into uselessness. In some countries, citizens now maintain parallel blocklist archives, comparing them week by week. The changes tell a story ministers prefer not to explain aloud.

Latency tells a story too. When network operators want to avoid public backlash, they rarely cut access outright. They simply make it painful. Video buffers endlessly. Voice calls crackle, then drop. It is censorship disguised as incompetence. The public blames ageing infrastructure, not policy. But latency can be measured, and when the same platforms slow down only on sensitive dates—elections, protests, court rulings—the coincidence stops looking accidental.

Appeal times offer another window into digital freedom. A citizen whose post is removed or whose account is suspended deserves a fair process, especially when platforms serve as public squares. In many countries, appeals languish for months, effectively silencing voices without judicial review. A right to speak is hollow if it depends on customer support queues. A simple metric—the average time to resolve a content dispute—can be more revealing than any press release about human rights.

Some indicators are even subtler. Watch for the disappearance of VPN servers, the sudden requirement for national ID numbers to register accounts, or the quiet removal of encryption features under the guise of "safety". Each one adds friction to dissent. Each one chills speech without arresting a soul. Measuring these changes is not paranoia; it is civic hygiene.

Yet monitoring alone is not enough. Citizens need benchmarks. What does a healthy, open internet look like in practice? It offers stable latency across political seasons. It allows a diversity of services—messengers, hosting providers, payment gateways—to operate without sudden, unexplained failures. It provides transparent moderation dashboards, publishes appeal statistics, and issues public explanations for takedowns that affect large audiences. It supports independent third-party audits of filtering systems. Freedom is not an abstraction; it is testable.

This raises a deeper philosophical point. Traditional liberties were defended in courts and parliaments. Digital liberties also require observatories, open-source measurement tools, and collaborative monitoring across borders. A single organisation cannot track a global network. But thousands of volunteers, researchers, and civic technologists can. They already do. When Egypt blocked social media during protests, it was outside measurement probes that detected the throttling. When a European country quietly experimented with DNS tampering, academic researchers surfaced the evidence before journalists could confirm the story. Transparency is now a distributed practice.

Of course, states will argue they are defending security, not silencing speech. Sometimes they are telling the truth. Platforms can be used for scams, foreign interference, and harassment. A healthy society balances openness with safety. The problem is not that states act; it is that they act without accountability. Measurement brings that accountability into daylight. If a government claims it blocked only terrorist propaganda, but the logs show opposition media on the list, the discrepancy becomes public fact rather than private suspicion.

Platform companies deserve scrutiny as well. Freedom does not vanish only at the hand of governments. Commercial throttling, arbitrary takedowns, and opaque recommendation systems can sideline entire communities. Measuring appeal times and tracing content removals is a way to see whether a corporation behaves like a neutral host or a political actor. When companies operate at the scale of nations, citizens should track them like governments.

The challenge is cultural as much as technical. Many people assume the internet simply "works". They assume delays are accidents, bans are rare, and their communications are private. The infrastructure is too complex to see, so it feels apolitical. Authoritarians rely on that invisibility. If no-one measures, no-one can prove what changed.

One day, civic monitoring may become normal: news outlets will publish monthly reports on latency patterns, universities will host censorship dashboards, community groups will investigate suspicious outages. These tools already exist in pieces. What they lack is recognition. Transparency is not only a virtue of governments; it is a demand of citizens armed with data.

The last century taught a lesson about democracy: rights without enforcement are illusions. The next century will teach a parallel one: digital freedoms without measurement are myths. The most important watchdogs may not carry microphones or placards, but packet sniffers and server logs.

Some will ask whether this vigilance risks paranoia. The answer is simpler. Healthy systems survive scrutiny. Open societies welcome it. Only those with something to hide fear measurement.

If the internet is the nervous system of modern civilisation, then monitoring its signals is a form of collective self-defence. A latency spike is not just an inconvenience; it can be the first sign of political pressure. A blocklist change is not just a technical tweak; it can be a warning that dissent is shrinking. Citizens who can read these signs do not wait for freedoms to disappear—they notice when the future begins to tighten.

And once you learn to listen to the network's heartbeat, silence becomes louder than sound.

Chapter 10

Institutions for Digital Borders

The collapse was quiet. One morning, users across a medium-sized European country woke to find their bank apps unavailable, government portals stalled at login, and messaging services timing out mid-sentence. It was not a cyberattack, nor a natural disaster. A single cloud provider suffered a routine configuration error, and half a nation's digital life fell to its knees. Schools could not issue attendance records, hospital receptionists returned to paper clipboards, and small businesses queued at banks because card terminals had gone dark. For a weekend, the country discovered that its sovereignty depended on a private status page and a team of engineers in a data centre that did not sit within its borders.

When systems behave like states—controlling identity, payments, and speech—the question becomes unavoidable: who governs the governors? National constitutions never anticipated a world in which a moderation policy feels as consequential as a court ruling, or where an outage can paralyse emergency services. Yet that is the world modern societies now inhabit, a world where digital borders are built and maintained by institutions that did not exist two decades ago. The uncomfortable truth is that power has shifted faster than oversight. The next phase of digital governance requires a new architecture—one designed not just for efficiency, but for legitimacy.

Legitimacy is no longer a philosophical indulgence. It is the only defence against a crisis of trust. When a platform suspends an account that organises food donations, or a payroll service freezes salaries because of a disputed content flag, people expect reasons. They expect a right of appeal. They expect remedy. These expectations are not radical; they are the same expectations democracies demand of any authority capable of inflicting harm. It is time the digital sphere caught up. The internet is no longer an experimental playground. It is civic infrastructure, and civic infrastructure requires institutions.

Some governments respond with blunt force—national firewalls, data localisation mandates, licensing regimes for cloud providers. Yet the instinct to centralise control often breeds fragility rather than strength. Real resilience comes not from autarky, but from institutional rules that limit power and invite scrutiny. That means independent oversight bodies capable of reviewing platform decisions without being captured by the very companies or governments they are meant to supervise. It means processes designed with due process in mind, so that users confront a system of rights rather than a black box. A border that is legitimate is one that can be challenged.

The same logic drives public interest engineering, a field still young enough to be defined. For decades, product design has answered to shareholders and market metrics; harm was an afterthought. Now the stakes are higher. When a recommendation algorithm amplifies rumours of ethnic violence, or a fraud detection system locks millions out of unemployment benefits, design choice becomes public policy. Organisations need engineers empowered to ask uncomfortable questions: Who is harmed if this fails? How will it be abused? What remedy exists for the innocent? Red-teaming is not just a security exercise; it is democratic hygiene.

Markets carry weight too. The purchasing power of governments and universities has always shaped standards—from environmental protocols to labour rights. The same leverage can demand open formats, data portability, and interoperable identity systems. Procurement may not sound glamorous, but it is often the fastest route to reform. A nation that insists its software contracts include export tools and public APIs does more for user rights than a thousand symbolic speeches. When public funds buy technology, public values should ride along.

None of this matters if citizens cannot recognise governance when it happens. Civic literacy has traditionally taught parliaments and courts; it must now teach feeds and firewalls. Children learn how a bill becomes law, but not how a content moderation team decides who may speak. Civics lessons explain voting, but not how digital blocklists shape access to information. The next wave of education must offer simple exercises: measure latency on election night; compare blocklists between networks; file an appeal and observe how the system responds. Democracy requires citizens who can see power clearly, even when it is encoded in software rather than written in statutes.

A future of digital borders will not be defined by grand speeches or sweeping treaties. It will be defined by institutions—independent, transparent, and accountable. These institutions may not resemble parliaments or courts, yet they will perform parallel functions: reviewing decisions, protecting rights, enforcing norms. Some will be global, others local. Some will evolve from industry groups, others from civil society. All will exist because the alternative is worse: a digital world ruled by arbitrary power, where outages and opaque suspensions carry the force of law without any of its safeguards.

The path forward is not about building a digital state. It is about ensuring that no single actor—corporate or governmental—can unilaterally redraw the map of online life. Power spreads across code, contracts, and cloud providers. So must accountability. The history of democratic institutions is the history of tools invented to limit harm. The digital age demands its own inventions. The only question now is whether societies will build them before the next quiet collapse reminds us why they are needed.

Independent Oversight

The livestream froze just as the chanting grew louder. Viewers assumed it was a bandwidth glitch until the channel quietly vanished from search results and the creator's account went dark. The protest in the street continued; the protest online was erased. Hours later, a corporate spokesperson insisted the removal was a routine application of policy. No explanation. No notice. No appeal. The user had lost their voice, and the platform had no obligation to answer to anyone but itself. The irony was brutal: a movement fighting for accountability had been silenced by a system without any.

Episodes like this are not hypothetical hazards. They are part of everyday digital governance. Suspension algorithms mute journalists during elections. Automated filters delete war-crime evidence because it resembles extremist propaganda. Payment platforms block dissidents under the guise of "risk." Decisions shape public life at the scale of nations, yet the institutions behind them remain private, opaque, and largely unaccountable. Traditional states learned centuries ago that unconstrained power corrodes legitimacy. Platforms, for the most part, have yet to learn the same lesson.

Independent oversight is not a luxury. It is the price of wielding authority. The challenge is clear: platforms operate globally, their decisions affect millions, and their incentives often tilt towards political protection or commercial convenience. The answer is not to hand control to states—many of which are eager to censor or surveil. Nor is it to trust corporate ethics committees that report to the same executives whose decisions they are asked to review. Real oversight requires independence, plural representation, transparent procedure, and enough institutional bite to matter.

One model is multistakeholder review bodies—hybrid tribunals composed of legal scholars, civil society advocates, technologists, and community representatives drawn from the user base itself. Their legitimacy comes not from hierarchy, but from diversity and independence. When such a body hears a case, it does not ask whether a decision was profitable or politically expedient; it asks whether it was fair. These panels can examine wrongful removals, algorithmic bias, or systemic harms. They can publish reasoned opinions and force platforms to explain themselves. The very act of articulation disciplines power.

Yet even well-designed bodies risk capture. Corporations may stack the membership with friendly experts; governments may push for seats that turn oversight into surveillance. The architecture must anticipate corruption. Funding should be ring-fenced, not dependent on executive goodwill. Terms should be fixed and staggered, so no single actor can reshape the bench. Deliberations must be documented and published, with dissenting opinions preserved. Independence is not a feeling; it is the outcome of design choices that make manipulation difficult and exposure likely.

Examples already exist, though they are imperfect. Facebook's Oversight Board was an early attempt to externalise review, with binding decisions on content cases. It introduced due process into a space previously ruled by unilateral moderation. But its scope remains narrow, its scale dwarfed by the platform's size, and its mandate limited by corporate charter. Still, the experiment proved a principle: powerful platforms can submit to independent judgment without collapsing. It also exposed the next frontier—oversight not just of individual cases, but of system design decisions, such as algorithmic ranking or data access policies.

A deeper model borrows from administrative law. Agencies act as stewards of public power, subject to standards of reason-giving, evidence, and appeal. Translating this to the digital sphere suggests oversight bodies with investigative authority: the right to audit moderation practices, inspect training data, and scrutinise risk assessments. Transparency is only meaningful when it is enforced. Without teeth, oversight is theatre—comforting, symbolic, ineffective.

Opponents raise predictable objections. They argue oversight slows innovation, burdens companies, exposes proprietary information. But these are excuses, not reasons. The financial sector already accepts independent regulators, audit trails, and disclosure. Airlines submit to safety boards with full access to systems. Pharmaceutical companies endure rigorous review because the cost of failure is measured in human harm. Platforms now carry similar stakes. When a recommendation model accelerates self-harm among teenagers, or a payment ban ruins a family business, the consequences are not digital—they are real, visceral, and often irreversible.

There is also the risk of state capture. Some governments will attempt to weaponise oversight to force censorship or compel data access. This is why multistakeholder composition matters: no single constituency can dominate. Civil society must have seats; academia must have seats; users from vulnerable groups must have seats. Review should occur in the open, with published reasoning and statistical reporting. A bad-faith actor can influence a backroom meeting, but it struggles to distort a public record.

Legitimacy is procedural before it is substantive. People do not expect perfect outcomes; they expect fair ones. A platform that can show evidence, offer notice, and provide appeal earns respect even from those who disagree with the result. Independent oversight creates a record of governance—case law for the digital public sphere. It also disciplines future behaviour. Companies that know their decisions will be reviewed are less likely to hide behind vague policies and more likely to invest in careful judgment.

The most radical idea is also the simplest: users deserve representation. In many online communities, people spend more time under platform rules than under those of their national governments. They deserve mechanisms to influence those rules—through councils, juries, or elected delegates with real authority. Representation does not mean crowd-pleasing populism; it means structured voice. Democracy in miniature, scaled to the spaces where people actually live their digital lives.

Some will insist that platforms are private property and owe nothing to their users beyond service terms. History disagrees. Any system that mediates speech, commerce, and social organisation inevitably becomes infrastructure. Infrastructure attracts expectations: safety, neutrality, transparency. Railways, postal networks, telecommunications grids—once they shaped public life, societies built institutions to oversee them. Digital platforms can pretend they are mere apps, but the world already treats them as utilities. Institutional reform is catching up to reality.

The question now is not whether oversight will emerge, but what form it will take. Will it be cosmetic committees issuing press releases, or independent bodies with subpoena power and public reasoning? Will it be captured by governments that crave control, or built by coalitions that defend freedom? Every design choice—how members are appointed, how cases are selected, how judgments are enforced—tilts the balance between legitimacy and domination.

Independent oversight is not the end of governance. It is the beginning of trust. It signals that power has limits, that reasons matter, that users are not mere product. It forces the invisible machinery of digital borders into the light, where it can be debated, criticised, and improved. And it raises a final, unsettling question: if private platforms can create institutions of accountability, what excuse remains for those that refuse?

Due Process Online

A schoolteacher in Cairo posted a satirical poem on her private account. By morning, she found herself locked out of her livelihood: her payment app refused access, her gig-teaching platform suspended her profile, and her cloud drive flagged her documents as "potentially abusive." There was no notice, no explanation—only automated emails advising her that "a decision has been made." She did not know who lodged the complaint, which rule she had broken, or whether she could contest it. In the physical world, such punishment without process would ignite public outrage. Online, it was a silent erasure. The infrastructure that governed her economic life behaved like a state, yet offered fewer rights than a parking ticket dispute.

This is the paradox of the digital border: millions live under systems that shape speech, commerce, association, and reputation—but those systems are structured around click-wrap contracts and opaque enforcement. Platforms have become de facto administrative authorities, issuing sanctions at the speed of automation. The questions they face sound familiar to any constitutional lawyer: Did a rule exist? Was it applied fairly? Can the person affected challenge the ruling? The answers are often: perhaps, maybe, and no.

Due process online is not a philosophical luxury; it is the operating system of legitimacy. A society that accepts opaque punishment builds resentment and fragility. A digital commons that embeds transparency, notice, and appeal builds trust. The challenge is to translate centuries of administrative law—crafted for courts and ministries—into procedures that function at internet scale without collapsing under their own weight.

Minimal procedural rights are neither extravagant nor vague. They begin with the simplest promise: if the platform takes action against you, you should be told. *Notice* is the first step. Without it, a user cannot defend themselves, correct errors, or even understand what went wrong. Notice is also a restraint on power: an unexplained decision must withstand later scrutiny. Yet many platforms treat silence as policy. A ban may arrive via a generic form letter; a demonetisation may appear as a downward arrow on a dashboard.

The second principle is *reasons*. In physical institutions, decisions must be explained with reference to rules. A council cannot revoke a licence by whim; a regulator cannot fine a company without citing evidence. Online, reasons are often replaced with vague assurances about "community standards" or "safety." A meaningful reason links rule to action: which policy, which clause, which behaviour. This is not merely informational. It allows the user to demonstrate that a mistake has been made, or to change their behaviour. It disciplines the decision-maker by forcing them to articulate their logic.

The third right is *appeal*. Every system makes errors. Moderators misread jokes as threats; automated filters treat archival footage as extremist propaganda; facial recognition wrongly flags innocent people. Without appeal, injustice calcifies. With appeal, systems learn. Appeals require three things: a channel to submit a challenge, a human review at some stage, and a timeline for response. Even the smallest bureaucracies provide these. Some platforms, to their credit, have begun experimenting with user councils or independent panels that hear appeals in complex cases. But too often, appeals vanish into a void—the digital equivalent of shouting into the wind.

The final right is *remedy*. If a platform is wrong, the user deserves more than an apology. Their account should be restored, their ranking repaired, their revenue reimbursed. Remedy creates accountability; it also changes incentives. When wrongful sanctions carry a cost, platforms invest in more accurate systems. Without remedy, errors become cheap, and cheap errors accumulate.

Critics argue that due process is incompatible with scale. Billions of posts cannot be individually reviewed; decisions must be automated; delays harm safety. The objection is understandable—but misguided. Large systems already manage due process at scale. Payment networks investigate fraud, telecommunications companies handle disputes, and courts process millions of parking violations with minimal delay. The trick is not endless paperwork; it is structured procedure.

Technology can help rather than hinder. Machine-generated notices can be specific without being verbose. Transparency dashboards can show users the evidence behind decisions. Appeals can be triaged—simple reversals handled automatically, complex cases escalated to human reviewers with domain expertise. Open audit logs can allow researchers to detect patterns of bias without exposing personal data. Due process is not bureaucracy; it is architecture.

The deeper issue is incentives. Platforms fear that too much transparency reveals their weaknesses. They worry that abusers will reverse-engineer enforcement. They prefer ambiguity, which gives moderators discretion and allows executives to shift blame. Yet opacity is costly. In the absence of explanation, communities assume the worst: censorship, favouritism, political pressure. Silence breeds conspiracy.

The public sector offers guidance. Centuries of administrative law distilled the idea that power must justify itself. Agencies rely on reason-giving not for charm, but to limit arbitrariness. Courts demand evidence so that future cases can learn from precedent. These safeguards exist because institutions without them become corrupt, incompetent, or both. Digital governance faces the same risks—only magnified by speed and scale.

There is also a human dimension. Behind every moderation decision is a person whose reputation, livelihood, or identity may be harmed. A merchant wrongly suspended during a holiday sale may lose a year's income. An activist silenced before an election may lose their community. A student locked out of an email account may lose scholarship applications. Due process transforms faceless enforcement into accountable judgment.

Some platforms experiment with quasi-legal innovations: advisory boards publish opinions; transparency reports quantify takedowns; terms of service are written in plain language. These steps matter, but only if they evolve into enforceable standards. A platform that cites "human rights principles" without mechanisms for compliance is offering branding, not justice.

There are also tougher dilemmas. Should due process apply when a platform removes terrorist propaganda, child abuse imagery, or real-time doxxing? Must notice and appeal still be offered? The instinctive answer is no—some content is so harmful that speed outruns procedure. Yet even in these extremes, precision matters. Automated filters routinely classify historical documentation, satire, and counter-extremism research as "terrorist content." Blind deletion destroys evidence used by human rights investigators. As with emergency powers in states, the exception must not swallow the rule. There can be rapid action without permanent erasure; urgent removal without irreversible harm; oversight even in crisis.

A harder question is anonymity. If due process requires notice and appeal, what if the user cannot be identified? In many contexts—journalism, whistleblowing, political dissent—anonymity is a shield against danger. Due process must protect anonymity, not abolish it. The solution is procedural creativity: encrypted channels for appeals, third-party ombuds services, or delegated representation through trusted organisations. Rights need not be traded against safety.

Ultimately, due process online is a test of power. Platforms that embrace it accept that they are custodians, not sovereigns. They acknowledge that mistakes are inevitable and that users deserve the dignity of explanation. They trade a little speed for a great deal of legitimacy. They also gain something practical: systems that learn from their errors, communities that trust their governance, and regulators who see accountability rather than impunity.

But the direction is not guaranteed. Economists speak of "path dependency"—systems calcify around the choices of their early years. If platforms normalise opacity, the next generation inherits a culture of unexamined authority. If they normalise due process, the digital commons can mature into something citizens recognise as fair.

The teacher in Cairo eventually regained her accounts after an international NGO intervened. It took six weeks, dozens of emails, and public pressure. The platform never explained what happened. She was grateful, but she did not trust the system. She moved her work to a different service and kept backups offline. Her sense of safety was not restored, only her access.

That story is replicated millions of times. Some users are reinstated; many are not. Most never learn why they were punished. The rule of law does not demand perfection. It demands procedure, transparency, and the chance to be heard. If platforms govern by analogy to states, they must answer to the same principles that civilised state power long ago.

And so the question lingers: if a digital border can throttle speech, freeze assets, or erase identity, what obligation does it owe the people it governs—and what happens if those obligations remain optional?

Public Interest Engineering

The room was silent except for the click of a projector. On the wall, a screenshot of a cheerful user interface: bright icons, quick onboarding, a single tap to share. Then the lead engineer pressed a button, and the same screen reappeared—this time showing how a hostile actor could use the tool to track political dissidents through correlation of check-ins, how a teenage prankster could trigger a panic by spoofing emergency alerts, how a corrupt official could quietly purge complaints about police abuse. The product team stared. None of them had intended harm. Yet harm was already present in the code, hidden not by malice, but by omission. Prevention required a different discipline, one that product management and traditional engineering had rarely embraced: public interest engineering.

Most technology firms behave as though civic values are externalities—good to mention in blog posts, awkward to embed in roadmaps. They prioritise growth, scale, and feature velocity. Safeguards are bolted on after public scandal or regulatory threat. But infrastructure that shapes speech, safety, and markets is too consequential to leave civic considerations to chance. Public interest engineering treats harm prevention as a first-class design requirement, not a charitable afterthought.

Some firms experiment with "responsible AI" teams or trust-and-safety units, yet these are often siloed, under-resourced, or pulled in only when a crisis erupts. What matters is not the vocabulary, but the authority and the process. Public interest engineering requires roles with genuine veto power—professionals who can say *no*, not merely draft slide decks. It expects harm reviews before launch, not retrospective autopsies on damaged communities.

A harm review mirrors ethical risk assessment in medicine or aviation. It demands specificity: who might be hurt, by what mechanism, under which incentives? The most dangerous harms are rarely hypothetical. Consider location-sharing apps that enable violent partners to stalk survivors; recommendation engines that amplify hate speech faster than moderators can react; automated filters that silence journalists documenting war crimes. The engineering challenge is not to imagine every possible misuse, but to identify plausible abuse pathways and design against them.

Red-teaming is a discipline borrowed from security. Instead of assuming good faith, it simulates adversaries. A red team asks: how would a troll brigade weaponise this ranking algorithm? How could a fraud ring exploit this payment flow? Could a government use this moderation API to erase dissent? When done well, red-teaming forces uncomfortable clarity. It turns abstract values into concrete design changes: stricter rate limits, audit logs that cannot be silently erased, kill switches that shut down dangerous features under emergency oversight.

Critics worry that such scrutiny slows innovation. They are half right. It does slow reckless innovation—the kind that launches without testing failure modes, the kind that treats users as beta testers for security. The goal is not speed at any cost, but progress with foresight. The history of public infrastructure is clear: bridges built without safety inspections collapse; medicines released without trials kill; markets trade on trust, and trust requires systems that anticipate harm.

Public interest engineering is not a rejection of entrepreneurship. It is an expansion of its ambition. A product that withstands adversaries, protects vulnerable users, and remains resilient under political pressure is more valuable than one that merely ships first. A social network that embeds due process, transparent ranking, and abuse mitigation will outlast a rival that grows quickly and implodes under scandal. Responsible design is competitive advantage.

The most compelling examples come from teams that integrate civic expertise into everyday development. A messaging service embedding journalists and human rights advocates into product review to detect state-level threats. A financial app subjecting new features to "misuse drills" where engineers must demonstrate how a money laundering scheme could be detected and throttled. A cloud provider whose internal dashboards track not only uptime, but the false positives of automated abuse systems, forcing teams to iterate until innocent users are no longer swept into punitive algorithms.

Public interest engineering also shifts how companies treat data. Instead of hoarding everything, teams ask what data is truly necessary and what can be safely deleted. They consider differential privacy, encryption defaults, and access logs that deter internal abuse. They bake consent into flows instead of burying it in legal boilerplate. They recognise that privacy is a form of safety, especially for dissidents, minorities, and at-risk youth.

This mindset upends a myth: that ethics is a constraint separate from engineering. Good civic design is engineering. A platform that allows mass harassment is not merely unethical; it is poorly architected. An identity system that locks users out during political crisis is not merely insensitive; it is brittle. A recommendation engine that drives people into extremist rabbit holes is not merely regrettable; it is a design failure. Civic values and technical excellence reinforce each other.

Governments and civil society play a role, but not by dictating every rule. The most effective interventions make harm visible. External red-teams composed of academics, journalists, and security researchers can pressure companies to fix systemic weaknesses. Bug bounties for ethical misuse—rewarding those who uncover civic vulnerabilities—mirror security bounties for software flaws. Independent audits that measure bias, censorship, or wrongful takedowns reveal where systems fall short of their public commitments.

Yet incentives matter. As long as metrics reward engagement over well-being, harm reviews will be outnumbered by growth experiments. As long as product deadlines outrank safety assessments, red-teams will be invited too late. Internal advocacy is necessary but insufficient. Boards, investors, and regulators must demand that civic values appear on roadmaps with the same prominence as quarterly revenue.

There is also the question of professional identity. Engineers building financial systems must meet licensing standards; architects sign off on physical safety. In software, the stakes are just as high, yet professional responsibility remains voluntary. Public interest engineering argues for a cultural shift: practitioners who see themselves as stewards of public safety, not merely builders of features. That shift does not require a licensing regime to begin; it requires pride in restraint, rigour, and public duty.

The alternative is a world where platforms repeatedly apologise for harms they could have foreseen. Where survivors of abuse, victims of fraud, and suppressed activists pay the price for someone else's KPIs. Where innovation sells itself as disruption while quietly replicating old injustices at machine speed. Public interest engineering does not pretend that all harms can be eliminated. It insists that foreseeable harms be confronted before they scale.

There is a deeper reward. When teams design for the public interest, they rediscover the original promise of technology: to expand human flourishing, not erode it. They build systems that people can rely on during crisis, trust during conflict, and critique without fear of retaliation. They create infrastructure that earns legitimacy rather than demanding obedience.

The engineer in that silent meeting pressed play again. The second demonstration showed fixes: rate limits, encrypted location tags requiring consent, anomaly detection, a panic button that severed data flows during crisis. The interface did not change. The values embedded in the system did. No press release announced the difference. Millions would use the tool unaware of the potential catastrophe that never occurred.

That is the quiet work of public interest engineering: invisible success, harms prevented, dignity preserved. And the most important question remains unresolved—will this become standard practice, or will it survive only in pockets of enlightened teams?

Procurement as Policy

A city government needed a new learning platform for its public schools. Three vendors bid for the contract. The first promised seamless deployment; the second touted cutting-edge analytics; the third offered a slightly less polished system that allowed students to export their work, teachers to move their classes to another provider at any time, and parents to see exactly what data was collected and why. The procurement officials chose the cheapest. Two years later, when the company was acquired and shut down its education arm, tens of thousands of students lost coursework, teachers rebuilt material from scratch, and parents discovered that their children's data had been quietly sold to advertisers. No law had been broken. A single purchasing decision had reshaped the rights of an entire school system.

Most debates about digital rights focus on legislation: bills, regulations, and court rulings. But governments already wield a quieter form of power that rarely makes headlines—procurement. Every public agency buys software: learning platforms, payroll systems, communication tools, cloud storage, identity providers. When the state purchases technology, it is not merely buying functionality. It is choosing values. Demand for open standards, auditability, portability, and due process does more to shift private markets than years of regulatory lobbying. Companies compete for public contracts; if governments insist on freedom of exit and transparency, vendors adapt or lose revenue.

Public procurement sounds bureaucratic, but it is one of the most potent policy levers in the digital world. Unlike legislation, it requires no parliamentary majority. Unlike enforcement actions, it does not depend on proving a violation after the fact. Procurement sets expectations at the moment products are built and deployed. Cities and ministries can insist that data be exportable in machine-readable formats, that APIs allow interoperability with alternative vendors, that audit logs record state access, and that users receive notification when decisions are made about their accounts. These are design requirements as concrete as encryption or uptime.

Some governments have begun to experiment. A European capital introduced a rule that any messaging platform used by the city's agencies must support open standards, permitting future migration. The rule did not dictate which vendor to choose; it merely ensured no department would be trapped. When companies realised that compliance opened doors to wider contracts, they implemented open protocols. Schools gained leverage they never had before. If one platform grew predatory or negligent, they could walk away.

The American federal government's procurement of cloud services moved markets in similar fashion. Early contracts demanded FedRAMP compliance, encryption at rest, and granular audit logs. Vendors initially protested, claiming such features were expensive and invasive. Then the contracts arrived—the largest in the industry. Within a few years, capabilities once marketed as premium extras became standard practice, available to private customers as well. Procurement reshaped the baseline.

Yet procurement is rarely treated as governance. Civil servants focus on price and feature checklists, not rights. Vendors emphasise "ease of use" rather than open exits. The result is predictable: lock-in, opaque decision systems, and citizens dependent on proprietary platforms they never chose. Migrating away becomes dangerously expensive, so governments tolerate weaknesses they would never accept in physical infrastructure.

Lock-in is not a neutral business strategy. When a state entrusts identity verification, voter roll management, or transit scheduling to a closed system, it effectively transfers sovereignty to a private firm. If the vendor collapses, sells itself, or changes policy, the state scrambles. If the contract ends in dispute, the public may lose access to vital services. A private corporation gains more control over citizens than the government that hired it.

Reversing this trend does not require heroic regulation. It requires procurement officers who ask better questions. Can the data be retrieved without penalty? Are APIs documented and stable? Is there a clear audit trail for government requests? Does the platform allow appeals and corrections? These are not ideological demands. They are basic safeguards.

Some jurisdictions have gone further, bundling public interest requirements directly into requests for proposals. A South American health ministry demanded that vendors submit a decommissioning plan: if the contract ended, all medical data had to be migrated to another system within ninety days at no additional cost, in a standard format, under cryptographic integrity checks. Firms that relied on proprietary lock-in withdrew from the bidding. New entrants demonstrated that openness was technically feasible and commercially viable. Patients benefited from continuity; clinicians gained tools that respected mobility.

Critics argue that these requirements raise costs and deter innovation. That fear is overstated. Open standards and portability do not stifle competition; they redefine its terms. Companies must win customers with service quality, security, and user trust, not coercive switching fees. Just as public building codes force architects to meet fire safety standards, procurement requirements force software developers to protect users. The market adapts.

Procurement can also safeguard speech and due process. When public institutions sign contracts with content moderation vendors—tools used in libraries, schools, or municipal communication portals—they can require that users receive notification if content is removed, that appeals are available, that blocklists are auditable. Without such terms, private moderation quietly replaces public accountability.

Flexibility matters in the face of political pressure. A news archive hosted on a proprietary platform may be one legal dispute away from deletion. By contrast, an archive stored on open, portable systems can migrate when threatened. Governments that value press freedom can build this resilience into procurement terms rather than pleading with vendors after censorship occurs.

The same applies to cybersecurity. If a vendor is compromised, the state must be able to cut ties swiftly. Open APIs and exportable data allow emergency migration. Closed systems trap agencies in dangerous limbo; every day spent negotiating access is a day of risk. Procurement that demands graceful exit reduces the blast radius of breach and failure.

There is philosophical clarity here. Procurement treats the public not as consumers, but as rights-holders. Citizens should not lose access to records, benefits, or communications because a vendor changes terms. Students should not forfeit their intellectual labour because a platform sunsets. Migrants should not depend on a single company to prove their identity. Public contracts can encode these principles, turning abstract rights into operational reality.

Some reforms are strikingly simple. Procurement offices can publish template clauses demanding: open data formats; documented APIs; transparent pricing for extraction and migration; published uptime and appeal metrics; regular third-party security audits; and the right to contract with multiple interoperable providers. None of this requires new law. It requires discipline.

Public interest groups and open-source communities often plead for transparency. Procurement can convert pleading into obligation. When a ministry pays for election systems, it can require that code be auditable and interfaces interoperable. When a district buys body-camera storage, it can require public export formats so defence attorneys and journalists can review footage. Vendors who refuse will lose business—not in theory, but on signed contracts.

Market influence scales beyond borders. A national government that demands open standards for identity providers inspires vendors to sell compliant versions everywhere. Municipalities that require portability in learning management systems create pressure for regional interoperability. Procurement is networked governance. One well-designed contract becomes a benchmark; others copy it.

Yet procurement can be captured. Vendors cultivate relationships; lobbying shapes requirements; public officials fear disruption. To prevent capture, procurement processes must be transparent, competitive, and open to civil society oversight. When terms are published and bidders ranked publicly, advocacy groups can scrutinise whether procurement protects rights or quietly erodes them. Sunlight disciplines both buyers and sellers.

There is a deeper cultural shift here. Civil servants often see themselves as risk-averse. But procurement designed for the public interest is not reckless; it is preventive. It builds safety and continuity into systems before crises arrive. It recognises that digital services are not consumer toys—they are the administrative backbone of modern society.

Most people never think about procurement, yet it shapes their lives. A young mother in a rural town uses an online portal to apply for benefits. A refugee checks their case status through a mobile app. A business owner pays taxes electronically. If these systems fail, thousands suffer. If they lock in, governance becomes hostage to private interests. If they respect openness, portability, and due process, citizens gain resilience without noticing.

There is an irony. Legislators can spend years arguing over digital rights, only to watch their own agencies sign contracts that quietly undermine the principles they defend. Procurement operates in the shadows; it deserves attention in daylight. When governments demand civic protections in every contract, the market listens.

The unanswered question is whether states will treat procurement as a strategic tool or remain captive to the cheapest bidder. Will they demand systems that citizens can exit, scrutinise, and trust? Or will convenience and cost savings continue to obscure dependence? Public purchasing can strengthen freedom without passing a single new law. Whether governments use that power remains uncertain.

Civic Literacy

A secondary-school teacher in Manchester once set her students a simple task. They opened their phones, refreshed their social feeds, and wrote down the first ten posts they saw. Then she asked a single, disarming question: *why these posts and not others?* Some shrugged; others muttered vaguely about "the algorithm". Not one could explain how recommendations were made, what signals counted, or which institutional choices shaped their information diet. Yet those feeds influenced their views on elections, health, immigration, and war. The class could describe how a bill becomes law, but not why a meme becomes viral. They knew how Parliament is dissolved, but not how a platform account is suspended. Their civics education had stopped at the border of a world they already lived in.

This is the central paradox of modern citizenship: children are taught about courts, constitutions, and councils, yet the systems that actually govern their daily lives—feeds, filters, firewalls, app stores, and identity providers—are treated as consumer conveniences rather than institutions of power. Civics in the twentieth century assumed that state action was the primary force shaping freedom. But for a teenager whose friendships, education, credit history, and future employment flow through digital systems, the constitutional order of platforms matters as much as the constitutional order of nations.

Civic literacy must evolve. It is no longer enough to memorise the branches of government. Citizens need to understand how ranking systems shape knowledge, how content moderation policies define visibility, how firewalls draw invisible borders, and how data brokers form dossiers that affect insurance, employment, and policing. These are not technical curiosities; they are the rules of a new public square. A platform that changes its recommendation algorithm can shift the tone of political debate in a week. A filtering contract between a ministry and a private vendor can silence dissidents overnight. A data breach at a health app can affect a generation's trust in healthcare. Civics that ignores these systems is civics in name only.

To teach this effectively, education must shed the idea that technology is a specialised field. It is governance. One can teach digital civics with the same clarity used to explain juries, budgets, and judicial review. A classroom exercise might begin with moderation. Students post fictional content—funny, controversial, benign, harmful. They vote on which rules should apply: should hateful speech be banned? Should misinformation be labelled or removed? Should appeals exist? Then the teacher introduces complexity: what if a wrong removal erases vital health advice? What if a delayed removal causes harm? Students role-play moderators under time pressure, forced to decide without perfect knowledge. The lesson lands: behind every takedown is real human judgment, fallibility, and institutional design. Moderation is not magic; it is a civic system.

Firewalls offer another powerful lesson. A teacher can divide students into groups, giving each group a different "internet" with a subset of websites. One group sees global news; another sees only local entertainment; a third sees neither international nor critical content. After fifteen minutes of browsing, groups compare what they learned. The disparities are stark. Some students can discuss world events; others cannot. They experience in miniature what millions live every day: informational inequality engineered by policy, not ability.

The point is not to frighten students but to empower them. Understanding breeds agency. When citizens realise that feeds and firewalls are designed, not inevitable, they can demand better: transparency, appeal rights, independent oversight. The democratic instinct extends to the digital domain.

Teachers often protest that they lack technical expertise. They do not need it. Effective civic literacy treats platforms the way traditional civics treats legislatures: as institutions with powers, responsibilities, and constraints. One can explain notice-and-appeal systems for content moderation using the same logic as due process. One can explain data minimisation using the same principles as privacy rights. Students learn to ask: who decides? who benefits? who can challenge? These are civic questions, not engineering ones.

Some schools have already begun. In Taipei, students compare different search engines' results for the same query, documenting discrepancies. In Helsinki, pupils simulate phishing attacks to understand why a single careless click can compromise a city network. In Nairobi, a community programme teaches teenagers how to download their platform data and see what is stored, what is guessed, and what can be deleted. These are acts of citizenship, not coding.

There is resistance. Some parents worry that teaching algorithmic awareness will encourage distrust. In reality, understanding fosters healthy scepticism, not paranoia. We teach students how advertising works so they can make informed choices; we should teach how recommendation systems work for the same reason. Others argue that this is too political. Yet civics has always been political. Teaching how a vote is counted does not endorse a party; teaching how content is sorted does not endorse a platform. It simply reveals the machinery of influence.

A society that lacks digital civics is vulnerable to manipulation. Conspiracies thrive when people do not grasp how virality is engineered. Disinformation spreads fastest among those who think platforms are neutral mirrors of reality. Digital literacy is often taught as a warning against scams or bullying. Civic literacy goes deeper: it teaches how power is exercised in networked systems, how rules are made, and how citizens can contest them.

Simple, low-cost exercises can illuminate this. One activity examines "shadow bans" and visibility rules without invoking real social conflict. Students create a small forum—perhaps a shared document or classroom platform—and assign moderators secret instructions: suppress posts from those who use too many emojis; boost posts that mention "science"; hide posts that criticise moderators. Students then reflect on how these hidden rules affected conversation and trust. The lesson is clear: governance without transparency invites suspicion, even if well-intentioned.

Another exercise focuses on portability. Ask students to imagine that their school email, cloud storage, or homework system vanished overnight. How would they retrieve documents? Could they move to another platform? This leads to discussion about open formats, export tools, and the right to exit—concepts most adults never learn until a crisis arrives.

Digital civics also needs history. Before the commercial web, protocols were open by necessity. The early internet worked because anyone could implement the same standards. This spirit persists in the open-source movement, where code is a public good. Students who build simple websites or contribute tiny edits to open software see cooperation as a civic act, not a technical one. It demystifies power: the internet is not a monolith but a series of human choices.

There is a deeper philosophical argument for digital civic literacy. Democracies survive only when citizens can recognise when power is abused. In the past, that meant understanding police, courts, and parliaments. Now it also means recognising when a platform silences critics under pressure from advertisers or governments; when a search engine buries marginalised voices; when a cloud provider enables mass surveillance. These actions shape public life as surely as legislation.

But civic literacy should also celebrate constructive power. Platforms can amplify marginalised voices, build movements, and connect communities that states ignore. Students can study moments when social media enabled accountability: police brutality filmed on phones; corruption exposed online; disaster relief organised rapidly through messaging apps. They see both danger and promise.

For civic literacy to matter, it must be practical. Schools can teach students how to file data access requests, compare privacy policies, and exercise appeal rights when content is removed unfairly. Universities can run clinics where students assist local organisations in securing communications or analysing platform transparency reports. Libraries can host workshops for older citizens to understand permissions and data tracking on everyday apps. Civics becomes lived, not abstract.

The greatest challenge is inertia. Traditional civics remains frozen in a world where power flowed through ministries and courts. The curriculum rarely acknowledges that a platform's automated recommendation engine can polarise a country faster than any parliament. When young people learn civics from textbooks rooted in the 1980s, they feel patronised. When they learn that civic power includes the right to audit, contest, and exit digital systems, they feel engaged.

Some countries are experimenting. Estonia teaches students how national digital identity works and why it enables rapid public services. South Korea includes media literacy not as a side topic but as central to democratic participation. Brazil's electoral court partnered with educators to explain how misinformation campaigns target voters, using real examples and data. These efforts remain isolated. They need scale.

There is a broader cultural shift here. Digital civics frames technology as part of the social contract, not a consumer gadget. It reminds students that platforms govern communities, whether they admit it or not. And it equips them to demand better governance: transparency instead of secrecy, accountability instead of arbitrary power.

Will schools embrace this shift? Or will another generation graduate fluent in constitutional doctrine but illiterate in the systems shaping their daily lives? The answer is still unwritten. Civic literacy is not nostalgia for democratic ideals; it is preparation for digital self-determination. The next citizens will need it.

Chapter 11

Designing for Dignity

A young woman reaches for a "delete account" button and finds none. She searches settings, taps menus, reads help pages. Every path loops back to the same trap: disable notifications, pause the account, reconsider. The system is designed to retain, not release. Her data stays where it is, her profile haunts the platform like an unburied shadow, and the company calls this "choice". It is not a technical limitation. It is a design decision, made by humans, and it tells a simple story: dignity was not a priority.

Dignity is not a poetic aspiration in digital systems; it is a measurable property. You see it when a person can leave a service without being harassed by pop-ups or threatened with losing years of memories. You see it when a non-native speaker can navigate a safety setting without stumbling through untranslated jargon. You see it when a survivor of abuse can make an online report without reliving trauma through endless forms. And you see the absence of dignity in the places users feel small: locked accounts without recourse, inaccessible interfaces, invisible surveillance, correction channels designed to exhaust, not assist. Digital life is now public life. Design has become governance.

For a decade, the dominant belief was that frictionless design was humane. One click to sign up, one tap to share, instant uploads, infinite scroll—an ethic of smoothness that framed friction as failure. But friction can be protection. A speed bump saves pedestrians. A confirmation step prevents mass harassment. A pause before forwarding a rumour can save someone's reputation. The platforms that promised frictionless delight discovered that abusers, bots, and propagandists also loved smoothness. Dignity requires thoughtful friction: circuit breakers for virality, cooling-off windows for angry messages, prompts that explain consequences before harm occurs. Friction by design is not inconvenience; it is respect for the humans on the receiving end.

Privacy belongs here too, not as secrecy but as power-sharing. A street without curtains tells you everything about the people inside but offers them no control. A social platform that demands radical transparency, tracks behaviour invisibly, or buries settings in dark corners creates the same imbalance. Privacy with dignity means giving users intelligible choices. Not legalese. Not deceptive toggles. Defaults that honour autonomy. Systems that do not punish those who opt out. When privacy is framed as something only hackers or paranoids care about, it reinforces a lie: that ordinary people do not deserve control. The truth is simpler. The less a system respects your agency, the less dignified your participation becomes.

Language and accessibility are often treated as kindness rather than justice. In reality, they are borders. A safety warning available in English but not in Urdu protects some and endangers others. An appeal process that requires sighted navigation excludes the visually impaired. A help page written by lawyers rather than educators assumes that understanding is a privilege, not a right. When platforms fail to translate, caption, or describe, they are not being negligent; they are drawing invisible lines between those who count and those who are on their own. Dignity is not a UX flourish—it is a distribution of power.

Repair matters as much as prevention. Every system makes mistakes: false positives, automated blocks, lost accounts, mislabelled content. Dignified design does not pretend this will vanish; it builds humane channels for redress. A user who is wrongfully suspended does not want a labyrinth of support tickets or auto-responses that say "we cannot comment further". They want clarity: what happened, how to fix it, who to speak to. Platforms often tolerate high error rates because victims are diffuse and powerless. But error without remedy is cruelty. Systems that treat users as disposable lose legitimacy, no matter how polished the interface.

And there is the ethics of exit. Digital borders often trap rather than protect. A platform that stores years of photos but lacks export tools holds memories hostage. A service that refuses account deletion, or quietly copies data into "inactive profiles", violates the elemental right to leave. Imagine a hotel where the doors only swing one way. No one would call that hospitality; it would be imprisonment by architecture. Many platforms operate this way, normalised by habit. Designing for dignity means permitting graceful exits: deletion that is real, portability that is functional, migration paths that do not punish autonomy.

The chapter ahead explores these threads not as abstractions but as responsibilities. It asks what happens when product design is treated as civic design, when engineers and designers see themselves as custodians of dignity rather than custodians of engagement metrics. It shows how friction can slow mobs, how privacy can equalise power, how language can include rather than exclude, how appeals can heal rather than frustrate, and how exit can be a right rather than a technical afterthought.

Designing for dignity does not promise a perfect internet. It offers something quieter and more radical: systems that treat people as adults, citizens, participants—never as targets. The most successful platforms of the next decade will be those that learn to put dignity first. Whether they will is an open question. The pages that follow ask what it would take.

Friction by Design

A politician posts a doctored video. Within minutes it spreads from phone to phone, leaping continents before fact-checkers have caught their breath. Journalists request a takedown; the platform hesitates. Nothing is technically broken—servers are healthy, algorithms operating as intended—yet the system behaves like a runaway vehicle. Everyone can see the crash coming, and no one can reach the brakes.

A generation of designers were taught that speed was kindness. One-tap sharing was celebrated as empowerment, and platform growth rewarded the smoothest path from creation to amplification. But smoothness has a darker twin. The same systems that let charity appeals reach millions also allow mobs, hoaxes, and coordinated harassment to spread with the velocity of adrenaline. The paradox is stark: frictionless design empowers both the brightest and the bleakest impulses of human behaviour. When a single retweet can summon thousands to target an individual, the absence of friction is not neutrality; it is acceleration.

Thoughtful friction sounds counterintuitive in an industry built on optimisation. Yet mature systems in the physical world embrace it. A motorway may be engineered for speed, but it still has speed limits, crash barriers, and signage. Public squares welcome protest, but they close roads and erect gates to prevent stampedes. Digital platforms are the only public spaces where millions gather without the equivalent safeguards. When the stakes are reputations, elections, and the safety of vulnerable people, adding friction is not censorship; it is responsible stewardship.

Consider *circuit breakers* for virality. In financial markets, circuit breakers pause trading when volatility spirals, giving participants time to evaluate risk rather than react to panic. Social platforms now face similar dynamics: sudden surges of outrage, misinformation, or abuse. A circuit breaker in a messaging service might limit forwarding when a message crosses a threshold—many countries requested just that during waves of mob violence triggered by viral rumours. The pause does not delete speech; it slows its acceleration, making space for verification, context, and cooling of tempers. Even a delay of minutes can change the outcome.

Rate-limiting abusive accounts is another quiet form of friction. Most harassment online is not a lone user typing furiously; it is coordinated messaging, automated scripts, or low-cost impersonation. Restrict an account from sending hundreds of replies a minute and the blast radius shrinks dramatically. A troll might still speak, but cannot drown others. Similarly, throttling newly created accounts until they build trust removes the cheapness of pseudonymous aggression. When abuse becomes slow and labour-intensive, it loses its advantage.

Not all friction needs to be technical. *Cognitive friction*—a moment of reflection—can be remarkably powerful. Fact-check labels prompt users to read before sharing. Confirmation screens ask: "Are you sure you want to send this to 5,000 people?" A banking app demands a two-step confirmation before transferring a large sum; few would call that oppression. Yet platforms routinely treat such prompts as burdensome, even though they are a modest tax on reckless behaviour. A misleading story that travels with a visible warning moves differently through the network; it can still be viewed, quoted, debated, but its viral thrust loses momentum.

There are deeper philosophical tensions beneath these tools. Critics argue that any friction is a restriction—a paternalistic intervention that assumes users cannot think for themselves. But what if the real paternalism lies in pretending that frictionless systems are neutral? No platform is a blank canvas. Ranking algorithms, recommendation engines, and push alerts are forms of silent choreography. They set the tempo of conversation and the visibility of speech. Friction does not create a controlled environment; it acknowledges we already live in one.

Moreover, friction is not only protective—it can be profoundly democratic. Imagine a small activist group facing a coordinated harassment campaign. Replies flood in faster than any human can read. Report queues overflow. Without friction, the attackers dictate the pace and scale of harm. With friction—rate limits, identity verification, or posting pauses—the defenders regain agency. Friction returns time to those who lack power.

Some platforms have discovered this reluctantly. After repeated outbreaks of harmful misinformation, messaging apps in Brazil and India limited forwarding to five chats at a time. The result: falsehoods still circulated, but the viral explosions became smaller. Disinformation campaigns had to work harder, spending more coordination, more labour, more money. When abuse is expensive, less of it happens. A frictionless network rewards the cheapest tactics.

The lessons extend to content moderation. A company could automatically remove borderline posts, but doing so risks overreach and political backlash. Introducing friction instead—demoting discoverability, prompting edits, slowing the rate of spread—offers a proportional response. It preserves speech while containing harm. Crucially, it recognises that the worst damage is often inflicted not by content existing but by content exploding.

Thoughtful friction also humanises dispute resolution. Consider user appeals. Many platforms treat appeals as a black hole: submit request, wait indefinitely, receive silence. Adding friction for the platform—mandatory explanation, timeline guarantees, human review—shifts power back toward the user. The inconvenience is productive; it forces accountability. Just as constitutional democracies build friction into government through checks, balances, and courts, digital systems require similar scaffolding to avoid arbitrary authority.

Friction can even foster healthier communities. Online forums that require newcomers to read before posting develop richer culture than those open to immediate shouting. Email newsletters that ask subscribers to confirm sign-ups stop bots and reduce spam. Rate limits on posting frequency push users to think instead of reacting. A three-second delay before replying to a comment seems trivial, yet studies show it can reduce impulsive harassment. Friction creates room for reflection, and reflection is the enemy of mob instinct.

There is, admittedly, a line between thoughtful friction and manipulative friction. Some companies deploy *dark patterns*—deliberate obstacles to leaving or opting out—to coerce users into staying. That is friction in service of capture, not dignity. The ethics here are clear: friction should protect users from harm, not trap them for profit. A friction that serves power rather than people is mere exploitation dressed as safety.

Critics also worry that friction disadvantages the marginalised—those with slow devices, limited literacy, or tight bandwidth. This is a real concern. Friction must be intelligently targeted: applied to mass forwarding, not private messaging; applied to automated accounts, not verified individuals; applied proportionally, with transparency. A speed bump in front of a school protects children; a motorway littered with random barriers would be chaos. The challenge is precision, not abandonment.

Interestingly, friction is not only defensive. It can be generative. Long-form writing thrives on slow creation. Scientific peer review is friction. Judicial due process is friction. These systems trade speed for legitimacy. Most societies accept that some decisions must be slow because they matter. Online platforms rarely acknowledge this. Every interaction is optimised for immediacy, as though slowness were shameful. But speed is not virtue. A public square where the loudest voice always wins is not a democratic space; it is a gladiator pit.

If the next decade of digital governance has a signature theme, it may be this: the courage to slow down. To accept that virality is not a right. To recognise that delay can be a social good. To build networks that resist weaponisation rather than enable it. The public rarely demands perfect algorithms—but they notice when systems make life worse. They notice when lies move faster than facts, when mobs gather faster than help, when abuse arrives faster than remedy.

Thoughtful friction will not prevent every crisis. It cannot solve polarisation or eliminate cruelty. But it can change the arithmetic of harm. It can make attacks harder, victims safer, and conversations more deliberate. In a world where speed is worshipped, the radical act is to pause.

And perhaps the lingering question is this: if our digital environments are the new public squares, libraries, and courts, do we trust them more when they are frictionless—or when they are designed with the humility of guardrails?

Privacy as Power-Sharing

A woman in a small town reports harassment to the authorities. Unknown to her, the police request location data from a major platform, and the platform hands it over without notice. Days later, the harasser learns she went to the police. He knows because the app he uses shows when his name was queried. The victim is now afraid to seek help again. Nothing was encrypted. Nothing was leaked. Privacy, as traditionally defined, was technically intact—and yet power shifted decisively against her.

For decades, corporations and governments framed privacy as secrecy: the ability to hide. If you had "nothing to hide," you supposedly had nothing to fear. But privacy is not a cloak; it is a lever. It determines who can observe, influence, predict, or coerce. When platforms store everything for ever, track everywhere you go, and infer what you will do next, secrecy becomes irrelevant. The real question is not whether you can hide from power, but whether power can hide from you.

In digital life, asymmetry is the defining problem. A platform often knows thousands of data points about a user. The user knows nothing about the platform's intentions, retention policies, human reviewers, or algorithmic models. A citizen navigating a social service cannot see the automated score that decides whether she is "risky" or "low priority." A migrant applying for a visa does not learn which keywords trigger extra scrutiny. Privacy is therefore not an argument for silence; it is a demand that power be shared rather than hoarded.

Negotiated control changes the frame. Ordinary people rarely want perfect secrecy. They want a say. They want to know who sees their messages. They want choice about whether third parties can profile them. They want the ability to correct errors, delete what feels invasive, pause data collection during crises, and understand who benefits from their digital footprints. In this sense, privacy becomes a civic relationship—forward-looking, mutual, conditional—rather than a locked vault of hidden facts.

Default settings reveal where allegiances lie. A service that automatically opts users into targeting, indefinite retention, or broad visibility has already answered the question of whose interests come first. Compare this with platforms that start from minimal collection, ephemeral storage, and local processing. The same feature—sharing a photo, sending a message, browsing a map—can exist with entirely different power dynamics. The engineering choice is not neutral.

Encrypted messaging illustrates this vividly. Some governments argue that encryption protects criminals and terrorists. But historically, asymmetric access to communication has harmed the weak more than the powerful. Whistle-blowers, journalists, dissidents, and domestic abuse survivors rely on protected channels to survive. End-to-end encryption does not guarantee safety, but it levels the field. It ensures that no company employee, no hacker, no corrupt official can quietly read private conversations.

Privacy, in this context, is not secrecy; it is the refusal to grant unilateral surveillance capacity to whoever owns the servers.

The same logic applies to location and behavioural data. A fitness app may collect GPS trails to map jogging routes. Lovely idea—unless that data is retained, sold, or breached. Soldiers at overseas bases learned this the hard way when a public heatmap revealed patrol patterns. Once again, privacy was not about hiding crimes; it was about preventing unintended exposure. A simple default—local processing rather than central aggregation—would have changed the outcome entirely.

Negotiated control also means visibility of watchers. Credit scoring algorithms that decide mortgage eligibility should be auditable. Content moderation systems that categorise certain dialects as "toxic" should publish metrics on error rates. Predictive policing tools should disclose training data and appeal processes. If a system can deeply influence a person's rights, freedoms, or opportunities, then secrecy is a form of domination. Privacy rights here demand transparency upwards as well as downwards.

Designers often claim transparency is technically difficult. Sometimes it is. Yet opacity is usually a choice. A platform that can deploy personalised advertising to billions in milliseconds could, if it wished, provide each user with a clear dashboard: what data was collected, what decisions it influenced, and what options exist to withdraw consent. Some have done exactly this. Others hide behind jargon-filled privacy policies that bury crucial details in footnotes.

Consent is weakest when it is demanded at the beginning of a relationship. When a service states, "Agree to everything or leave," the user has no bargaining power. Negotiated control requires continuous consent—revocable, comprehensible, granular. A privacy setting should not be a trapdoor: tick once, and surveillance begins. Better is the model where permissions expire, where apps request access only when needed, and where silence after a period of inactivity returns power to the user.

Laws have begun to acknowledge this. The European Union's GDPR introduced rights to data portability, deletion, and access. California followed with similar provisions. Yet legal rights are only half the battle. If the interface buries them, if the process takes months, if the appeal requires a lawyer, formal rights become meaningless. The real frontier is design: making privacy rights as easy to exercise as sending a message.

In some places, activists have demonstrated how defaults shape behaviour. Browsers that block third-party tracking by default dramatically reduce the surveillance economy. Messaging apps that delete messages after 24 hours by default change the psychology of conversation: less paranoia, less reluctance, less fear of permanent records. Crucially, these defaults do not ban persistence; they make it an active choice rather than an invisible assumption. Power shifts accordingly.

Privacy-as-power-sharing also challenges data monopolies. When a social platform can see your social graph, contact list, private messages, purchasing habits, and location, it possesses leverage no individual can match. Data portability—exporting your history, messages, and friends list—breaks that monopoly. It allows community migration without amputating the social bonds that anchor people to platforms. For many, the threat of losing memories and relationships is more coercive than any contract. Portability transforms exit from self-harm into self-respect.

There are tensions here. Public institutions need data to deliver services effectively. Hospitals require medical records. Transport authorities need usage statistics. Privacy by design must balance collective intelligence with individual autonomy. Federated systems offer one way forward: data stored locally and aggregated only when essential, with privacy-preserving computation that reveals patterns without revealing identities. The result is a population-scale benefit without population-scale vulnerability.

Some critics argue that privacy obstructs innovation. But the opposite is true. Innovation thrives when people trust systems enough to use them. Medical researchers cannot work with patient data if citizens fear misuse. Online education stalls if students believe their behaviour is mined for surveillance capitalism. Democracies weaken when private conversations feel unsafe. The health of digital society depends on consent, not coercion.

Perhaps the deeper issue is that many people feel privacy is already lost. They suspect that data brokers know everything, that governments listen to calls, that corporations track every heartbeat. Fatalism is a powerful enemy. But fatalism is inaccurate. Small changes—shorter retention, encrypted backups, anonymous analytics—shift the balance. For ordinary citizens, meaningful privacy is not perfection; it is protection from predictable harms. It is the difference between being observed and being exposed.

The most compelling vision of privacy is therefore relational. It recognises that every exchange of data is a negotiation of trust. It accepts that some vulnerabilities are necessary for connection. It respects that consent must be renewed as contexts change. It understands that the dignity of digital life rests on the humility of systems that collect less, reveal less, retain less, and disclose more about themselves.

If privacy were merely about hiding, it would be a relic of the pre-digital age. But if privacy is about *sharing power*, then it becomes a foundation of digital citizenship—a guardrail for autonomy, a shield for dissent, a prerequisite for equality.

And that leaves a final question hanging: if platforms claim to empower people, why do so many design choices still concentrate power on one side of the screen?

Language, Accessibility, Inclusion

A young mother tries to apply for welfare benefits on a government website. She speaks fluent Arabic, but the portal is only in English and French. The form times out after fifteen minutes, wipes her progress, and demands she upload PDFs she cannot generate from her old phone. She abandons the application. Somewhere in a government dashboard, a statistic will record that she "chose not to complete". In reality, a system that should have served her quietly excluded her—no guards, no guns, just interface decisions.

Digital borders often appear without warning. They are rarely announced, and never debated in parliament. They sit in dropdown menus, error messages, and unreadable captchas. They are formed when a platform supports eighteen European languages but ignores indigenous dialects. They emerge when someone who uses a screen reader is blocked by unlabeled buttons, or when a deaf student joins a video lecture with no captions. These are borders drawn not by politicians, but by developers, designers, and product managers who rarely notice the frontier they are building.

The assumption that the internet is inherently inclusive is one of the great illusions of our age. In truth, the web can replicate every social barrier—class, language, disability, geography—only faster and more quietly. A public service available in law may be inaccessible in practice. A right granted on paper may be denied by a loading spinner that never ends on low-bandwidth devices. In this sense, inclusion is not a slogan; it is engineering.

Human dignity hinges on whether systems acknowledge difference. For someone with dyslexia, a wall of dense text with no spacing is not a page—it is a dead end. For the visually impaired, a beautifully designed infographic without alt text is a blank screen. For those navigating low-cost devices, a webpage that assumes unlimited data is a luxury, not a service. And for those whose first language is not the platform's default, every interface becomes a test they never asked to take.

Language remains the most visible frontier. English-language platforms dominate global discourse. Yet billions of people operate outside English, with regional dialects, scripts, and cultural idioms that machine translation mangles. A hate speech classifier trained on American slang will miss caste-based slurs in India or targeted harassment in Nigeria. A moderation queue staffed with English-only reviewers will misinterpret satire as threat, or threat as banter. When linguistic minorities are ignored, they are not simply underserved—they are left unprotected.

This is not theoretical. Sri Lankan activists raised alarms for years that social media companies were failing to detect inflammatory posts in Sinhala. When violence later erupted, politicians blamed platforms for complacency. The deeper truth was simpler: the language was never prioritised. If a platform earns revenue from a region, it inherits a duty to understand its words, its threats, and its context. Pretending otherwise is negligence disguised as neutrality.

Accessibility is the other great test. The World Health Organization estimates more than a billion people live with disabilities. Many depend on assistive technologies: screen readers, voice input, magnifiers, captioning, simplified layouts. When these fail, entire populations are locked out. Accessibility, when done well, is profoundly practical. It means every image has alt text. Every video has captions. Buttons are large enough to tap. Text can be resized. Forms can be saved mid-way. Colour contrast is sufficient for those with low vision. These are not luxuries for niche users; they are basic requirements of a public square.

Some companies treat accessibility as a compliance chore—something to file under legal risk. Others embrace it as a design imperative. Apple redefined mainstream accessibility by integrating features into every device: VoiceOver, guided access, switch control. What once required specialist equipment is now built-in. That shift is philosophical. It recognises that accessibility benefits everyone: commuters listening rather than reading, older adults with declining vision, parents typing with one hand while holding a child. Universal design is not charity. It is competence.

Inclusion goes beyond disability and language. Consider literacy. Billions of people are entering the internet with limited reading skills. For them, text-heavy platforms are unusable. Voice interfaces, simplified navigation, pictorial instruction, and low-bandwidth modes are not optional extras; they are gateways to civic participation. When disaster strikes, a weather warning written only at a university reading level is a moral failure.

Connectivity itself is an axis of exclusion. A government service that assumes 4G streaming will fail in rural areas. A messaging app that loads ten megabytes of content on startup will punish those with expensive data plans. Optimising for low-bandwidth users—delayed image loading, offline access, compressed files—turns technology into a lifeline rather than a tax.

Practical design choices can dismantle invisible borders. A civic platform that handles multiple scripts, from Amharic to Urdu, signals that those voices matter. A website that works on old Android phones respects economic reality. A service that provides human support for those who struggle with forms offers dignity rather than shame. And a moderation system that hires reviewers fluent in local dialects protects vulnerable communities rather than abandoning them.

There are predictable tensions. Translation is expensive. Accessibility requires resources. Localisation can slow feature launches. But these costs must be compared with the cost of exclusion: lost trust, misinformation, discrimination, and public outrage when invisible harms become visible tragedies. When a platform claims to connect the world, accessibility is not a favour—it is a promise.

The rhetoric of inclusion often collapses under its own vagueness. Everyone nods. Everyone agrees. Nothing changes. Progress begins when inclusion becomes operational. Platforms that take inclusion seriously build checklists into their release process: Are captions available? Is the text machine-readable? Are navigation elements accessible via keyboard? Does the app work on 2G networks? Is the privacy policy written at a reading level a teenager can understand? Has this feature been tested on older devices? Are help articles available in local languages?

Public institutions can lead by example. The UK Government Digital Service built comprehensive accessibility guidelines and required compliance for all public websites. That framework forced agencies to adopt semantic HTML, alt text, keyboard navigation, and readable content. It changed the culture from "accessibility if time allows" to "accessibility by default". When governments raise the bar, private companies often follow.

Civil society has also begun to audit digital borders. Volunteers test banking apps with screen readers. Activists document government portals that block access to those using VPNs. Researchers track where machine translation fails, particularly for minority languages. These investigations expose barriers that would otherwise remain invisible. Over time, they build pressure for reform.

There is a philosophical dimension here that deserves clarity. Inclusion is not mere politeness. It is a claim about who counts in a digital society. Platforms that dismiss accessibility as niche are declaring which bodies and languages deserve recognition. Systems that ignore screen readers, captions, and translation are making a political choice: some voices matter more than others. Digital infrastructure inevitably encodes values, and exclusion—whether intended or not—is a value.

At the same time, inclusion cannot mean perfection. Languages evolve. Dialects multiply. Needs change. The aim is not universal comprehension, but universal respect. A platform that listens to users, adapts to feedback, releases in beta for under-served communities, and iterates rapidly can achieve remarkable gains. Failure is forgivable; indifference is not.

The broader lesson is stark. Borders are not only checkpoints and walls. They are form fields that refuse non-Latin characters. They are "invalid" errors when a name includes an accent. They are autocorrect systems that erase indigenous place names. They are captcha tests impossible for the visually impaired. These barriers do not appear in political speeches. They do not inspire protests. They are quiet, constant, and devastating.

And so we circle back to dignity. The measure of a digital system is not how it treats the fluent, the wealthy, the literate, and the able-bodied. It is how it treats everyone else. Designing for inclusion is rarely glamorous. It requires patience, humility, and the willingness to test products in conditions far from Silicon Valley campuses. It asks teams to think not only about edge cases, but about the edges of society.

Yet the reward is profound: a digital commons that does not shrink to the size of the privileged. A world where citizenship does not depend on English fluency, eyesight, or the latest hardware. A public square where the disabled are not trapped outside the gates, and where language is not a border but a bridge.

If language and interface can quietly exclude millions, they can also quietly welcome them. The only question is whether those who build our digital structures are willing to see the borders they already control—and take responsibility for dismantling them.

Repair and Redress

A woman wakes to find her small business page deleted without warning. Years of customer reviews, invoices, and photographs vanish overnight. An automated notice claims she violated a policy she has never heard of. She appeals through a form that replies only with scripted platitudes. No human ever speaks to her. The digital equivalent of a clerical error destroys her livelihood, and there is no desk to knock on, no official to call, no right to be heard. The page simply does not exist anymore.

This is the silent cruelty of many online systems: the border is not built of barbed wire, but of indifference. When things go wrong—and they inevitably do—most users discover that the modern internet has abundant mechanisms for punishment and almost none for repair. Appeals disappear into a black box. Suspensions linger without explanation. Mistaken bills and erroneous blocks take hours to impose, and weeks to undo. The speed of enforcement dwarfs the speed of mercy.

Every complex institution makes mistakes. Courts acquit the innocent. Airlines lose luggage. Banks reverse fraudulent charges. What distinguishes a civilised institution is not that it never errs, but that it provides a clear path back to justice. Digital platforms now carry responsibilities once held only by governments—identity systems, marketplaces, payment rails, public communication. Yet when harm occurs, the mechanisms for redress look less like modern governance and more like a customer support queue in permanent collapse.

This matters because errors online rarely stay digital. A mistaken ban can cost a person their voice in a political protest. A frozen account can trap money a family needs to pay rent. An algorithmic flag can mislabel someone a spammer, extremist, or fraudster—with consequences that spread to employers, banks, and border agencies. If platforms wish to be taken seriously as infrastructure, they must take repair as seriously as enforcement.

The most basic demand is clarity. When an action is taken against a user—deletion, removal, shadowban, demotion—there should be a reason given in plain language. Not a cryptic code, not a reference to a policy that has changed fifty times, but a sentence an ordinary person can understand. The principle is ancient: a person deserves to know the charge against them.

Without transparency, people cannot correct errors, learn from mistakes, or contest abuse.

Some platforms have begun to move. After years of public pressure, a few large services now provide notification dashboards, pointing to policies violated and evidence used. But clarity is still uneven. For millions of smaller companies, clarity is a luxury. And for governments offering digital services, the situation is often worse: welfare applications rejected without explanation, immigration portals that time out, forms that cannot be resubmitted, and phone lines that lead nowhere. When public services move online, opacity becomes a democratic flaw, not merely a technical inconvenience.

Appeals are the next frontier. In most systems, an appeal is symbolic: a form that leads to a dead inbox. Yet appeals are where legitimacy is earned. The opportunity to tell one's side of the story is central to justice. A fair process does not guarantee a favourable outcome, but it guarantees dignity. The least a platform can offer is a second look by a human who can interpret context, nuance, and cultural meaning that algorithms cannot.

Proper appeals demand independence. If review teams are measured solely on the volume of tickets closed per hour, they will not spend time reading nuance. If the same department that enforces rules reviews complaints, it has every incentive to defend its own decisions. Some companies have experimented with external review boards—the closest thing to courts the digital world has produced. Their existence is imperfect, but conceptually important: a recognition that users deserve not just customer service, but due process.

Speed matters too. A wrongly blocked business account restored six weeks later remains a tragedy. A journalist removed during an election is repressed no less because reinstatement eventually arrives. The timeline of harm is rarely the timeline of redress. Digital systems demand something closer to emergency medicine than leisurely correspondence. Errors should be reversible within hours, not months.

Some governments have begun to model humane digital support. Estonia's e-government platform, famous for its transparency, allows citizens to see exactly what inquiries are made about their data and by whom. When systems fail, users can contact an accountable public agency staffed by professionals trained in service, not scripted apologies. In contrast, many other states outsource digital portals to low-cost contractors, where support tickets circle endlessly through underpaid staff who lack authority to fix anything.

Citizen expectations are shifting. When banks freeze a card due to suspicious activity, they often allow immediate confirmation via text message. That is repair in action: fast, clear, reversible, humane. Platforms have no excuse for building systems that can erase a user in seconds and take weeks to fix the damage. The asymmetry reveals priorities: enforcement is automated; redemption is manual.

There is also a deeper question of empathy. For decades, platforms optimised for scale and frictionless automation. Support was treated as a cost to be minimised. Yet when mistakes involve identity, livelihood, or safety, automating humanity out of the equation becomes a moral failure. Humane support recognises that behind every ticket number is a person with limited time, limited patience, and possibly limited literacy. It means offering help in multiple languages. It means designing interfaces that do not presume legal or technical fluency. It means that someone whose account was hijacked should not need to write a dissertation to prove who they are.

Repair and redress also apply to content. When misinformation spreads, platforms often delete harmful posts. But deletion alone is not repair. When rumours destroy reputations or fuel violence, communities deserve context, correction, and transparency. Some media organisations issue visible corrections; platforms should do the same. Instead of silently removing content, they can annotate it: "This post contained inaccurate information; here is a correction." Repair acknowledges the harm while teaching users how misinformation spreads.

There is a philosophical tension here. Platforms fear that acknowledging error undermines trust. In reality, silence corrodes trust far faster. Mature institutions admit mistakes, compensate victims, and change procedures. They publish transparency reports, not as public relations, but as accountability. They learn from failure and share what they learn. When platforms refuse to admit error, they signal that they are tools, not institutions.

Many of the world's worst digital injustices persist because they are invisible. Users silence themselves, lose income, or lose access without making headlines. A gig worker deactivated by an algorithm rarely has the power to challenge the decision. A refugee denied access to an online identification system cannot file a lawsuit. In these cases, repair is not merely a matter of support; it is a matter of power. Appeals must be accessible not only to the loudest, but to the least powerful.

Civil society has begun documenting these harms. Researchers track shadowbans, suspension rates, and demographic disparities. Journalists investigate cases where appeals vanish. Some activist networks even run parallel support systems, helping victims navigate messaging platforms or marketplace suspensions. Their work exposes the gap between corporate slogans about community and the lived reality of user abandonment.

The strongest systems design for reversibility. Instead of permanent deletion, they use soft-deletion that can be restored. Instead of automatic demotion, they allow administrators to override. Instead of triggering cascades of punishment across linked services, they isolate the damage. These architectural choices make repair cheaper than harm. They assume that users will occasionally be wrongly accused, hacked, or misunderstood.

Redress also includes compensation. When a platform's failure causes material loss—lost sales, frozen funds, reputational damage—users deserve remedies, not apologies. A responsible institution does not merely undo the error; it compensates for its consequences. Today, few platforms even acknowledge this duty. They hide behind terms of service disclaimers, declaring they owe nothing. That may satisfy lawyers, but it erodes legitimacy. The law sets a floor, not a standard. Institutions earn respect by doing more than the minimum.

There are practical models to emulate. Consumer banks offer chargebacks, fraud insurance, and customer service lines. Airlines compensate for lost bags and delays. Even public agencies often provide ombudsman services. Platforms could create rapid-response teams for account recovery. They could provide binding timelines for appeals. They could publish data on error rates and fixes. These steps do not require new laws—only willingness.

The deeper insight is simple: digital systems are now part of the social contract. Rights mean little without remedies. A platform that can silence, exclude, or confiscate must offer a pathway to fairness. Without repair, rules become arbitrary; without dignity, governance decays.

And so we return to the woman whose business disappeared. She does not demand miracles. She asks only that someone listen, investigate, and fix what went wrong. She seeks the opposite of a labyrinth: a door, a person, a remedy. The true measure of a digital institution is not how it behaves when everything works, but how it behaves when something breaks.

One question lingers: if platforms can automate enforcement at planetary scale, could they not also automate compassion? Could they build systems where mercy is as swift as accusation, and where repair is not a privilege reserved for the well-connected? Until they do, the internet's borders will remain not only technical, but moral.

The Ethics of Exit

The most revealing moment in any relationship is not the beginning, but the end. A user tries to delete an account that has served them for a decade. The platform responds not with a goodbye, but with a gauntlet: endless confirmation screens, guilt-inducing messages about "losing precious memories", warnings that friends will miss them, hidden buttons, broken export tools, and a final demand to phone customer support during office hours. The message is unsubtle: you may enter freely, but you may not leave.

This is the dark heart of the modern internet. Platforms speak of empowerment, freedom, and choice. Yet the right to exit—once taken for granted—has been quietly dismantled. Accounts can be created in seconds, but escape requires negotiation. Data portability is promised, but export files arrive corrupted, incomplete, or formatted so cryptically that only specialists can understand them. Deletion exists in legal theory while backups, shadows, and machine learning embeddings keep traces forever. The greatest trick platforms ever pulled was persuading the world that choice exists while designing systems where leaving feels impossible.

Exit matters because power matters. When departure is easy, loyalty is earned. When departure is painful, loyalty is coerced. The freedom to walk away is the bedrock of dignity—offline and online. In physical life, one can change schools, switch banks, move neighbourhoods, or buy from a different shop. The difficulty of doing so varies, but the right is fundamental. In digital life, that right has become conditional, obscured behind interfaces engineered to discourage autonomy.

Tech companies often justify their hostility to exit by claiming users will inadvertently harm themselves—lose photos, lose messages, miss important notifications. The paternalism is revealing. Like any monopolist, they insist that the product is too important to abandon. Behind the gentle language sits a harder reality: users are a source of data, and data is currency. Losing users means losing leverage, losing precision, losing profit. Dark patterns are not accidents; they are business models rendered in pixels.

Consider portability. In principle, a social network user should be able to export their posts, messages, connections, and media in a standardised format that can be imported elsewhere. In practice, portability is treated like a courtesy, not a right. Exports arrive as giant compressed archives without metadata linking messages to senders, comments to threads, or images to albums. The user receives a puzzle, not a passport. The theory of interoperability exists; the implementation is sabotage by complexity.

Email offers a rare counterexample. A person can switch providers while keeping their contacts and forwarding rules. The protocol survived decades of corporate consolidation precisely because no single company controlled it. It is a reminder that portability is not utopian—it is normal when the architecture allows it. Where platforms resist portability, it is a design choice, not a technical obstacle.

Deletion is similarly contested. When a user deletes an account, they expect disappearance. Yet many systems merely hide data from the user while retaining backups indefinitely. Speech that was supposedly erased persists in machine learning models, recommendation engines, and cached profiles. To delete is to request a kind of digital mercy; the platform decides how literal that mercy is.

In financial services, deletion has legal teeth. Banks must erase data when accounts close, subject to regulatory retention rules. Telecom companies must do the same. If a mobile phone provider secretly retained call lists or text messages after a contract ended, it would be a scandal. Online platforms rarely face such scrutiny. They hide behind jargon: "We retain certain information to improve user experience", "We cannot erase data used for training", "Some information may persist in backups." The result is a vast archive of ghosts—past users who thought they had left, but whose data remains in the afterlife of servers.

And then there are the users who cannot leave at all. Gig workers whose income depends on a single platform cannot simply exit without losing their livelihood. Immigrants using digital identity services to access healthcare or benefits cannot opt out without risking survival. Children whose schools require centralised learning platforms are locked in by design. When participation is mandatory, the right to exit becomes symbolic. The platform has ceased to be a service and has become a gatekeeper.

The ethics of exit rest on a simple rule: no system should hold a person hostage. Yet hostage-taking has become normalised. Subscription cancellations require phone calls that mysteriously drop. "Deactivation" hides data but does not erase it. "Account closure" requires five different screens of emotional blackmail. "Are you sure? Your friends will miss you." "Are you sure? You will lose access to your favourite brands." "Are you sure?

You will never recover your memories." Leaving a platform should not feel like leaving a cult.

Some jurisdictions have begun to intervene. The European Union's General Data Protection Regulation enshrines the right to data portability and erasure. But rights on paper are not rights in practice. Enforcement is slow. Penalties are rare. And platforms have become expert at compliance theatre—appearing to obey while quietly undermining the spirit of the law. Regulators move at the pace of paperwork; platforms move at the pace of code.

Design offers a deeper solution. The most ethical systems build exit into their architecture. They separate identity from service so that users can switch providers without losing themselves. They allow one-click export and deletion that is truly deletion. They create APIs for migration, plugins for interoperability, and handoffs for continuity. They assume that users are citizens, not customers trapped in a casino.

Open-source platforms often lead here. A user who tires of a Mastodon server can migrate to another and bring their followers. A person running their own email server can move hosts without changing address. These systems treat exit as a design constant, not an afterthought. Their model is not perfect—migration can be clumsy, incomplete, or confusing—but it expresses the right principle: power-sharing, not power-hoarding.

Of course, exit raises moral tension. Total deletion may erase evidence needed for investigations into harassment or fraud. Total portability may expose private conversations of other participants. Portability and deletion are not absolute; they are negotiated rights in a shared environment. Ethics requires balancing the autonomy of the individual against the safety of the collective. Yet platforms often invoke these complexities to justify indefinite retention and restrictive exports. The burden of ethical nuance should not consistently resolve in favour of corporate convenience.

Exit also reveals inequality. Digital natives may know how to navigate menus, download data, or switch services. Others do not. Disabled users, non-English speakers, the elderly, and those with limited digital literacy are the easiest to trap. Ethical design must begin with them: large buttons, plain language, no hidden menus, no emotional manipulation. If leaving requires legal literacy, technical fluency, or psychological stamina, the system is failing its ethical duty.

Even when exit works, there is the problem of social gravity. People stay where their friends stay. A platform with a billion users can neglect exit rights knowing that few will leave, because leaving means social exile. This gravitational force is invisible but immense. It is why true exit requires interoperability. Just as a citizen can change phone companies yet keep their number, a user should be able to join a new platform without losing their social identity. Without interoperability, exit becomes lonely.

Some platforms experiment with deletion windows—grace periods where a user can restore an account before data permanently disappears. These are sensible: they provide reversibility for mistakes and emergencies. But reversibility is different from obstruction. Grace periods should be 30 days, not forever. The deletion button should be visible, not hidden at the bottom of a help page.

Dark patterns flourish because they are profitable. Designers know that even small frictions—an extra step, a guilt-inducing phrase, a deceptive layout—can deter departures. Regulators could ban such patterns outright, calling them what they are: coercive design. Consumer protection agencies already ban misleading advertisements and unfair contract terms. Extending this logic to digital exits would be straightforward.

The stakes are moral as much as technical. A society that respects exit respects autonomy. A platform that embraces exit becomes worthy of trust. The paradox is that when leaving becomes easy, staying becomes meaningful. Compliance driven by force produces resentment. Loyalty born of freedom produces legitimacy.

The ethics of exit point to a future where digital systems resemble public utilities: accountable, interoperable, and humane. Not because every platform is regulated like a water company, but because users demand dignity. They demand the right to take their data with them, to delete what they no longer wish to share, to walk away without resistance.

The question is whether platforms are willing to loosen their grip. Those who fear exit fear accountability. Those who welcome it believe they can earn their users every day.

Some day soon, a platform will advertise not how easy it is to join, but how easy it is to leave. That may become the highest signal of integrity in the digital world.

And perhaps the most uncomfortable question remains: if a platform truly respected its users, would it still be so afraid to let them go?

Chapter 12

A Field Guide to Digital Frontiers

A student journalist in Manila posts a story about illegal logging, naming a well-connected company. Within hours, the article disappears from her university's website, her mobile provider throttles her data connection, and a string of anonymous messages warns her to stay quiet. None of these acts looks like formal censorship. Yet together they achieve the same effect. The borders of speech had shifted—not through a law, but through a mesh of technical decisions, private actors, and quiet pressure points.

Stories like hers are common, but what makes them so unnerving is the uncertainty. Who pulled the strings? Was it a regulator abusing its authority, a platform enforcing opaque policies, a network operator responding to an unofficial request, or a security vendor's filter set too tight? Something happened, but the chain is invisible. Many activists, journalists, educators, and public servants face the same puzzle: when a digital freedom is breached, where do you even start? The age of borderless communication has not eliminated control; it has merely wrapped it in layers.

This chapter is written for anyone forced to navigate this ambiguity. In traditional geopolitics, borders are concrete: fences, checkpoints, stamped passports. On the internet, borders are software, protocols, terms of service, data flows, and business contracts. They are subtle until they are not. And when they emerge, the instinct is often to shout, legislate, or litigate. Sometimes that is necessary. Often, it is not. The smartest actors—campaigners, policymakers, engineers, even product managers—begin with diagnosis, not outrage. They want to know: where is the gate, who controls the key, and what tools might unlock it?

The first practice is deceptively simple: identify the layer. Many digital conflicts masquerade as ideological battles when they are really problems of identity, inspection, or enforcement. A protest livestream blocked on one platform may work perfectly on another, not because of politics but because of automated filters or authentication failures. A payment gateway that refuses donations to a charity may be following a risk-scoring algorithm written by a third-party vendor on the other side of the world. Before fighting a monster, one should learn its anatomy. Misdiagnosis wastes energy and empowers those who rely on confusion.

Once the layer is clear, the actors come into focus. Digital borders are rarely enforced by a single hand. They are the product of chain reactions: regulator to telecom, telecom to platform, platform to content-moderation contractor, contractor to automated filter. Mapping these actors is a discipline, not an art. It reveals leverage: who can intervene, who can escalate, who is merely following orders. In some countries, the key decision-makers are public. In others, they are a tangle of subcontractors. When activists learn to map the system, they stop shouting at the wrong door.

The temptation in moments of digital repression is to draft new laws. Laws feel definitive—statutes, penalties, permanence. But legislation is slow, blunt, and often obsolete the moment it passes. Sometimes transparency is stronger than prohibition: forcing disclosure of filtering policies can change behaviour without a single courtroom. Sometimes procurement achieves what parliaments cannot: a government that insists on open standards and data portability can shift an entire industry. Sometimes standards bodies build interoperability that sidesteps monopolies. Not every problem is a law-shaped problem.

Yet digital power never stays still. The moment one barrier is lifted, another appears. Messaging apps build encryption; states demand metadata. Platforms allow content appeals; trolls learn new tactics. Each advance produces a counter. Nothing is static, and the most agile societies accept that control systems evolve. This is why pilot programmes matter: small, reversible experiments that reveal what works without committing a nation to permanent mistakes. Sunset clauses, kill switches, and staged rollouts are not signs of weakness; they are signs of wisdom.

This idea—reversibility—is rare in digital governance. Politicians like permanence. Ministers cut ribbons; they do not celebrate the graceful rollback of failed policy. But on the internet, rigidity is a liability. The cost of a bad decision is global: once a filtering mandate is deployed, it can spread across networks; once a platform's trust and safety model shifts, its effects are felt by millions. Designing for reversibility is a civic safety net. It allows innovation without authoritarian drift.

A field guide is not a manifesto. It is a tool. This chapter is meant to equip those confronting digital borders with something better than outrage:

orientation, strategy, and leverage. It shows how to diagnose the layer of control, how to map the actors who enforce it, how to choose the right instrument for the job, how to anticipate adaptive countermeasures, and how to build systems that can be rewound when they go wrong. The goal is not romantic heroism. It is competence.

The deeper lesson is that digital power is decentralised. Few battles are won by pressuring a single ministry or shaming a CEO. Change happens when the network of actors—technologists, civil servants, educators, city councils, standards bodies, funders, journalists—understand where to push. A telecom that refuses a government's unlawful request. A city procurement officer who demands accessible design. A platform engineer who builds export tools not as an afterthought, but as a user's right. These are small acts. Together, they redraw borders.

The digital frontier is not a frontier at all. It is a landscape of overlapping sovereignties, some democratic, some not. Those who learn to navigate it will not eliminate conflict, but they will turn panic into strategy. The student journalist in Manila could have asked the right questions: which layer failed, who made the call, and what instrument might change it? Perhaps her story would still have vanished. But she would not have been lost in the dark.

The chapters ahead offer a compass for those moments. Not theories, but practices. Not speeches, but steps. Because power that hides in code and contracts can only be challenged by those who know where to look—and how to move when the ground shifts beneath them.

Identify the Layer

A medical charity in West Africa tried to purchase cloud hosting using a mainstream payment processor. The transaction failed. A second provider rejected them as well. When they asked for an explanation, no one could tell them why. Their website finally went back online only after a volunteer routed payments through his personal account. The problem was labelled "technical." In fact, it was political. Somewhere in the chain—identity checks, risk engines, sanctions filters, vendor policies—an automated system had quietly categorised them as dangerous. No single human decided to silence them. The border emerged from code.

This is how modern control often works: a blockage without a culprit; a right denied without a villain. When a livestream vanishes mid-broadcast, when a messaging app refuses connections, when a donation platform suddenly freezes a fundraiser, the first instinct is outrage. Yet shouting at the obvious target—usually the visible platform—frequently misses the real point of failure. Digital repression, or even accidental harm, rarely operates at one layer. It moves through identity systems, inspection systems, and enforcement systems. Only by diagnosing which layer is failing can the right remedy be applied.

Identifying the layer is not an academic exercise. It is a practical skill for activists, policymakers, engineers, journalists, and anyone who works in contested digital spaces. Misdiagnosis leads to wasted political capital, performative outrage, and technical fixes that achieve nothing. A protest network throttled by a telecom cannot be rescued with a content appeal to a platform. A journalist mistakenly flagged by a credit-card processor cannot be freed by new encryption standards. Without clarity, righteous anger becomes theatre.

Three layers dominate the anatomy of digital borders: identity, inspection, and enforcement. Each has its own logic, its own decision-makers, its own vulnerabilities, and its own remedies. Learn to distinguish them and half the puzzle becomes solvable.

Identity failures are the most basic. Who are you? What device are you using? Are you allowed to be here? These questions are asked constantly, often invisibly. A citizen in Cairo finds that her messaging app works only when using a foreign SIM card; the local telecom has tied national identity to network permissions. Migrant workers in Singapore discover that welfare portals reject logins unless names exactly match passport spelling, turning clerical variation into exclusion. A student trying to join an online protest is blocked because her account is "unverified." These are borders created by credentialing.

Identity-based blockages often masquerade as technical glitches. But the tell-tale signs are clear: some users can access the service while others cannot; VPNs or alternate accounts restore functionality; similar content succeeds in a different namespace. The remedy is rarely content appeals. The relevant actors are authentication providers, telecoms, certificate authorities, and account-verification systems. When identity is the layer, the solution is escalation to the gatekeepers of access, not the moderators of speech.

Inspection failures occur when systems look inside packets, messages, or files and decide that something is dangerous—or appears so. These are filtering engines, malware scanners, copyright bots, terrorist-content detectors, and government-run deep packet inspection boxes that sit inside network infrastructure. A video might never upload because its hash resembles extremist propaganda. An academic paper might vanish because an automated filter misread a keyword. A charity website might be inaccessible in one region because a vendor's threat classifier marked it "risky." Here, appeals must reach those who control the inspection logic: the platform's trust-and-safety teams, the filtering vendors, the standards bodies that define what counts as malicious.

Inspection failures create the tightest feedback loops. The more platforms automate content analysis, the greater the risk of false positives. The quieter the censorship, the harder it is to contest. When activists cannot diagnose inspection as the layer, they may spend weeks arguing with a hosting provider that is merely inheriting decisions from an upstream threat feed. Meanwhile, the true arbiter—often a security vendor three countries away—remains untouched.

Enforcement is the final layer. Something is allowed to exist, recognised as legitimate, and still removed or throttled. Here one finds the visible acts of power: takedown orders, penalties, suspensions, temporary or permanent bans. A government demands the deletion of a cartoonist's post. A telecom blocks an opposition website during elections. A platform suspends a whistleblower for "violating community guidelines." Enforcement is where political pressure is most visible, and yet even here the chain can be complex. A platform might act voluntarily, fearing regulatory retaliation. A telecom might comply with a vague state directive. A moderator may enforce a policy written under legal threat. Enforcement failures appear obvious, but they are often the product of half-seen coercion.

The question that stitches these layers together is simple: where did the intervention occur? When a message fails to send, was the failure at identity (you were not recognised), inspection (your message was flagged), or enforcement (your account was punished)? Each layer has a different diagnostic path. Activists now share checklists: test with alternate accounts; inspect error codes; record timestamps; compare behaviour across networks; try different DNS resolvers. In heavily controlled regions, citizens become amateur network forensics experts, learning to trace their own blockages.

Some might argue that these distinctions do not matter—that all forms of restriction are equally harmful. That view is philosophically tidy and practically disastrous. If a livestream stalls because of identity misconfiguration, no amount of political campaigning will fix the packet headers. If a teacher's remote classroom keeps dropping because of deep packet inspection, no appeal to a platform will restore her lesson. Precise diagnosis reveals the right leverage: a regulator for telecom coercion, a vendor for faulty blocklists, a platform for wrongful enforcement, an identity provider for exclusionary verification systems.

There is another reason diagnosis matters: complexity allows denial. When a government wishes to silence critics without overt censorship, the easiest method is to nudge a telecom or payment processor behind the scenes. When platforms censor content but fear political backlash, they can hide behind automation. Every actor can claim, sincerely or not, that the problem lies elsewhere. The more ambiguous the layer, the harder it is to fight. Clarity becomes power.

For officials who want to defend digital rights, identifying the layer changes how interventions are designed. Instead of passing blunt legislation, they can require detailed transparency reports from telecoms and filtering vendors. Instead of mandating backdoors, they can invest in independent audits of inspection systems. Instead of pressuring platforms to remove content, they can strengthen appeal rights and remedial pathways. When the target is precise, policy becomes surgical rather than symbolic.

For engineers, the skill is equally vital. Systems designed without layer-awareness routinely create accidental harm. A payment gateway that flags charities as risky. A content filter that confuses satire with extremism. A user-verification flow that excludes the stateless or undocumented. If technologists understand how identity, inspection, and enforcement interact, they can build guardrails: human review of appeals, transparent error messaging, public logs of decision pathways, and kill switches for runaway automation.

And for activists, the discipline of diagnosis prevents despair. Most blockages are not permanent. They are maintained by brittle code, rushed policy, and bureaucratic inertia. Once an activist knows where the blockage sits, they can lobby the right decision-maker, mobilise public pressure, or switch to alternate routes—mirror sites, federated platforms, domain fronting, or community-run networks. The enemy is not always a monolith. Often it is a chain of small failures.

There is a philosophical insight here too. Digital borders are not always the product of intentional tyranny. Sometimes they emerge from carelessness, risk aversion, or business incentives. Engineers optimise for safety; lawyers optimise for liability; platforms optimise for profit. In that mix, the rights of users can evaporate. Identifying the layer reveals which institution is shaping the border and forces it to justify its choices.

But clarity does not guarantee victory. Some states premise their power on ambiguity. They scatter responsibility across actors so no single institution can be blamed. A telecom throttles connections "to protect network stability," a platform removes posts "out of an abundance of caution," a filtering vendor blocks domains "due to risk," and a government quietly applauds the result. If every actor sees the others as the decision-maker, accountability dissolves.

This is why the diagnostic skill must be paired with public expectation. Citizens, civil society, and the press need to normalise the question: which layer failed? Only then can the fog lift. When a livestream drops during a protest, journalists should ask whether identity, inspection, or enforcement was at fault. When a crowdfunding page disappears, lawyers should demand disclosure from upstream payment processors. When an activist's account is suspended, appeals should be accompanied by technical forensics.

For years, digital borders were portrayed as inevitable consequences of sovereignty. But much of what feels inevitable is simply unexamined. The right to connect, speak, trade, and organise now depends on the willingness of societies to scrutinise how control is built into infrastructure. Identifying the layer is not glamorous. It is work. But it transforms helplessness into strategy.

Some will claim the complexity is too great. They underestimate how much ground can be gained through methodical inquiry and persistent transparency. Every court order leaves a trace. Every filtering vendor has a client. Every telecom has a regulator. Every platform enforces a policy. Borders built from software and contracts can be exposed with enough light.

The question that remains is whether societies will cultivate this habit. Will journalists treat network interference as seriously as legal censorship? Will regulators demand technical audits rather than political theatre? Will platforms expose their decision pipelines instead of claiming inscrutable automation?

The next chapter of digital sovereignty will be written not only in parliaments but in debugging logs, procurement contracts, standards documents, and appeal forms. Those who learn to identify the layer will have the leverage to challenge digital borders before they harden into permanent walls. Those who do not will continue shouting into the void, certain that someone is to blame, but never quite knowing who.

Map the Actors

When a journalist in Jakarta discovered her investigative podcast had vanished from a major streaming service, she assumed the government had forced its removal. Yet the regulator denied involvement, the platform claimed the takedown was an automated copyright strike, and the hosting provider insisted it was simply complying with a notice from a cloud security vendor. It took a month of emails, public pressure, and back-channel lawyers to locate the culprit: a private brand-protection contractor in London, hired by a foreign corporation, whose filter had falsely flagged the show's theme music. The censorship was accidental, the silence was global, and the responsibility was nowhere in sight.

This is the paradox of digital power. It can be overwhelming, but it is rarely concentrated in a single hand. Instead, it is dispersed across a web of actors: regulators, telecom carriers, platforms, infrastructure vendors, and the public who legitimise or contest their actions. Control emerges from coordination—sometimes deliberate, sometimes incidental. Understanding who actually made a decision is often harder than the decision itself.

Mapping actors is therefore not a bureaucratic exercise. It is the essential first step in making digital governance accountable. If you cannot name who holds the pen, you cannot ask why they wrote the rule. Nor can you change it.

Many civil liberties campaigns fail not because they lack evidence or moral force, but because they aim pressure in the wrong direction. A regulator is blamed for a takedown caused by a platform's automated moderation. A platform is condemned for a blockage enforced at the telecom level. A telecom is denounced for a ban demanded by a sovereign state. Without a clear map, advocacy becomes noise.

The actors are not mysterious. They are familiar institutions playing unfamiliar roles. Regulators write rules, but also whisper unofficial expectations. Carriers transmit packets, but also throttle and prioritise. Platforms host communities, but also adjudicate speech. Vendors supply the invisible plumbing—filters, analytics, identity systems—quietly shaping what is permitted. And hovering above them all is the public, whose outrage or indifference determines the space in which each actor moves.

Begin with regulators. They do more than pass laws. In many countries, they operate as shadow censors, issuing informal requests that companies treat as binding. When Pakistan's telecom authority "requests" a platform to remove blasphemous content, no statute is cited, yet refusal risks licence renewal. When India demands user identities for encrypted messages, courts may not have ruled, but companies calculate the cost of resistance. Mapping the regulator means tracking not just legislation but directives, threats, and whispered expectations. The remedy is legal challenge, transparency, and coalition: governments act differently when forced into the light.

Carriers, by contrast, rarely claim overt regulatory power. They speak of "network management," "traffic shaping," or "security." Yet they sit at the junction of every packet. When Egypt disrupted encrypted messaging during political unrest, the government did not block apps directly. It simply leaned on carriers to degrade their quality. When the Venezuelan authorities wanted to stifle news of protests, they did not censor websites; they slowed them to unusability. Throttling is censorship that looks like congestion. Carriers obey because they are licensed. Pressure here looks different: regulators must be compelled to justify any interference, and carriers must be forced to publish logs of government requests.

Platforms are the most visible actors, and often the easiest to blame. Yet many platform decisions are not truly voluntary. They sit between governments demanding compliance and users demanding freedom. When Nigeria ordered Twitter to be blocked, carriers obeyed. Twitter eventually negotiated partial restoration, but the real leverage was not diplomacy—it was public pressure at scale. Platforms respond to reputational threat more quickly than legal argument. Users who understand this can mobilise attention towards opaque moderation practices, force the publication of transparency reports, and demand appeal rights.

Vendors are the quietest actors and sometimes the most powerful. A single content-filtering company can shape what millions read. A threat-intelligence firm can blacklist domains that vanish from the internet overnight. These decisions are made in private contracts, audited by no-one, and justified by vague claims of "risk management." When a human-rights group in Myanmar found its email server inaccessible, the problem was not the local telecom, but a Western security vendor who misclassified its domain. The telecom simply imported a blacklist. Activists who mapped the chain revealed the true leverage point: the vendor's international clients, who did not want to be complicit. Within weeks, the blacklist was corrected.

Mapping vendors requires detective work—tracing certificate authorities, payment gateways, filtering lists, identity providers, and cloud subsidiaries. But the payoff is immense: once the true actor is found, they can be pressured, sued, embarrassed, or forced to justify their decisions. Anonymity is a privilege, and it evaporates under scrutiny.

And then there is the public. Citizens are not passive recipients of digital borders. They co-create them. When a tabloid campaigns for "online safety," platforms tighten rules and collateral damage follows. When parents panic about misinformation, lawmakers rush to regulate encryption. When silence is tolerated, control spreads. The public is both subject and sovereign: the ultimate source of legitimacy for every other actor.

Mapping the public means identifying who can shape opinion—journalists, educators, community leaders—and recognising that digital governance is a cultural project as much as a technical one. Pressure applied without a public constituency is ignored. Pressure backed by voters, consumers, and the press becomes irresistible.

There is a deeper value in mapping the actors. It forces humility. The internet is not governed by a villain. It is governed by incentives, risk calculations, fear, and convenience. Regulators fear chaos. Platforms fear liability. Vendors fear lawsuits. Carriers fear losing licences. The public fears harm to children and democracy. Each actor believes it is acting responsibly. Sometimes they are right. Often, they are not.

When all actors believe someone else is accountable, abuses flourish. Platforms blame governments for coercion; governments blame platforms for inaction; vendors hide behind clients; carriers hide behind regulators. In this fog, no-one raises their hand. Mapping breaks that cycle. It restores lines of responsibility.

The most effective activists do not waste time on moral grandstanding. They build spreadsheets. They list every actor in the chain: regulator, carrier, platform, vendor, and public. They mark leverage points: public relations risk, contractual vulnerabilities, regulatory obligations, financial pressure, political costs. They identify where silence hurts most. Then they target, systematically and relentlessly.

Engineers can learn from this discipline as well. When something breaks—an access path, a domain name, a payment flow—the instinct is to fix the fault closest to hand. But digital harm is often upstream. Vendors supply poisoned data. Regulators impose quiet threats. Platforms deploy inherited policies. Without mapping, engineers patch the symptom while the cause persists.

Officials who care about democratic oversight need to map too. If a telecom insists that a blockage was compelled by law, demand the statute. If a platform claims that a takedown was automated, demand the human review path. If a vendor claims a domain is dangerous, demand the evidence. Public authority means public justification. Mapping actors exposes where explanation is absent.

There will always be actors who prefer to stay invisible. Some vendors thrive on obscurity. Some regulators rely on informal pressure. Some carriers enjoy a monopoly and feel unassailable. Yet invisibility is only sustainable when the public does not ask questions. When journalists treat obscure filtering decisions as newsworthy, the costs of secrecy rise. When legislators demand disclosure of vendor relationships, accountability follows.

The frontier of digital rights is not defined by technology alone. It is defined by power and responsibility. The internet is a political system run by companies, states, and communities. Like any political system, it can be studied. It can be mapped. And when it is mapped, it can be changed.

The lingering question is whether societies will embrace this work. Will they demand transparency from vendors who shape what they can read? Will they hold carriers accountable for secret censorship? Will they insist that platforms justify their speech rules? Or will control remain nebulous—every actor pointing at another, while the public loses ground?

The next battles will be won not by those who shout the loudest, but by those who see the full board. When you know every player, you can change the game.

Choose the Instrument

A politician once demanded a law to "stop the internet from being rude." Parliamentary draftsmen tried to translate the sentiment into statutory language. Telecom operators asked how they were meant to filter rudeness without reading private messages. Platforms warned that automatic filters would kill satire, whistle-blowing, and edgy humour. Civil liberties groups prepared legal challenges. Months of debate produced only embarrassment, because the original instinct—to legislate first—was the wrong instrument for the problem. The appropriate tools were transparency reports, targeted content standards, and user empowerment features, not criminal law.

This is a pattern that repeats itself around the world. Confronted with digital harms—misinformation, extremist content, privacy violations, fraud—governments reach instinctively for statutes. But law is a blunt tool, slow to adapt and expensive to enforce. It is essential in some cases, pointless or counterproductive in others. The deeper discipline is diagnostic: matching the instrument to the problem, and refusing the reflex to regulate when pressure, incentives, and sunlight can do the work more effectively.

Digital governance offers a surprisingly rich toolbox: transparency obligations, technical standards, procurement requirements, regulatory nudges, platform self-governance, public-interest engineering, and, when necessary, formal law. The order matters. The lightest interventions often achieve the strongest results.

Transparency is the simplest and most underused remedy. When platforms began publishing content removal numbers, automated takedown rates, and error statistics, public debate shifted from speculation to evidence. Patterns emerged: disproportionate impacts on minority languages, overzealous copyright bots, police requests without warrants. Once data existed, journalists and civil society could investigate, litigators could build cases, and parliaments could hold hearings. Transparency did not solve abuse, but it made it visible—and visibility changes incentives. Companies adjust when silence becomes scandal.

Standards are the quiet workhorses of governance. They are technical agreements about how systems interoperate and how safeguards are implemented. After a wave of SIM-card fraud in several African countries, regulators did not rush to criminalise mobile penetration. They convened carriers to adopt a shared authentication protocol, making mass registration fraud far harder. When browsers rejected weak cryptographic certificates, insecure websites were forced to upgrade. No new law was needed; the standard itself was regulatory pressure. Standards thrive because they are flexible, incremental, and enforceable through market power.

Procurement, though unglamorous, is often the sharpest instrument. Governments buy vast amounts of software, cloud services, and data infrastructure. When a city requires open file formats for public records, vendors either comply or lose the contract. When a national health service demands data portability, the market reconfigures. And when a school system insists on accessible design as a procurement condition, entire product lines become more inclusive. Procurement shapes behaviour quietly and quickly, without a single amendment to statute books.

Even informal regulation—soft law—has surprising influence. A regulator that publishes advisory guidance can shift industry norms without drafting penalties. A telecom authority that demands annual transparency reports on network shutdowns can deter political misuse. A consumer agency that pressures platforms to simplify privacy settings can transform user experience. These tools work because compliance is easier than defiance when penalties are social, reputational, or contractual rather than criminal.

There are still moments where formal law is essential. Data protection statutes, anti-discrimination rules, and competition law all exist for good reason. But law should be the final instrument, not the first. When legislators write criminal offences for ill-defined harms such as "disinformation," they hand future administrations a weapon. When they demand blanket filtering technology, they incentivise invasive surveillance. And when they regulate at the application layer what belongs at the network layer, compliance becomes impossible. Over-regulation is not merely clumsy; it creates collateral censorship.

One can see the spectrum of instruments clearly in the fight against algorithmic discrimination. Activists could have insisted on banning algorithms outright. Instead, they demanded transparency audits, access to training data, and standards for accuracy and fairness. Companies responded with external review boards, red-teaming exercises, and bias testing frameworks. Legislators then layered law on top—but only once evidence and standards existed. The law that emerged was narrower, more practical, and less vulnerable to political misuse.

The wrong instrument can cause damage even when intentions are noble. After a terrorist attack, a European government demanded a backdoor in messaging apps. Engineers explained it was technically impossible without weakening encryption for everyone. Civil society argued it would endanger dissidents. Instead of stepping back, the government doubled down. The proposed law was quietly shelved months later, but the damage was done: trust eroded, global companies considered relocating, and users migrated to foreign services. A transparency obligation to disclose lawful interception requests would have achieved more, with none of the harm.

Choosing the instrument also requires anticipating adaptation. Powerful actors will evade the strictest controls. Criminals migrate platforms.

Propagandists open new accounts. Authoritarian states develop national firewalls. Light-touch tools—standards, procurement requirements, and transparency—are easier to update. Law is brittle; traps are not.

For activists, matching the instrument to the problem prevents wasted energy. If the issue is opaque censorship by a filtering vendor, legislation aimed at platforms will do nothing. The correct tool may be procurement pressure on public institutions that use the vendor's services. If disinformation spreads through virality incentives, mandating user identity verification may worsen surveillance while ignoring the true cause. Circuit breakers or friction-by-design features can reduce the damage without undermining anonymity.

Officials face similar choices. During the pandemic, governments confronted a flood of misinformation. Some threatened criminal sanctions. Others asked platforms to promote authoritative content and label dubious claims. A few supported public education campaigns to teach citizens how to assess sources. The most effective interventions were not punitive; they increased reliable visibility and strengthened civic resilience. The lesson is not that law is irrelevant, but that it is only one instrument among many—and often not the best.

Markets respond to signals long before they respond to statutes. When a small European country required government contractors to support data portability, tech providers implemented export features for all users, not just public clients. When a U.S. city insisted on open procurement for police surveillance tools, vendors released transparency frameworks to compete for contracts. Procurement shaped behaviour faster than any national privacy law.

None of this means that law should be timid. When necessary, it must be bold: banning bulk surveillance, enforcing competition, protecting encryption, guaranteeing accessibility. But bold law works best when other tools have laid the groundwork. Transparency produces evidence. Standards demonstrate feasibility. Procurement builds market capacity. Soft law stabilises expectations. Legislation then locks in gains.

There is a deeper philosophical principle here. Digital governance is not a war to be won, but a system to be tuned. Every instrument has trade-offs. Transparency risks aiding adversaries. Standards risk locking in flawed designs. Procurement can entrench incumbents. Law can chill speech. The art is not maximalism but proportionality: enough control to protect the public, enough restraint to preserve innovation and freedom.

Political impatience pushes leaders to legislate first, but wisdom demands a slower hand. Ask questions before wielding power. Is the harm measurable? Can transparency fix it? Can standards prevent it? Can procurement shape it? If these fail, then, and only then, reach for law.

The future of digital rights may hinge on this choice. Will societies default to criminalisation and surveillance, or will they master the lighter tools that preserve freedom while managing risk? Will governments build legal monuments they cannot amend, or regulatory ecosystems they can adapt?

Choosing the instrument decides what kind of digital world we build: punitive or participatory, rigid or resilient. The question now is whether leaders and citizens alike will learn to reach for the right tool, instead of the loudest one.

Anticipate Adaptation

The police in Nairobi seized a server farm they believed was powering a wave of financial scams. For a week, the fraud stopped. Victims stopped reporting mysterious withdrawals. Banks congratulated themselves. Then, on the eighth day, complaints surged again. The scam had reappeared, routed through a different service provider, using fresh SIM cards and anonymised routing. Law enforcement had treated a digital crime like a physical one—remove the equipment and the harm disappears. But digital actors adapt. They move, fork, reroute, and reconfigure faster than any courtroom or committee. The lesson was painful: a solution that works once is not a solution.

Every intervention in the digital sphere triggers a countermove. It is the defining strategic fact of online governance—and yet the one most frequently ignored. Policy-makers, activists, and platform designers still behave as though every rule is a finishing point rather than the first move in a shifting contest. If filtering rules become strict, adversaries encrypt messages. If platforms clamp down on abusive accounts, bad actors automate account creation. If governments block a website, the website migrates to a new domain. It is a dance of escalation, but only one side usually acknowledges the choreography.

The most effective digital governance accepts that no control is permanent. Adaptation is inevitable, so interventions must be designed for flexibility, experimentation, and reversal. That is why pilot programmes and sunset clauses matter: they shift governance from grand declarations to iterative learning. Instead of building legal monuments that cannot be changed, societies can build scaffolding—structures that are sturdy enough to act, but light enough to dismantle.

Consider the early days of automated copyright filtering on video platforms. Rights-holders demanded immediate takedowns. Platforms deployed broad filters. But the filters frequently misidentified legitimate content: educational clips, open-licence material, independent creators. Every time a rule tightened, adversaries found ways to evade it—editing audio, adding overlays, splitting content into fragments. The solution that finally stabilised the system did not come from harsher punishment. It came from test beds, incremental rollout, user appeals, and audit teams analysing false positives. The lesson was clear: the system needed flexibility more than force.

Pilot programmes prevent hubris. They expose failure when failure is still cheap. When a European regulator experimented with age verification tools for adult websites, they rolled it out only in one region, measured circumvention rates, monitored privacy risks, and halted the project when evidence showed it was easily bypassed and dangerously intrusive. Without a pilot stage, that mistake would have become national policy, difficult to unwind, harmful to millions. The cost of humility was a temporary embarrassment; the reward was avoiding a lasting error.

Sunset clauses do a different kind of work. They build expiry dates directly into law or policy, forcing a moment of reflection. Without them, emergency measures linger forever: surveillance systems built to fight terrorism persist in ordinary policing; pandemic tracking apps become generic monitoring tools; temporary shutdown powers become permanent habits. A sunset clause is an admission that good intentions often grow teeth. It demands evidence before renewal. It forces governments to justify continued intrusion.

Digital actors adapt because they are not anchored in geography. When a Southeast Asian government demanded that platforms remove disinformation within hours, troll farms simply broke their networks into smaller units and spread content across closed messaging channels. Moderators could not see it, regulators could not measure it, yet influence continued unimpeded. The intervention changed the visible surface without touching the underlying structure. A pilot phase could have revealed this predictable adaptation before political leaders presented the reform as a triumph.

Anticipating adaptation also protects democratic norms. Consider internet shutdowns. Governments justify them as emergency measures to stop unrest or misinformation. Citizens adapt by using VPNs, satellite connections, or mesh networks. The shutdown harms the innocent while barely slowing the determined. Over time, shutdowns become symbols of insecurity, not control. If governments studied each shutdown as a temporary, reversible measure—with audits, sunset clauses, and pilots—they would learn that the consequences almost always outweigh the benefits. The refusal to anticipate adaptation creates policy that is performative rather than effective.

The pattern repeats in moderation of violent content. When platforms began removing extremist propaganda, extremist groups responded with code words, emojis, and layered symbolism. Bans forced them underground, where detection became harder. Researchers now argue that platform policies need not only removal mechanisms but "resilience engineering": tools for context analysis, language-scanning, and cross-platform cooperation. In other words, adaptation forced innovation—but only after years of reactive policy.

There is a philosophical shift embedded in this approach. Traditional governance is built around permanence: law is fixed, standards endure, constitutions resist change. Digital governance rewards the opposite. Systems evolve. Threats mutate. Users discover unintended behaviours that turn features into vulnerabilities. Instead of finality, the wisest digital policies are provisional. They are not weak; they are self-aware. They recognise that certainty in a dynamic system is naïve.

This is why kill switches, audits, and reversibility matter. A platform introducing a new ranking algorithm can deploy it for 5% of users, measure impacts on harassment, misinformation, or engagement, and roll back instantly if harm emerges. A government adopting biometric border controls can require automatic deactivation if error rates exceed a threshold, with mandatory independent evaluation. Such reversibility protects not just the public, but the legitimacy of the institution implementing the change.

Adaptation is not only malicious. Ordinary users also respond to incentives. When a messaging app limited broadcast forwarding to curb political spam in India and Brazil, ordinary users began taking screenshots and circulating them as images. The problem resurfaced in a new form. The lesson was not that forward limits were useless, but that interventions must be layered. Technical friction is helpful, but must be paired with public education, civic literacy, and better reporting tools. Solutions evolve just as harms do.

Platform designers are learning this. Fraud detection systems now include adversarial modelling, anticipating how criminals might react. Content moderation teams engage in red-teaming exercises to test loopholes. Even product designers run "misuse workshops" to imagine how a feature might be exploited. These practices are signs of a maturing field—an acceptance that no policy survives first contact with a motivated adversary.

Activists, too, benefit from anticipating countermoves. When campaigners demanded data portability from financial apps, companies complied—but exported data in formats so obscure that migration was impossible. Activists adapted. They demanded human-readable, machine-readable formats, mandatory documentation, and independent audits. The campaign succeeded because it treated compliance not as a checkbox but a battlefield.

The deeper point is that the digital space punishes arrogance. Grand solutions fail not because they are ill-intentioned, but because they assume static behavior. A law that makes perfect sense on paper collapses in the face of a clever programmer or a motivated propagandist. Systems without feedback loops decay into irrelevance.

Pilot programmes and sunset clauses are the antidote. They acknowledge uncertainty. They let societies try new ideas without committing to them forever. They create space to learn, revise, and sometimes abandon. Most importantly, they convert governance into an iterative craft rather than a one-shot decree.

There is a generational shift happening. Older legal and regulatory systems were built on physical metaphors: borders that could be policed, documents that could be verified, behaviour that could be observed. Digital systems are different. You can change your identity in seconds. Content can spawn infinite copies. Networks react like living organisms, not mechanical machines. Governance must evolve accordingly.

The future belongs to those who embrace adaptive policy. Imagine content moderation rules that expire every year unless evidence justifies renewal; encryption laws that must be reauthorised after independent privacy audits; biometric systems that shut off automatically when accuracy degrades. Imagine a world where regulation is not a hammer but a set of adjustable instruments, tuned and retuned as reality shifts.

Will leaders accept this? Or will they cling to the illusion that rules can be permanent, and that adversaries will sit still? The story of digital governance is being written in real time. The question now is whether societies are ready to govern like gardeners rather than generals—pruning, adjusting, and learning as systems grow.

The digital world will keep changing. The only choice is whether policy keeps pace.

Build for Reversibility

In the winter of 2020, a major social network launched a ranking update designed to surface "meaningful interactions". Overnight, political outrage went viral. Local news collapsed beneath celebrity spats. Researchers later discovered that the tweak rewarded inflammatory language and punished nuance. The harm was not intentional, but it was swift—and, crucially, it was reversible. Engineers quietly rolled back the change within days. The platform recovered not because it was wise, but because it had the technical humility to press an undo button.

Not every system is so lucky. Cities have installed predictive policing tools that keep running long after error rates are exposed. Governments have deployed biometric databases with no mechanism for deletion, retention limits, or independent evaluation. Platforms have launched automated content moderators that silently remove legitimate speech with no fallback plan. These systems calcify. They trap societies in permanent mistakes. In the physical world, bad infrastructure lasts decades; in the digital world, bad infrastructure can mutate beyond visibility.

Reversibility is not a luxury. It is the ethical and operational backbone of responsible digital governance. A system that cannot be paused, audited, or undone becomes a danger—to rights, to trust, and to legitimacy. The question is no longer whether mistakes will happen; it is whether those mistakes can be detected and corrected in time.

Modern engineers know this intuitively. They rarely deploy new code to every user at once. They stagger releases, run A/B tests, monitor error logs, and watch dashboards for anomalies. Yet the moment digital systems become political instruments—border filters, identity checks, misinformation detectors—that humility disappears. Governments lean toward permanence. Platforms fear admitting error. Vendors prefer contracts that lock in clients. Irreversibility becomes a business model.

The alternative is simple: build systems with kill switches, auditability, and rollback paths. This is not techno-utopianism; it is routine practice in safety-critical industries. Nuclear plants and aircraft software include fail-safe modes. Financial trading systems can halt exchanges when volatility spikes. The same philosophy should govern digital borders and algorithmic enforcement.

A kill switch is not sabotage; it is a contract with the public. It says: if this system harms, we will stop it. When a major ride-sharing company deployed algorithmic driver ratings that penalised workers unfairly, public outrage forced the company to suspend the system temporarily. But suspension required a frantic scramble, because no one had designed for shutdown. A policy that could be activated in minutes took weeks to unwind. People lost income for no reason except that reversibility had been forgotten.

Audits work the same way. They allow institutions to change course before the public is harmed. When the Dutch government's automated welfare fraud detector was audited by independent researchers, the system was found to disproportionately flag immigrants and low-income families. Because the audit was mandatory and publicly disclosed, the programme was shut down before its discrimination became political poison. The audit did not weaken the government; it protected its legitimacy.

One might argue that designing for reversibility undermines deterrence. If a system can be turned off, won't bad actors simply wait for weakness? But deterrence built on brittle systems invites catastrophe. A content moderation rule that cannot be paused when misinformation databases misfire risks silencing entire communities. A biometric system that misidentifies thousands of travellers but has no rollback capacity invites lawsuits and diplomatic crises. Strength is not rigidity. Strength is adaptability.

Reversibility also protects democratic accountability. Laws that mandate audits and sunset provisions force public debate. They prevent quiet entrenchment. They give citizens visibility into whether a system is doing what it promised. And they give legislators evidence instead of ideology. In 2019, an Australian state introduced a facial recognition trial for retail theft. Civil liberties groups sounded alarms. Instead of doubling down, the government paused the trial, commissioned a third-party review, and did not renew the programme when efficacy was unproven. That decision preserved trust, not weakness.

The philosophy behind reversibility can be boiled into a single principle: design like you might be wrong. Policy-makers often assume their intentions will match outcomes. They rarely do. Digital systems interact with human behaviour in unpredictable ways. Introduce a friction measure, and users may find shortcuts. Deploy an identity check, and adversaries may buy stolen credentials. Launch a misinformation warning, and conspiracists may claim censorship and gain followers. When systems can be reversed, experimentation becomes safe.

This approach also encourages innovation. A city that fears being stuck with a surveillance system forever will hesitate to experiment. A platform that knows it can roll back a moderation rule will try it earlier. A regulator with sunset clauses can test ambitious reforms without political suicide. Reversibility liberates decision-makers from paralysis.

There is a deeper ethical layer too. Permanent systems violate a basic principle of justice: errors must be repairable. If an algorithm wrongly flags a student as a cheat, a citizen as a criminal, or a refugee as a risk, the harm should not be locked in. A humane system offers remedy, not resignation. It gives people the dignity of correction.

The tools already exist. Product teams use feature toggles—only needing to flip a switch to deactivate harmful changes. Database designers build versioned schemas so data transformations can be rewound. Security engineers rely on immutable logs so investigators can see exactly what a system did and when. These are not radical inventions. They are everyday safeguards that the public sector has been slow to adopt.

Opponents of reversibility claim it is expensive. That is true—at first. Building two code paths is harder than one. Designing auditing pipelines requires skilled teams. But the alternative costs far more. Irreversible systems lead to courts, protests, public distrust, and political overcorrection. In the long term, reversibility is cheap insurance.

The history of technology is full of irreversible mistakes. Cities built motorways that cut through neighbourhoods and spent generations unpicking the damage. Governments installed surveillance tools that outlived the crises that justified them. When institutions fail to build for reversibility, the public becomes the safety valve: whistle-blowers, activists, and journalists fight to expose harm that could have been prevented with a switch and an audit.

The digital sphere gives us an opportunity the physical world never had. Code can change overnight. Databases can roll back. Models can be retrained. If we do not take advantage of that, the failure is intentional.

Progress requires humility. The systems shaping identity, speech, mobility, and opportunity must assume they will sometimes do harm. They must be designed to stop, rewind, and learn. If not, mistakes become policy, accidents become precedent, and temporary harms become permanent scars.

The question for every builder, regulator, and civic leader is brutally simple: when this system fails—and it will—can we undo it? If the answer is no, the system is not ready for the public.

About the Author

Ayaan Chowdhury writes about the invisible rules that govern our digital lives. Raised between Kolkata and London, he brings the sociologist's lens to questions usually left to engineers and lawyers, asking not only how systems work but who they serve. At the Oxford Internet Institute, his research explores AI governance and the global digital divide, with a focus on how infrastructure choices shape everyday freedoms. He is driven by a simple mission: to make complex technology legible to citizens and accountable to the public interest. A childhood memory of crossing India's Howrah Bridge lingers in his work: a reminder that passage is never just a route, but a relationship between power and possibility.

www.ingramcontent.com/pod-product-compliance
Lightning Source LLC
Chambersburg PA
CBHW021215250926
51852CB00006B/31